ICT for Dialogue and Inclusive Decision-Making

WARSAW STUDIES IN POLITICS AND SOCIETY

Edited by
Radosław Markowski

VOLUME 6

PETER LANG

Anna Przybylska (ed.)

ICT for Dialogue and Inclusive Decision-Making

PETER LANG

Bibliographic Information published by the Deutsche Nationalbibliothek
The Deutsche Nationalbibliothek lists this publication in the Deutsche Nationalbibliografie; detailed bibliographic data is available in the internet at http://dnb.d-nb.de.

Library of Congress Cataloging-in-Publication Data
A CIP catalog record for this book has been applied for at the Library of Congress.

INSTYTUT SOCJOLOGII

UNIVERSITY OF WARSAW FOUNDATION

The National Centre for Research and Development

This publication was financially supported by the Institute of Sociology at the University of Warsaw and the University of Warsaw Foundation. It is a result of the project entitled "New perspectives for dialogue: the model of deliberation and IT tools for social inclusion in decision-making processes" financed by the National Centre for Research and Development in Poland.

Proof-reader: Laurence Taylor
Reviewers:
prof. Jerzy Bartkowski, University of Warsaw
prof. Todd Davies, Stanford University
dr Marek Średniawa, Warsaw University of Technology

Cover illustration: Marianna Wybieralska, mariannawybieralska.pl

ISSN 2193-3774
ISBN 978-3-631-74810-7 (Print) E-ISBN 978-3-631-74811-4 (E-PDF)
E-ISBN 978-3-631-74812-1 (EPUB) E-ISBN 978-3-631-74813-8 (MOBI)
DOI 10.3726/b13935

Peter Lang – Berlin · Bern · Bruxelles · New York · Oxford · Warszawa · Wien

This publication has been peer reviewed.

www.peterlang.com

Table of Contents

Anna Przybylska

Introduction: ICT and Dialogue in Democratic Innovations

In this book, we discuss the theoretical premises and the institutional context of the *inDialogue* software's development. It has been designed to intervene in the practice of public consultations, which is a weak but institutionally embedded form of civic participation in political decision-making. We are concerned with the quality of public consultations, both their input and output. This is why we have followed the deliberative public consultation model, which recognizes the value of social inclusion in knowledge-sharing for open political community building.

Certainly, the Polish socio-political environment, which has influenced the inDialogue software's design, is distinctive in some respects, but the issues of the interventionist role of ICT in deliberative democracy and democratic performance, which we apply in our analysis, remain relevant to other democratic countries. Therefore, this book is not only about Poland, but it does set an applied experiment in democratic innovations in a Polish background to offer original empirical data to feed discussion across borders.

Conditions for the Transformative Role of ICT in Politics

In regards to strengthening trust in political institutions and decision-making, much attention has been accorded to the mechanisms and institutionalized practices that serve to justify political actions. The interest in the transformative role of communications as well as the transformation of communications due to the advancements in ICT has been manifested in academic publications and institutional documents alike. But, already in the 1980s, it was observed that even the use of technology with its unprecedented potential for interactivity would not, alone, remodel political processes; instead, it demonstrated how the functions and features of technology depend on the model of democracy favored by politicians (Van Dijk 1996).

ICT is a function of institutionalized politics: the model of democracy at large and the model of civic participation in decision-making through, for example, referenda, public consultations, participatory budgeting. Christopher F. Arterton (1987) proposed a division of communication tools, which were developed to strengthen civic participation in politics, along two axes, where the first refers to plebiscitary vs. deliberative politics, and the second refers to the different degrees of interactivity among participants. The fact of who is the organizer of a communicative situation has additional consequences for the ICT's design.

Coding for democracy always starts with the model of action. The software used in public consultation can differ due to several factors; among them, the role and responsibilities of the principal user in politics and political communication; the stage or stages in public consultations where ICT is applied; and the standards and methodology adopted for public consultations. Going more in-depth, the influence of the choice of methods and techniques for the organization of debates on available ICT tools—especially participant selection, group formation, moderation and incentives—can also be observed.

The aforementioned decisions made on the procedural aspects of public consultations are of prime importance to the design of ICT and to the results collected—the information about the needs and preferences of citizens that should have an impact on political decisions. It may be that the overall aim—strengthening public participation—is shared by different stakeholders, but variations in its operationalization bring about an array of tools that allow for disparate modes of political communication and participation. Approaching the issue of the software design from the other side, it can be said that the software carries within itself the information about the political norms of the principal users who recommend it.

Proponents of deliberative democracy propose a set of methods for public consultations. By means of their comparison, it is possible to draw conclusions about some of the general characteristics, which in combination, constitute the model of deliberative public consultation. This model is already helpful for those who intend to develop tools to implement deliberative norms. Debates based on the knowledge accessible to all and an exchange of arguments without social prejudice are within their focus. But, designing specific ICT functions and features requires further reflection on the institutional, socio-political and technical environment.

There have been many projects in which scholars, public servants, or social activists have attempted to develop software for implementing the norms of deliberation. The references to the model of deliberation are direct, but can be indirect when linked to the open data resources, knowledge sharing, and collaborative problem-solving for better public governance (Davies and Gangadharan 2009; Noveck 2009; Lathrop and Ruma 2010; Stromer-Galley et al. 2012; Coleman and Shane 2012; Nabatchi 2014; Klein and Convertino 2015). Each project has been a particular contribution to our understanding of deliberation in practice. Let us provide two examples that bear some similarities as well as differences.

The *Deliberatorium*[1] software launched by Mark Klein (Massachusetts Institute of Technology), highlights the importance of argumentation in finding solutions to complex problems by multiple users who bring in different competences. Each user follows the discussion, observing and contributing to the development of a graph of argumentation. Contributions are organized by topic, and a moderator can check them for structural errors and eliminate irrelevant posts. The participants can rate individual inputs, as the aim is to select the best ideas. The Deliberatorium application can be used by anyone at any time—an institution, a group, or unallied individuals.

In the *Online Deliberation*[2] software, Weiyu Zhang (National University of Singapore) proposes debates among randomly selected participants who are obliged to go through educational materials before joining a debate. They are encouraged by a system of incentives to contribute to discussions, for example, they are rewarded for being active participants. The formation of opinions is supported by a visual representation in the form of a mind-map that is generated by a moderator; otherwise, moderators do not intervene in the organization of the topic-structured deliberation. The Online Deliberation application is not linked to any particular institutional user or category of users, but, a large scale random sampling of participants supported by the system suggests that it is meant for governmental bodies or large institutions and concerns issues relevant to considerable populations.

Our own inDialogue application shares some features with Deliberatorium (threaded discussions and argument visualization in text debates, moderators in an intervening role) and some with the Online Deliberation software (access to educational materials and participant selection, threaded discussions and argument visualization in text debates), but also differs from both of them. Sometimes the difference concerns an approach to the use of a particular element in the functional system rather than to the presence or absence of it, for example, mind-map creation (who creates them and how).

Undoubtedly, setting a matrix of analytical criteria to compare various applications that support deliberations, especially if accompanied by a justification for the solutions adopted, brings valuable information to developments in the area under scrutiny (for some examples of categories and criteria of deliberative design see Davies and Chandler 2012). The major difference between the two aforementioned applications and the inDialogue software is that the latter is meant

1 http://cci.mit.edu/klein/deliberatorium.html (accessed September 5, 2017).
2 http://onlinedeliberation.org/ (accessed September 5, 2017).

to change the practice of institutions and the behaviors of participants in regards to public consultation within the existing institutional framework. Our efforts are directed towards the institutionalization of its use. This is why the interface is less universal and flexible (defined institutional users, compulsory actions within a process that is composed of several phases), but, at the same time, the software is more complex in addressing the issue of the quality of public consultations.

ICT for Public Consultations in City and Town Halls

In Poland, the ICT services for public consultations once developed by the national government either are no longer in use, which highlights the ephemeral character of this kind of project, or they do not fulfil their role. The supra-local initiatives for creating online tools for local governments have been promoted by NGOs, sometimes in cooperation with units of the national government. Projects like "I have an opinion" and "Citizens decide" deserve special mention. The large city halls develop their own internet platforms dedicated to public consultations that are used in parallel to traditional face-to-face data collection or as the sole place for public hearings. Some cities experiment with websites supporting participatory budgeting (mainly to provide information about projects and to facilitate voting), the use of maps in locating problems within the city space combined with dialogue and polls. But the software available for public consultations is mostly mono-functional. It facilitates the following: internal communication within the city or town hall and the circulation of documents (the preparatory phase), and the annotation of documents; or participation in synchronous or asynchronous text debates; or collecting the answers to polls (the implementation phase). Even if several tools for conducting public consultations are at the disposal of a city or town hall, they are rarely used in combination.

The growing importance of the internet for public communication requires profound reflection on the tools. The quality of discussions on forums managed by public institutions usually do not meet the criteria of deliberation at all; meaning that they are not grounded in reliable information and participants rarely use arguments supported by facts during the exchange of posts. We are convinced that to increase the quality of public consultations and public dialogue it is necessary to provide education about their standards. This is why the inDialogue software, which we have presented in this book, helps institutional organizers to understand the methodology of public consultations. Its innovativeness can be explained, among other things, by its multiple functions. It offers a set of tools that can be used not only to conduct but also plan public consultations. It exemplifies an attempt to introduce some standards of deliberation into institutionalized politics and involve citizens in meaningful and task-oriented debate.

Due to the fact that the set of tools in the inDialogue software serve for public consultations' planning in the local government, the interface for the clerk is more complex than the interface for the citizen. The inDialogue software facilitates internal communication (within the city or town hall) to make the external communication (with citizens) efficient. It supports planning and reporting of both online and offline debates, as public consultations have to be socially inclusive and not all citizens use the internet or have adequate internet competences. The debates are threaded, and moderators can intervene to make sure that the discussion focuses on the topic and sub-topics. The rating of posts in text debates is possible only after gathering all the proposals and arguments that can be automatically transformed into an argumentation map. In addition to these functions, the inDialogue software also archives consultations and makes it possible to use data gathered across multiple consultations as input to strategic documents in public policy development.

The model for the inDialogue software was based on research findings that involved potential beneficiaries, that is, local government administration. The survey carried out on the methodology of public consultation was followed by online group debates that offered explanations for identified problems, and then a series of case studies in which the role of academics was not only to observe but also to intervene in the procedures and practice of the public consultations that were carried out. Local government administration partners were consulted about the model before coding started in 2014. The second stage of the project results' evaluation took place in 2015 after the prototype was ready for use. The tests were carried out in two municipalities: Nowa Dęba, a city of approximately 11,000 inhabitants in the Podkarpacie region; and Olsztyn, a city of approximately 173,000 inhabitants in the Warmia-Mazury region.

Interdisciplinary applied research in the area of social informatics conducted in the tradition of action research, with its demand for developing practical knowledge in participation with social partners as well as for an ongoing circle of action and evaluation (Reason and Bradbury 2008) are rare as they require time, resources, and make researchers responsible for the results in a different way to primary research projects. One important characteristic of our project is that it has both analytical and applied aspects. Another is that it is value based. When we observe the practices of public administration critically or when we promote specific patterns of behaviors during public consultations, we have adopted the particular perspective of a scientist who favors deliberation in political communication and decision-making. However, the rigor and transparency of the research design contribute to the scientific objectivity of the results.

The inDialogue software is a result of the project "New Perspectives for Dialogue: A Model of Deliberation and ICT Tools for Social Inclusion in Decision-making Processes" conducted between the years 2014 and 2017 by the Centre for Deliberation at the Institute of Sociology, University of Warsaw (leader); the Warsaw University of Technology; the Association of Polish Cities; the MIT, an ICT training company; the Foundation of Free and Open Software, replaced by the Association of "Cities in the Internet" (late 2015); and the Polish Forum of Disabled Persons, replaced by the Association for Deaf People in Łódź (2016). It received financial support from the National Centre for Research and Development within the framework of the "Social Innovations" Program.

Team Perspectives on the InDialogue Application

In this volume, we discuss the factors that have influenced the inDialogue software's development. We also share some of the preliminary results from its implementation in two communities. The authors who have contributed to this book are researchers from the disciplines of computer science and social sciences, as well as practitioners in the areas of local government, electronic administration services, and Web Content Accessibility Guidelines (WCAG) 2.0. In their chapters, they analyze various aspects of the inDialogue application's functions from the perspectives of their professional competences and interests. In doing so, they document the complexity of the work carried out in an applied interdisciplinary project.

In the preceding paragraphs from "Introduction: ICT and dialogue in democratic innovations," the background information that is meaningful to the inDialogue application's conceptualization and goals was presented. By describing the main tools and functions of the inDialogue software, I have attempted to position it in relation to other ICT software used in public consultations and deliberations.

In chapter 1, "Social Research and Public Consultations," Jacek Haman argues that although similar cognitive goals impose common methodological requirements on social research and public consultations, specific political functions and legal restrictions must be taken into account when we plan consultations. Thus, although it is necessary to adhere to the rules of social research methodology when preparing good consultations, given the formal limitations, it is also important to make the public aware of what knowledge is achievable. This approach implements the idea of the citizen as subject in public consultations, which makes these consultations distinct from the majority of social studies in which the researcher is the subject and a community only the object of research. We have adopted this as a guideline in our project.

The following chapter, "ICT Solutions for Public Consultations: Methodology and Design of the InDialogue Platform" shows how the model of deliberative public consultations and the norms defining deliberation have informed the design of the inDialogue application. Anna Przybylska links the development of specific functionalities and features of the software to the results of evaluation studies that were based on deliberative standards and demonstrated the weaknesses of public consultation practice. All the flaws that were identified in the planning and conducting of public consultations have been responded to in the design of inDialogue's tools. The inDialogue software is a middle-solution between a hard (legal) and a soft (advisory) measure. It guides institutional users through the public consultation procedure and does not allow them to omit crucial elements that serve transparency, proper methodological planning, and the legitimacy of processes and results.

The use of anonymity in public consultations, as compared to social sciences, is discussed by Maja Sawicka and Anna Przybylska in chapter 3, "The Online Anonymity Controversy: Theoretical Considerations and Practical Implications for the InDialogue Platform." The authors present a set of conceptual approaches to the issue of anonymity as well as the social and political consequences of the disclosure or the lack of disclosure of personal data of participants in public consultations. They also discuss practical solutions for the process of verifying participants, which can include their geo-localization, the use of systems operated by e-administrations, or identity numbers. In the inDialogue platform the ID number is an essential, although not always used, component in the verification of participants; its use depends on the subject matter and the data gathering methodology. Citizens can be anonymous or, if the circumstances warrant it, known to each other by their names and surnames.

For the software to meet the accessibility requirements for people with disabilities and, in fact, the requirement of openness of participation without prejudices; it is essential that developers work hand-in-hand with experts in the WCAG field. Even though ICT accessibility standards are publicly acknowledged and formally adopted by institutions, they are not always respected or applied to ICT tools for group communication. Bartosz Stępień and Jacek Zadrożny in chapter 4, "Where ICT Meets Disability," present these standards, explain what they mean for the software's design, show the results of preliminary tests of the inDialogue application, and recommend solutions for the problems found. The problems that were diagnosed related to the contrast level of a few of the elements on the page, and the visibility of the focus frame. Resolving these errors has improved the accessibility of the platform.

Further, in chapter 5, "ICT Solutions for Voice Moderated Debates," Robert Bembenik, Anna Przybylska, Aneta Świercz, and Jacek Zadrożny describe the criteria that they have adopted to assess the ICT applications supporting voice communication, along with the results of their analysis. The evaluation criteria have been divided into—technical aspects that have consequences for the accessibility of ICT tools, especially for people with disabilities; cost; and some features that may strengthen deliberation during online meetings. The tool that has met more criteria than any other is the open source, TeamTalk 5. The project team recommended its integration with the inDialogue platform after the optimization of some features. These improvements concerned, for example, accessibility for blind people through labelling function buttons so that they could be recognized by screen readers, as well as some indications concerning the order of participants wanting to join a debate, which facilitates turn-taking.

Paweł Tymiński and Marta Kołodziejska in chapter 6, "Usability Testing of the InDialogue Platform," posit that usability testing is one of the most effective methods of verifying how real users experience a piece of software. They outline the design and results of tests conducted on the inDialogue application. Among those who tested the first version of the platform were clerks from partner towns or city halls responsible for public consultations as well as people with different categories of disabilities. The tests were the basis for the prototype's further development. The chapter concludes that certain elements (buttons and fields), functions (the actions of the citizen) and sequences of actions (i.e., the in-built procedures) of the platform were incomprehensible and/or inaccessible, or that their purpose was unclear to users. Users' suggestions as well as reported issues, were then used to improve the prototype of the software, which led to the creation of the pilot version of the inDialogue platform.

The software's usability is evaluated not only from the point of view of its proper features but also from the point of view of its adaptability. Tomasz Kulisiewicz discusses this practical issue in chapter 7, "Integrating the InDialogue Platform into the Local Administration ICT Environment." He studies the main aspects of the interoperability between the inDialogue software and the ICT systems used in local public administration, in particular document management systems (DMS). He points out that the integration of the inDialogue software with IT systems like DMSs would increase the efficacy of information circulation processes and information availability, as well as the quality of the processed information due to the use of proofing tools and the avoidance of typing errors. The main obstacle to this is the established practice of dealing with all tasks separately, as well as the high rate of non-machine readable documents used in public administration.

The usability tests applied to the inDialogue software in laboratory conditions were followed by tests in a real-life environment. These were performed during public consultations in partner institutions; one of these was Olsztyn's City Hall. Radosław Sierocki, in chapter 8, addresses the question of "How ICT Tools Intervene in Public Consultations" using data from the Olsztyn case study. The author compares the ICT tools created on demand for the local authorities in Olsztyn with the inDialogue application to draw conclusions about the consequences of their use for the public consultations processes and their results. He notes that participants using the inDialogue tools contributed to the debate with substantive arguments and obeyed the rules of civil dialogue, which was not necessarily the case in previous internet debates. At the same time, he observed a low number of participants. Further investigation is needed to see if both effects will continue; and if there is a method to encourage participation.

The mass media is still the prime source of information on local issues in medium and large cities. But do they perform the role of educators or watchdogs where new modes of institutionalized public participation are concerned? Does the idea of public journalism engaging the local community in local issues and projects, appeal to them? Marta Kołodziejska and Klementyna Świeżewska in chapter 9, "Public Consultations in Media Narratives. The Case of Olsztyn and Nowa Dęba," analyze the local media's discourse on public consultations in two Polish municipalities that participated in the testing of the inDialogue software. The key finding is that public consultations are represented in local media narratives, not as a multi-level process, but rather as a single event; and that media, while focusing on the basic facts about the consultation, neither engage citizens in a democratic debate, nor contribute to their knowledge about the purpose and meaning of public consultations.

In chapter 10, "Opportunities and Barriers to the Use of the InDialogue Platform by Local Government Administration," Tomasz Potkański discusses the applicability of the inDialogue tools for public consultations from the perspective of a local government practitioner who represents an association of cities. He briefly describes models of governance in public administration in order to analyze how our proposed ICT tools for public consultation correspond with the changes in the functioning of Polish city halls. He expects local public administration to make the necessary initial investment in time to learn the new procedures in order to substantially improve internal communication as well as the preparatory process and the reporting of results from public consultations. These improvements would be particularly beneficial in the areas of spatial and investment planning. The author concludes that the new approach to public consultations that are based on deliberation is a must in order to rebuild social trust and overcome the social, economic, and ecological problems in our communities.

In the closing remarks, "Factors for the Absorption of Innovation," Anna Przybylska traces the course of action after the In Dialogue project finishes. By the end of 2017, pilot studies in eight municipalities will have been completed, and the implementation version of the inDialogue software will have been prepared. The fact that the software has been developed in communication with potential institutional users facilitates amendments to it. Based on prior experience, we share with the readers of this volume some valuable information on the factors that are important to inDialogue's implementation in public administration. These concern establishing partnership relations with local government administration, a clear division of roles among institutional partners and inside city or town halls, ongoing evaluation and the actions based on its results, the involvement of mass media and social organizations for scaling-up effect in the larger public sphere, choosing a long-term strategy for support by a national *umbrella institution* or a network of regional institutions in regards to servicing and development of the inDialogue platform along with changes in the law or other IT systems.

References

Arterton, F. Christopher. 1987. *Teledemocracy. Can Technology Protect Democracy?* Newbury Park: SAGE.

Coleman, Stephen, and Peter Shane, eds. 2012. *Connecting Democracy. Online Consultation and the Flow of Political Communication*. Cambridge, MA: The MIT Press.

Davies, Todd, and Reid Chandler. 2012. "Online Deliberation Design: Choices, Criteria, and Evidence." In *Democracy in Motion: Evaluating the Practice and Impact of Deliberative Civic Engagement*, edited by Tina Nabatchi, John Gastil, G. Michael Weiksner, and Matt Leighninger, 103–131. Oxford: Oxford University Press.

Davies, Todd, and Sweeta Pena Gangadharan, eds. 2009. *Online Deliberation. Design, Research, and Practice.* Stanford, CA: CSLI Publications.

Klein, Mark, and Gregorio Convertino. 2015. "A Roadmap for Open Innovation Systems." *Journal of Social Media* 2 (1). Accessed June 18, 2017. http://www2.mitre.org/public/jsmo/pdfs/02-01-roadmap.pdf.

Lathrop, Daniel, and Laurel Ruma, eds. 2010. *Open Government. Collaboration, Transparency, and Participation in Practice.* Sebastopol, CA: O'Reilly.

Nabatchi, Tina. 2014. "Deliberative Civic Engagement in Public Administration and Policy." *Journal of Public Deliberation* 10 (1), Article 21. Accessed June 18, 2017. http://www.publicdeliberation.net/jpd/vol10/iss1/art21.

Noveck, Beth. 2009. *Wiki Government. How Technology Can Make Government Better, Democracy Stronger, and Citizens More Powerful.* Washington, DC: Bookings Institution Press.

Reason, Peter, and Hilary Bradbury, eds. 2008. *The SAGE Handbook of Action Research. Participative Inquiry and Practice.* London: SAGE Publications.

Stromer-Galley, Jennifer, Nick Webb, and Peter Muhlberger. 2012. "Deliberative E-Rulemaking Project: Challenges to Enacting Real World Deliberation." *Journal of Information Technology & Politics* 9 (1): 82–96, DOI: 10.1080/19331681.2012.635971.

Van Dijk, Jan. 1996. "Models of Democracy: behind the Design and Use of New Media in Politics." *Javnost/The Public* 1: 43–56.

Jacek Haman

Chapter 1. Social Research and Public Consultations

Introduction

To answer the question about the relationship between social research and public consultation, we must first answer an auxiliary question—how do we understand the term *research*. By the term research we refer here to the process of acquiring knowledge carried out according to the rules of scientific methodology. So research is distinguished, firstly by a specific, strictly cognitive goal, and secondly by the specific rules governing it; subordinated to the objective of getting reliable and systematic knowledge—because these are the foundations of scientific method.

Conducting *social research*, as it is understood, is not the exclusive domain of academic institutions. Public opinion polls or market research conducted on behalf of commercial entities by commercial, specialized research centers, also meets the above definition. A good consumer survey, in terms of methodology, will not differ much from a scientific study: the aim of both is to gain reliable knowledge. The differences between academic and commercial research are: the reasons why this knowledge is being collected, its subsequent use, and its availability to others. The results of scientific studies are made available to the public, but when done for commercial purposes, often kept a company secret.

However, there are some differences between the rules for conducting commercial research and scientific research. In the case of commercial research, there is sometimes a relaxation of certain methodological rules. This frequently has a negative impact on the quality of the results. Accepting a loosening of methodological requirements is often an effect of customer ignorance; good methodology in many cases also means more expensive methodology, but the savings often turn out to be illusory. On the other hand, in some circumstances, the entrepreneur or manager does not need very detailed or precise information and will accept data that is collected faster and cheaper, but less accurately. So reducing the costs of research, even at the expense of its quality, may be legitimate business as long as the contractors are fully aware of the consequences of their choices. The latter case, however, requires an especially good methodological knowledge to really measure what is more profitable.

I have started with a comparison between academic and commercial research because public consultations are, in many ways, closer to commercial research (market research and opinion polls) than to classical university research, but at the same time, and in several aspects, it is closer to academic research. Consultation does not concern *fundamental issues* or very general questions, but specific issues usually related to the consumption and availability of *public goods*. In this respect, consultations are close to consumer surveys (often including the temptation to relax methodology). However, they are conducted by entities acting in the interests of society, and even, more precisely, the interests of the communities participating in the consultation. This makes them closer to academic studies, which are also conducted in the broadly defined public interest—to expand general knowledge.

But above all, what I want to emphasize in this chapter is that public consultations are something fundamentally different from social research, at least in some respects.

Research and Consultation: Similarities and Differences

Public consultation is a way of acquiring knowledge about the views, opinions and needs of citizens, usually in relation to the provision of some form of public goods. Such public goods can be public services, cultural institutions, infrastructure, but also the landscape and the environment (requiring protection), public safety (requiring assurance), etc. In this sense, consultations provide similar information to consumer research. Whether the subject of the study is to examine the needs of consumers with respect to washing detergent, or the needs of residents in relation to public space, is of little importance to the ways in which these needs are tested. Just as a secondary point, the purpose of commercial consumer research is to increase business profits, and the goal of the consultation is to determine the best choice for local authorities concerning what is most favorable for residents. In both cases, valuable information can only be obtained if the study or consultation is being conducted in accordance with state of the art methodology and practice. Also, the dilemmas faced by the researcher or the consultation organizer that are related to ensuring the representativeness of the study, or ensuring anonymity, data protection, and so on, will be the same.

Consultations are a form of research, but they are also more than just research. There are three important areas where consultation differs from social and market research:

- *Legal environment*. The principles of consultation and the consultation's functions, as a part of the system of local democracy, are often governed by separate legal regulations; we may agree with them or not, but we must respect them.
- *Purpose*. The aim of scientific research is strictly cognitive—to provide information. The objectives of the consultation are broader: consultations are a form of participatory democracy. So next to the cognitive aim, consultation contributes to objectives of a political nature.
- *Subject*. The subject[1] of research—both scientific and commercial—is always the researcher. The subject of consultations are citizens, the local community.

I will not deal with particular legal issues; instead, I will turn our attention to some broader problems. Of course, when conducting social research, we have to obey the law (for example the law on the Protection of Personal Data)[2] but in general, it is not for the legislature to decide who, how and for what reasons, research will be done. These are decisions for the investigator, subject to his scientific curiosity or business needs. In the case of a public consultation, the situation is different in two respects.

First, it is the law that forces public authorities to conduct consultations in certain situations. In Poland, the obligation of public consultation is provided by various laws, including, for example, the law concerning local self-government at the municipality,[3] county,[4] and regional levels[5] (the obligation to consult with residents on projects for combining, splitting or other changes to local government units), the act for principles of development policy[6] as well as the law on spatial

1 In this chapter, subject/subjectivity is used in the following specific definition: *a subject*, broadly meaning an entity that has agency, meaning that it acts upon or wields power over some other entity (an object); *subjectivity*: the quality or condition of something being a subject, as in the above meaning (see https://en.wikipedia.org/wiki/Subjectivity, accessed February 22, 2017).

2 In the Polish case: "Ustawa z dn. 29 sierpnia 1997. o ochronie danych osobowych" ("Personal Data Protection Act of August 29, 1997") as amended (*Journal of Laws* of 2016 item 922).

3 "Ustawa z dnia 8 marca 1990 roku o samorządzie gminnym", *Journal of Laws* of 1990, 16, item 95 as amended.

4 "Ustawa z dnia 5 czerwca 1998 roku o samorządzie powiatowym", *Journal of Laws* of 1998, 91, item 578 as amended.

5 "Ustawa z dnia 5 czerwca 1998 roku o samorządzie województwa", *Journal of Laws* of 1998, 91, item 576 as amended.

6 "Ustawa z dnia 6 grudnia 2006 roku o zasadach prowadzenia polityki rozwoju", *Journal of Laws* of 2006, 227, item 1658 as amended.

planning,[7] and a number of other legal acts (Zychowicz 2014, 34ff). By imposing this obligation it may also impose certain restrictions or formulate mandatory guidelines as to how they are to be conducted.[8] As a result, this can lead to a situation where a solution (e.g., consultations using a random sample, and therefore excluding non-sampled residents), whilst being methodologically justified, is in direct conflict with the law, or could be the basis for legal action taken against the authority conducting the consultations. Even if the case was eventually won in court, it could be associated with a deterioration in the atmosphere surrounding the consultation or result in a lower level of social trust. This in no way means that the representative method (or any other scientific and reliable method) should be ruled out as a tool for public consultation. We need to be aware, however, that its use may be associated with problems that would not be faced by the researcher conducting research for cognitive purposes only.

On the other hand, the public body must not only act within the law, as any other institution or individual must, but must also undertake their initiatives after having justified a legal basis for them. As for the researcher–scientist, or researcher–marketing specialist, the law is merely the factor that defines limits that should not be exceeded and they can draw inspiration for the study from their own interests or needs; while in contrast, the public authority conducting a consultation must consider whether a particular action is directly authorized by law. For example, although Polish law permits local authorities to carry out consultations concerning matters of importance to local communities, and determining how they should be conducted, the organizers of the consultation may, however, lack a legal basis for taking certain actions, such as imposing on the participants of the consultation an obligation to take additional measures or to meet certain conditions, even if this would foster a more reliable selection of authorized participants and obtain more reliable results.

But let's leave the legal issues to competent lawyers and instead concentrate on the consequences of the differences in purpose and subject between research and consultation.

---

7 "Ustawa z dnia 27 marca 2003 roku o planowaniu i zagospodarowaniu przestrzennym", *Journal of Laws* of 2003, 80, item 717.

8 For example: the law on spatial planning in art. 11. determines how to consult with residents about local plans. The law on the principles of development policy in the art. 6 rules on the consultation of the development strategy. In both cases, the law provides for compulsory publicly announced and consulted projects, with a call for opinions and desiderata. Thus, in these cases, the use of, for example, a representative method as a tool for consultation is excluded from the outset.

The similarity between the objectives of research and consultation determines the similarity of the measures applied and the need to adapt them to the same methodological requirements. However, consultation sets itself much broader goals than research. Consultation, in addition to delivering public information about the needs and views of citizens, also has a political function. It is a form of participatory democracy, a tool for the implementation of citizens' subjectivity and their right to influence the decisions and actions of public authorities and express their opinions and demands. This means that the consultations' assumptions, their organization and the course they follow must be set for the fulfilment of these objectives.

Can both these objectives—to provide information (for a public authority), and to enable citizens to participate in the exercise of power—be carried out simultaneously without harm to each other, or are they in conflict? I do not think that there is a fundamental contradiction between the two, but the implementation of the *political function* requires the commitment of additional financial and organizational resources, when taking into account that *political constraints* may limit the use of certain methods.

Perhaps the most important difference between research and consultation, is the difference in the subject of the action. While the *host* of a study is the researcher, in the case of a consultation the organizer acts only as an agent for the entire community and is responsible to it.

Even if the final objective of a study is to benefit the local community, its subject is the researcher:

- This researcher defines the objectives of the study and determines the choice of tools.
- The outcome of the researcher's effort—the survey results—are evaluated only by other competent specialists, and their assessment is primarily substantive.
- The researcher should abide by the general law and relevant codes of ethics,[9] but basically has a lot of flexibility in proceedings with the respondents (as long as he does not act to their detriment) e.g. he or she does not always have to inform them in detail of what is being done or why.

The subject of consultations are citizens—the local community:

- The consultation's organizer determines its goals and procedures, but the results and the legitimacy of the consultation are subject to the entire community, and its assessment can be of a political nature.

9 For example, the code of ethics by ICC/ESOMAR for market researchers, or the code of ethics by the International Sociological Association.

- The consultation process must be fully transparent and (if possible) fully understood by the participants, which often involves people who are not experts in methodology or social research. Even methodologically perfect consultations are of no value if the participants do not have the feeling that their voice counts.

In many cases, especially when the research concerns socially sensitive issues, or those in which the respondent may have a vested interest in giving a specific (albeit not necessarily true) answer to the question, more reliable results can be obtained using non-direct questions—in some cases without revealing the actual purpose of the study. For example, if we want to determine whether residents will use a planned public facility (e.g., a park, or sports stadium) often enough to socially justify the public spending, then we must take into consideration the fact that the respondents, knowing that the investment will only be completed based on their responses, will express a much greater interest in it; after all, it is nice to have a park in the neighborhood, even if one visits it only a few times a year. In such situations, more reliable results are obtained by asking the questions in a context that suggests there is no relation between the study and the planned investment. It is a completely correct way, also in ethical terms, of conducting research, but it seems completely inappropriate for public consultation.

Similarly, the fact that the host of the public consultation is a community, not a researcher, excludes tools that require the use of sophisticated statistical analysis or psychological manipulation: the results can be simply incomprehensible to members of the consulted community, and its members may raise doubts as to whether the conclusions of the consultation have been drawn correctly. On the other hand, in the case of scientific research we can expect the same level of professionalism from its critics as is expected of the researcher, while in the case of consultations the whole process should be understandable for the average person.

Consequently, we have a much wider choice of research tools for conducting research than is the case for public consultation. This could lead to higher costs (e.g., when a representative poll has to be given up for an exhaustive survey) or a lower quality of results (when a less adequate tool has to be used) and often, both.

Research and Consultations: Common Methodological Issues

To achieve the *cognitive goals* of the consultation, its procedures must meet the same methodological requirements as scientific studies. A full description of these would require writing of a complete handbook on the methodology of social research, but let's look at the problem from the other side. There are *critical errors* that would prevent, or at least significantly restrict, the ability to interpret the results of consultations; these we have to avoid.

Each research procedure (and thus also public consultation if they are also to be treated as a way of obtaining knowledge about the views and needs of citizens) must be preceded by defining the objectives of the study and the formulation of research questions. A common mistake committed by inexperienced researchers is to confuse *research questions* with the *questions posed to respondents*. The research question is the question that a researcher sets themselves, and to which the researcher has to provide answers to by analyzing the data obtained in the study (qualitative or quantitative). If we are interested in simple facts, perhaps the questions posed to respondents will refer to them directly, but in many cases the relationship between the research questions and questions in the questionnaire will be much more complex. For example, if the research question is "What is the optimal network for trams?", do not ask the respondent "What network of trams do you consider optimal?" It is much better to ask which routes the respondent travels most frequently. On the basis of answers to such questions, we will be able to answer the question about what network connections best meet the needs of passengers. So, to construct a proper grid of connections would require the involvement of engineers who are specialists in public transport; it should, therefore, be obvious that it makes no sense to put such questions directly to people who, although they have a vested interest in the operation of public transport, have neither the knowledge nor the data necessary to give them a meaningful answer.

The above example may seem unrealistic, but unfortunately this type of error may be encountered surprisingly often in social studies. In the case of public consultation the risk is even greater. To ask the question "What should be the final decision?" and not finding the reasons for its adoption can serve as a way for the officials responsible (and being paid) for taking it, to avoid responsibility. Meanwhile, asking people questions that they cannot competently answer is both a methodological error, and an operation only illusorily consistent with the spirit of democracy.

Another critical error that, as a rule, makes a study worthless is the use of inappropriate methods for investigating a given research question; in particular the case of attempting to answer a *quantitative question* using qualitative methods. I will discuss this problem in detail in the section devoted to the issue of representativeness in research and consultation. Often the opportunity for committing such mistakes occurs when we need to know *exact numbers* (i.e., *how many* of the respondents share a particular opinion), but we do not have the technical or financial capacity to carry out a quantitative study on a *representative sample*.

Unfortunately, in such cases we must simply accept the fact that the question cannot be answered, and even if we try to answer it using inappropriate methods, the numbers and data we get in return will be useless.

The Representativeness of Research and Consultation

The concept of *representativeness* is essential for the assessment of both social research and public consultation in all the cases where the research or consultation has not covered the whole community. Representativeness means, generally speaking, the generalization of findings that are formulated on the basis of research or consultation with a part of a community so that it refers to the whole community (Frankfort-Nachmias and Nachmias 2008, 167).

We should remember, however, that the research questions may vary and, consequently the research methods that entitle the generalization of answers to certain questions, may not entitle a generalized response to other questions. There is therefore no single, universal meaning of representativeness.

If the research questions are qualitative in nature, and therefore relate to the mapping of needs and views, the indications of problems existing in the community, or a description of the positions of various disputing parties or interest groups; but with no intention of determining their coverage, or even a relative comparison of their popularity; it is enough that the sample is representative in *qualitative terms*. The sample (i.e., invited or authorized participants in the consultation) is required to cover all the significant positions in the (potential) dispute, groups of interest, and types of stakeholders; but there is no requirement for the proportions of individual types in the sample to correspond exactly to their participation in the community.

By conducting qualitative research, we can use a *purposive sample*; that is one in which the researcher or the consultation's organizer, after initially identifying the existing types of stakeholders, invites the stakeholders' representatives to participate in the study, but taking care to ensure that all categories of the participants are represented. In this case, *self-recruitment* of the consultation participants is also acceptable, as long as reliable information about the planned consultation is provided to all those who are potentially interested. Auto-selection is one of the natural solutions used where participants have an interest in participating in a study, and the essence of the public consultation is precisely that they relate to issues potentially important for those being consulted. In the case of research not related to issues that are directly relevant to the participants, an appropriate form of selection will involve increased activity for the investigator.

On the other hand, the purposive sample, or the sample selected by self-recruitment, does not authorize the formulating of any conclusion of a quantitative nature. Even if 90% of the people in our sample are in favor of option A, it does not entitle us to conclude that the majority of the entire community support solution A. It is possible that such high support within the sample resulted from the fact that the supporters of solution A were easier to reach, or it may be that proponents of solution A are better organized, or it could even be that they were deliberately organized and motivated by someone concerned about the result of the consultation. A generalization of the result obtained through such a sample would expose the researcher, on the one hand, to an accusation of manipulation (perhaps unintentional), if the over-representation of supporters of one of the positions has been allowed; while on the other hand, the risk of manipulation by a better-organized group of interests. But even if the proponents of position A were actually overrepresented in the sample, and even if it was the result of someone's deliberate action, we are fully entitled to conclude that within the community there are those who support solution. A who use such and such arguments (Of course, even in a strictly qualitative study in situations where the sample proportions are significantly different from what is happening in the population, this is definitely unfavorable).

However, if the questions are of a quantitative nature (for example, how many people advocate a particular position or what is the ranking of the proposed solutions) the requirements for the representativeness of the sample are substantially greater.

The sample can be reasonably regarded as representative (in a quantitative meaning) only if it is a *random sample* or if the survey is exhaustive (i.e., covers the entire community). A random sample is a sample chosen in such a way that *each unit belonging to the surveyed population has a known and non-zero probability of being selected* (Lissowski et al. 2011).[10] The probabilistic character of a random sample allows for the results to be generalized and applied to the entire community by applying the rules of statistical inference and, therefore, also to the statistical evaluation of the uncertainty associated with the fact that we have not examined the entire population but only part of it (determination of confidence intervals and standard errors). A substitute for the random sample is the *quota sample*, in which participants are selected in a way that their particular categories (e.g., age groups, gender, education, place of residence) are represented in the same proportions as they are in the general population. However, the quality of such a sample is always limited and uncertain—we do not know what criteria finally decided

10 For a description of different kinds of random (probabilistic) samples and non-random (quota or purposive) samples (see, e.g., David and Sutton 2004, 226ff; Babbie 2016, 191ff).

the inclusion of the units in the sample. Surveys based on a quota sample are in many cases much less expansive and easier to conduct than those based on the classical random sample, so the decision to use a quota sample instead of a random sample may be the effect of a reasonable *cost–quality* deal. In contrast, purposive samples, *snowball samples*, various forms of *accidental selection*, or samples based on self-recruitment can never be accepted as a representative sample for quantitative analysis or for answering questions of a quantitative nature.

It should be realized that *quantitative representativeness* can only be found where the collectivity is defined in a clear manner, and when the *weight* or *importance* of each individual in the community is strictly defined (in most cases all are equal). It a priori, excludes representative (quantitative) research and consultations on many issues; for example, if we want to determine the support for local investment, which brings social benefits to all but is also burdensome for the nearest neighbors, we need to accurately define the community in which we are committing the study: whether the opinion of the inhabitants of neighboring buildings should have the same weight as that of a person who lives two streets away. If we are not able to resolve such issues clearly, we should not attempt to answer the quantitative questions. We have to limit ourselves to qualitative analysis and qualitative questions so as to gather existing positions, describe the reasons behind these differing opinions, but without trying to describe how they are distributed.

The reference to the representativeness achieved by the use of a random sample means that part of the community (those not drawn in the sample) seem not to be included in the study. How can a procedure in which we ask for the opinion of just some of the concerned residents, while others are not allowed to speak, be considered a form of the implementation of participatory democracy based on the principle of the equality of citizens? Can this be reconciled with the universality of the right to participate in consultation? I can indicate arguments for the fact that this right is not violated: anyone could be drawn, also, everyone is represented in the consultation at least by randomly selected people with similar views or interests; a priori, the procedure itself does not favor anybody. Research carried out on representative samples—especially on random samples—provides knowledge about the *entire* population, including those who were not sampled. Moreover, in many cases (when an exhaustive study is not feasible) this is the only way to provide reliable data on the distribution of opinion in the population.

The tradition of social research based on random samples has also been accepted in the theory of democracy in the form of the concept of *mini-publics* or *mini-populus*, first postulated by Dahl (1989, 340) and developed by the theorists of deliberative democracy (see Grönlund et al. 2014). But the acceptance of this approach, not only as a research method, but also as a legitimate method of the democratic expression of opinion (and even decision-making) by the major theorists of democracy does not guarantee that it will find full understanding by the *ordinary citizens*. In the case of a public consultation it is not only important that the researcher is right, but also whether the community can be convinced that the researcher is right. The procedures referring only to the testing a random sample, even if methodologically correct and justified, may not raise sufficient confidence among citizens in some cases. In the worst-case scenario such a procedure may even be questioned by lawyers.

The issues of selection and self-selection in research and consultation are essential both for the results obtained, as well as for the correct implementation of the political functions of consultation. Unfortunately, what is good for the cognitive objectives, is sometimes bad for achieving political goals, and vice versa. The selection of respondents can rely on a random sample or on a purposive sample, and if properly carried out this is a methodologically correct procedure for obtaining reliable results, which can then be generalized to reflect the entire population. The self-selection of respondents generally makes the results impossible to interpret or to exclude any interpretations, except the most general conclusions of a qualitative nature. A selection carried out by the organizer of the consultation—especially a purposeful, non-random selection—may, however, limit its value as a tool in participatory democracy. At the same time, the self-selection of participants, when resignation from participation in a consultation is the free decision of the individual, is politically, absolutely acceptable.

The preservation of the representativeness of a quantitative poll requires that the opinions of persons not selected for the sample be absolutely disregarded. On the other hand, every citizen should have the right to express their opinions. The solution to this dilemma seems to be to combine the quantitative and the qualitative approaches: for quantitative analyses, only data (answers) collected from persons selected for the sample should be used; but everyone should have the opportunity to express their views, and each statement should be included in the qualitative analysis. In this way the methodological rules will be maintained, and the organizer of the consultation will be protected against the dangers of a legal challenge against its actions.

Anonymity

In social research the anonymity of respondents is a common principle. This rule is supported by practical, ethical, and legal arguments (processing anonymous data does not need to be adapted to the requirements of the troublesome protection of personal data). Finally, in many cases, thanks to the guarantee of anonymity, we can count on the sincerity of the respondents.

However, should the same rules apply to consultation? Here I do not want to formulate too explicit an opinion. This issue is largely a matter of law, and each case should be examined by a lawyer who is competent in personal data protection law. However, it seems that there are substantial differences between research and consultation that justify a different approach to the issue of anonymity.

In my opinion this results from the following reasons:

- Participation in a consultation is a form of participation in the exercise of power—and with power comes responsibility. In the case of participation in a survey (scientific or commercial) the participant does not have any obligation to the investigator, nor shall they be liable to accountability.
- The results of a consultation can determine whether a public authority adopts conclusions that may be favorable to part of the community and negative for others. This creates a risk that the course of the consultation will be manipulated by interest groups. It must, therefore, be possible to verify whether the persons who participate in a consultation are authorized to do so.

On the other hand, the consultation process can be likened to an election procedure in which the principle of the secrecy of voting—beyond the verification of the right to vote—is of fundamental importance. Any information about the political views of citizens, including their position on issues of local politics, are treated as *sensitive data* and are subject to special protection. A public authority is not allowed to collect data, or demand any information that would help it *to identify* supporters or opponents. On this basis the Polish judiciary favors the anonymity of consultation procedures, as in the examples of the judgments by the Supreme Administrative Court of 5 November 2015 (Ref. II OSK 518/14) and the Constitutional Court of 26 February 2003. (Ref. K 30/02). If their positions are not too radical—which can be a matter of discussion—but only theoretically, the law must be followed.

However, it is important to realize that the very notion of anonymity in social research is operationalized in different ways: there are various *levels* of anonymity.

The first distinction concerns *anonymity* versus *confidentiality*. Anonymity implies that the identity of the respondents is not known to the researcher at all, or more precisely that the researcher does not have any way of linking the data to a specific person. Confidentiality implies only that the respondents have guarantees that the information that allows a specific person to be associated with specific data collected in the study will never be publicly disclosed (see Babbie 2016, 67). From the point of view of a researcher, applying the principles of confidentiality in place of anonymity can both simplify the research procedures and facilitate the validation of the survey.

It is also important, that data can be anonymous even if the research has not been anonymous from the very beginning. The data can also be anonymized in a later phase of a study (i.e., after the end of the fieldwork, or after the end of the validation of the fieldwork) so in the earlier phases subjects had guaranteed confidentiality of their data, but when the personal data are no longer needed, they are destroyed and the data collected in the study becomes anonymous data.

Such practices carried out by academic researchers may become the basis for the development (in consultation with lawyers) of the procedures for public consultation, which will guarantee both the effectiveness of the consultation process, limit the risk of manipulation by organized interest groups, and at the same time be in accordance with the law (and the expectations of the courts). Let's add the fact that neither the requirements of the law, or practices of the courts should be treated here only as ballast and limitations; they serve the very important task of protecting individual rights to privacy and to participate freely in public affairs.

The case, therefore, is not clear and each situation should be analyzed separately. It seems, however, that you can reject the position of demanding a full guarantee of anonymity of anyone who requests it in any situation.

Conclusion

The dichotomy of research–consultation is not an absolute one. Some activities may be difficult to classify clearly, especially if you look from the perspective of an outside observer. I omit here issues of a legal nature, so perhaps in certain situations, whether the action is considered a *consultation* or *research* may stem from the law. Such a distinction is not relevant if we are interested in the value of the information obtained and if correct methodological procedures are applied.

Similar cognitive goals impose common methodological requirements on social research and public consultations. At the same time, specific political functions and legal restrictions have to be taken into account when we plan any process of consultation. The fact that certain things cannot be done does not mean, however, that it is acceptable to omit them. If, due to legal reasons, for example, we reject the possibility of implementing a consultation on a random sample of citizens, we must, therefore, accept its failure to obtain answers to questions of a quantitative nature.

A study in which the researcher is the subject, and a community only the object of research, does not meet the political objectives of consultation, and they are not a form of the implementation of the subjectivity of citizens. Consultations may be less efficient at answering research questions due to the restrictions I have mentioned above. Thus, neither does research replace consultation, nor are consultations a substitute for research. Although their goals overlap, and although they may employ similar methods, there are still significant differences between the two.

It is necessary to adhere to the rules of social research methodology in preparing good consultations, but not all of its requirements can be met over the course of the consultation. Knowing what you can and what you cannot achieve within the given procedures, however, is as important as knowing how to act in order to achieve what is achievable.

References

Books and articles

Babbie, Earl. 2016. *The Basics of Social Research*. Balmond, CA: Wadsworth, Cengage Learning.

Dahl, Robert A. 1989. *Democracy and its Critics*. New Haven, CT and London: Yale University Press.

David, Matthew, and Carole D. Sutton. 2004. *Social Research: An Introduction*. Los Angeles, CA: SAGE.

Frankfort-Nachmias, Chava, and David Nachmias. 2008. *Research Methods in the Social Sciences*. New York: Worth Publishers.

Grönlund, Kimmo, Andrè Bächtiger, and Maija Setälä, eds. 2014. *Deliberative Mini-Publics: Involving Citizens in the Democratic Process*. Colchester: ECPR Press.

Lissowski, Grzegorz, Jacek Haman, Mikołaj Jasiński. 2011. *Podstawy statystyki dla socjologów*. Warsaw: Scholar.

Zychowicz, Zbigniew. 2014. *Konsultacje społeczne w samorządzie*. Szczecin: Instytut Rozwoju Regionalnego.

Legal sources

"Ustawa z dnia 8 marca 1990 roku o samorządzie gminnym." *Journal of Laws* of 1990, 16, item 95.

"Ustawa z dnia 29 sierpnia 1997 o ochronie danych osobowych" (as amended). *Journal of Laws* of 2016, item 922.

"Ustawa z dnia 5 czerwca 1998 roku o samorządzie powiatowym." *Journal of Laws* of 1998, 91, item 578.

"Ustawa z dnia 5 czerwca 1998 roku o samorządzie województwa." *Journal of Laws* of 1998, 91, item 576.

"Ustawa z dnia 27 marca 2003 roku o planowaniu i zagospodarowaniu przestrzennym." *Journal of Laws* of 2003, 80, item 717.

"Ustawa z dnia 6 grudnia 2006 roku o zasadach prowadzenia polityki rozwoju." *Journal of Laws* of 2006, 227, item 1658.

"Wyrok z dnia 26 lutego 2003. Zgodność z Konstytucją oraz Europejską Kartą Samorządu Terytorialnego art. 2 ust. 1 ustawy o referendum lokalnym, Ref. K30/02". *Orzecznictwo Trybunału Konstytucyjnego. Zbiór Urzędowy*, 2A, item 16.

"Wyrok z dnia 5 listopada 2015 Ref. NSA II OSK 518/14". Accessed July 11, 2016. http://orzeczenia.nsa.gov.pl/doc/64FA4075EC.

Others

ESOMAR and International Chamber of Commerce. 2016. "ICC/ESOMAR International Code on Market and Social Research". *esomar.com.* Accessed July 11, 2016. https://www.esomar.org/uploads/public/knowledge-and-standards/codes-and-guidelines/ICCESOMAR_Code_English_.pdf.

International Sociological Association. 2001. "International Sociological Association Code of Ethics". *isa.sociology.com.* Accessed July 11, 2016. http://www.isa-sociology.org/en/about-isa/code-of-ethics/.

Anna Przybylska

Chapter 2. ICT Solutions for Public Consultations: Methodology and Design of the InDialogue Platform

Introduction

The aim of this chapter is to reflect on the design of the inDialogue software, which has been developed to intervene in the organization of public consultation processes. The design of the platform has been informed by the results of empirical studies. In these studies, we evaluated the practice of public consultations in Poland, referring to the norms that constitute a model of deliberative consultation. The inDialogue software is expected to respond appropriately to the problems revealed during the evaluation.

This chapter starts with an overview of some of the theoretical assumptions and associated research findings that are relevant to the institutionalization of deliberation in public consultations. The following section analyzes the empirical data collected from Polish local governments. Against this background, I discuss the tools and procedures of the inDialogue software.

Deliberation in the Institutional Setting

Public consultations are a weak but institutionally embedded form of civic participation. Their value is dependent on methodological design and a particular concern for collecting citizens' opinions that would refer to reliable information and competing arguments (Fishkin 2009).

In considering deliberative public consultations, I will address three areas of tension. First, tension occurs when the institutions of representative and participatory democracy are being integrated (Edwards 2012). Second, in the institutions of representative and participatory democracy, tension becomes apparent between the ideal of deliberation and the results of its implementation (Johnson and Gastil 2015). Lastly, tension occurs when attempting to create a consolidated venue for public dialogue in a world of dispersed communication channels (Gastil 2016).

The model of participatory democracy gives significance to the participation of ordinary citizens in public problem-solving. The main rational is that they have the best knowledge concerning the needs of their communities and that they are the most efficient source for finding and applying adequate measures to achieve the public good. This can be done independently from government through civil society initiatives or in cooperation with government when it allocates tasks to civic organizations (Held 2006).

Meanwhile, in the public discourse, we also hear voices demanding the empowerment of lay citizens, particularly in local communities, by leaving to them decisions within particular areas of public life or within the frames of particular public projects, for example, participatory budgeting. This approach blurs the line between representative and direct democracy. It is possible that this ambiguity regarding the roles and competences of public institutions, vis-à-vis the society, is particularly characteristic of our times, with our new centers of power as well as new forms of social mobilization and communication (Marody 2014).

Arthur Edwards (2012) writes that civic participation can be perceived as a threat, especially in the absence of objectified and publically explained models of action, the division of roles and competences. He adds that the tension between representative and participatory democracy can be reduced by developing formal connections between one and the other. Public consultations can be of this form of connection. They embody a compromise between the aspirations of lay-citizens to influence politics directly and the public officials' responsibility for the well-being of different socio-economic groups (Budge 2000; Raciborski 2011).

During public consultations, the role of citizens is to provide public officials with information about their needs and preferences regarding various aspects of public policies. There are several general norms that characterize a responsible approach to public consultations. First, the public availability of information on the subject and the methodology of consultation is the realization of the norm of transparency in democratic, participatory mechanisms. Furthermore, a clear link between a citizen's input, the outcome of public consultations, and a political decision is an element of the procedure that cannot be ignored. The public justification of decisions made in view of the collected data and arguments is necessary for the legitimacy of public consultations.

On the one hand, public consultations can be beneficial to decision-making only if public officials perceive the social contributions as pertinent, and collect them using socially and methodologically justified means. But, on the other hand, it is also important that citizens contribute meaningfully to public debate. In the opinion of scholars who have developed the model of deliberative public consultations, it is possible to meet these conditions. I would suggest that there is more interest in public consultations among scholars who refer in their work to deliberation, than among those who are concerned with civic participation—and not without reason. While the proponents of civic participation in democracy focus on the level of involvement of ordinary people in politics and their positioning in it, the proponents of deliberative democracy focus on the conditions that are conducive to good quality input into decision-making.

The research on deliberation can be divided into three areas that correspond with the organizational levels of political communication: macro (inter-institutional), meso (intra-institutional) and micro (interpersonal). Studies on public consultations can be mostly located at the meso level, even if they have conceptual links with the other two levels. Our interest in the institutionalization of deliberation in public consultations focuses on local government.

Although public consultations are initiated by political representatives, who also make the binding decision on the issue under consideration, they are governed by public administration. The stress put on political or social aspects of public consultations matters substantially to their methodology. This is discussed more broadly by Jacek Haman in Chapter 1 of this volume. The paradox of the political, open process of public consultations with minimal intervention from the official organizers is that it is often discriminatory as the voices of the disempowered are rarely heard or taken into account.

In the model of deliberative consultations, there is a clear tendency towards the use of social research methodology for reasons to do with the social inclusion and social validity of the collected information. Thus, our concern is about the level of general knowledge on social research methods and techniques among public administration staff, as well as their understanding of the need to create an environment in which participants would be capable and willing to reflect on public policy issues and express their opinions without any constraints other than respect for others.

In considering the model of deliberative consultations, several conditions have to be met in order to receive results of good quality. These encompass the following: the careful selection of participants that are representative of the different socio-economic groups, their access to impartial information, moderation providing participants with an equal chance to contribute to discussions, and the open and reciprocal exchange of arguments (for a comparison of methods see, e.g., Gastil 2008).

The moderation guidelines for methods of deliberative consultations may differ in some respects, but they also have some features in common. First, moderators are responsible for including all participants in a debate. Second, unlike focus groups in market or social research, moderators are concerned with the educational aspects of meetings. They should not, usually, introduce new information into a debate, but they should check if participants are acquainted with the information materials, refer them to the relevant information, or help them formulate questions to experts. Thus, the level of knowledge about the issue under discussion is monitored. Another important component in deliberations is the scenario in which a meeting is held that includes a set of questions or points that a moderator uses to guide participants through the discussion. It serves the aim of collecting information from participants that corresponds with the general topic and can contribute to the decision. Only then can policy-making be responsive to the views presented (Gastil and Levine 2005).

There has been an array of studies in experimental settings to verify various hypotheses about good conditions for deliberation and their results (Nabatchi et al. 2012; Geissel and Joas 2013; Grönlund et al. 2014; Coleman, Przybylska and Sintomer 2015). Many confirm at least some positive effects resulting from an environment conducive to deliberation (procedures and tools), on the behaviors of participants in public consultations (processes), and their results (knowledge gains and well-informed opinions).

These positive effects cannot be diminished by the arguments of critics saying that deliberation in public consultations, or elsewhere, is rarely observed without the intervention of various combinations of public officials, academics, and social organizations. I would argue, after Johnson and Gastil (2015), that the tension between the value-based model of deliberation and practice feeds innovation. The intervention is necessary to achieve a short-term goal of good communicative conditions, and a long-term goal for the habitual use of deliberation in various institutional, social and cultural contexts.

Along with technological development, the possibility of ICT acting in a mediating role in deliberations has also been scrutinized. Some specific conditions for online deliberations have been described in regards to, for example, synchronous vs. asynchronous communication, the different modes for expressing emotions, tools of moderation, and manifestations of social exclusion (Davies and Chandler 2012; Zhang 2015). The studies monitoring the developments in online government brought some critical issues to our attention such as the marginal role of deliberation and the dominance of e-administration over e-democracy (Melitski, Holzer et al. 2005). Then, importantly, the influence of methodology and design on the quality of results was demonstrated in empirical studies concerning local governments (Åström and Grönlund 2012). Finally, various initiatives that aspire to implement the model of online deliberative consultations have been presented and tested (Davies and Gangadharan 2009; Coleman and Shane 2012).

There are multiple examples of software that have been developed to encourage civic participation; among them are tools that can be used during public consultations and deliberations. Their general typology is presented in the introductory chapter of this volume. In these times of potentially unlimited number of channels of communication, it is not easy to recreate a public sphere that would be a meeting point for different social groups. Yet, this task has been given to the inDialogue platform, along with the task of supporting public consultation methodology planning.

The Quality of Consultation Practice in Context

In what follows I will reflect on some of the empirical findings derived from our studies on public consultations in Polish local governments that have inspired us to design ICT tools to plan and organize public consultations that are favorable to deliberation. The most substantial observations come from the period 2011 to 2014. I will refer to the results of a survey conducted in 2011, an analysis of official websites carried out in 2014, and the opinions expressed by the clerks responsible for public consultations that were collected during the workshops that took place in-between.

In Poland, some acts of law address public consultations and embed them in the institutional system of representative democracy. Acts of national law on issues of ecology or spatial planning oblige public authorities to organize public consultations, whereas the Act on Municipal Government of 1990 only recommends the inclusion of local communities in decisions regarding all issues that are of high public importance. An attempt at codifying public consultations in a separate act of law (2011/2012) was opposed by city halls, who defended their independence regarding the establishment of rules for public consultations; in fact, in past years we could observe local governments adopting resolutions that regulate the modes and methods of the conduct of public consultations. The scope of the issues that are consulted is broader than has been established by national law.

The resolutions on public consultations issued by local governments provide information about who is entitled to initiate and participate in public consultations, as well as their overall procedure. They may also enumerate methods for information gathering among citizens. Next to polls, public debates and even specific methods of deliberation like citizens' juries, are sometimes referred to in these documents. Nevertheless, these documents do not give more specific explanations about the methodology of public consultations. Thus, the quality of public consultations depends largely on the knowledge and skills of the organizers in administration as well as the level of importance that policy-makers attribute to the consultations. The latter decide on the distribution of resources, that is, time and finance for the realization of these tasks.

There are several critical points to consider in regards to the organization of public consultations by local governments. First, only in some city halls are there units or posts dedicated to public communication and consultations, functioning under different names. The distribution of tasks between these units and other units dealing with specific areas of public policies differ from one municipality to another. What is more, the position of these units within the administrative structure is unstable and can be subject to change after elections. Further, the clerks who are assigned the tasks of organizing public consultations are often also responsible for the city hall's PR (public relations) service. This can be slightly problematic as public consultations and public relations are modes of communication with divergent goals—whereas one serves knowledge building, the other serves persuasion. They also require distinct competences and the use of different tools.

The lack of regulation on the use of personal data by local governments for the purpose of public consultations is a problem for the selection of participants and in achieving representativeness. Due to this legal obstacle, and current practice, the recruitment of citizens for consultations is of a mostly open character. In these circumstances, it is difficult to plan for small group moderated deliberations. The organizers of public consultation complain, on the one hand, about the unpredictability of the level of participation, and on the other hand, about the unrepresentative group of citizens who are always eager to voice their opinions independently of the issue and its real relevance to them personally.

The quality of public consultations has been measured by various institutions, among them the Centre for Deliberation at the Institute of Sociology of the University of Warsaw. The measures adopted by researchers may have differed, but the conclusions are similar—there is a need to reflect on the standards of public consultations. When even the most rudimentary elements of the procedure are not always respected, public consultations can do more harm than good to democracy.

The answers to the questionnaires that we collected from the clerks responsible for public consultations in the 270 city and town halls (2011) informed us that 56% of those who had had at least one project that had a profound impact on a local community during past several years, had also organized at least one consultation concerning these projects. In total, public consultations were organized in connection with 27% of the projects mentioned in the study. In 54% of public consultations, inhabitants had access to relevant information at least one day before the consultation; however, the information package did not necessarily present basic facts, the constraints on possible actions, or their proposals.

According to the respondents, the methods of organizing public consultations included the following: face-to-face meetings (70%), paper questionnaires (17%), written or oral comments on a published document delivered individually by inhabitants to the city or town hall (15%), online questionnaire (6%), online debates (6%), sending an opinion via an email or online form (5%), and online voting (1%). In up to 15% of cases, public consultations did not meet the basic standard of two-way communication, as the procedure was limited to providing information on a project. Judging by the descriptions of the methodology provided by city and town halls, only seven of them demonstrated any attempt to organize parallel online and offline discussions. Overall, they failed to apply the same strategy to all their public consultations.

In regards to the management of discussions, in ten of the methodology descriptions, there was an easy to identify scenario for meetings that went beyond the format of a public hearing. Moderation was mentioned six times in the descriptions. As our conclusions regarding moderation are not precise due to the fact that we did not ask a specific question about it, but instead drew our conclusions from an open question on the methodology, it is important to refer to the results of another survey. In this other study, 15% of municipalities declared that the meetings had been moderated by professional moderators (Stocznia and SMG/KRC 2011). In turn, the results of our monitoring of local governments' websites (2014) demonstrate that only 6 out of 912 cities (less than 1%) moderated text discussions, and in two of these 50% and 8% of debates were moderated.

In my understanding of the deliberation process, it is not necessary to have an external moderator to manage debates; however, it is important that the moderator has moderating experience. Self-managed groups that hold discussions without the intervention of a moderator are easily subjected to group processes that produce biased opinions. If additionally, the information materials are missing, it becomes even more probable that the opinions collected will not necessarily contribute to good decisions, being rather a reflection of the will of a powerful minority.

The lack of a questionnaire or even the unwillingness to have one was explained to us by one of the clerks as a reluctance to impose limits on the participants and the ideas that they may bring up. He did not see a problem with the fact that the majority of the ideas would be irrelevant, indicating that relevant ideas would be selected post-debate. This understanding of participants' empowerment is rather inconsistent with the model of deliberative consultations. Other comments that we have collected on the organization of meetings show no reflection on the usefulness of a scenario that goes beyond the division of a meeting into two sections: a presentation by the city or town hall, and comments from the participants gathered in the room.

Finally, our survey from 2011 revealed that the consultation results were published in 60% of cases, and information on how the citizens' opinions had been included in the decisions appeared in 58% of cases. It does not require an explanation to see that the lack of response to peoples' voices in the form of a report, whether there are 10, 50, or 100 participants, is disrespectful. But, the decision-makers, in order to justify their disregard for the consultations' results, sometimes use the argument that the small scale of participation is disproportionate to the population. As the conversations seemed to suggest, this approach, among other things, can be the effect of a misconception of public consultations and ignorance regarding qualitative methods of data collection and analysis.

In monitoring the official websites of all the city and town halls (2014), we intended to deepen our knowledge on the use of ICT in public consultations, in particular for dialogue. The study revealed that only in 20 out of the 912 cities (approx. 2%) did authorities use ICT tools for public consultations including some forms of dialogue accessible to several or more participants. This means a decrease of 2–3%, if we compare this result with results of previous studies done by other institutions and organizations, for example, the association Cities in the Internet. Going further in-depth in our analysis we found that only in five out of the eight municipalities that organized online dialogue with citizens, was the subject of consultations problematized (an average 68% of consultations), while in four there was access to a report from the consultations (an average 73% of consultations).

The meetings with representatives of public administration seem to suggest that the use of ICT in communicating with inhabitants is still thought of in terms of the presence or absence of an ICT tool. Reflection on the platform's design, which could have consequences for the inclusion of citizens in a meaningful debate, is not obvious. New trends in the use of ICT in local government are as follows: to bring participatory budgeting online in order to enlarge the number of votes, or to use social media to track attitudes among inhabitants. A handful of the largest cities have invested in offline or online quantitative research panels that systematically measure satisfaction with different aspects of life in their cities. It was not evident to us if local politicians or clerks connect the procedural transparency of public consultations with the level of citizens' participation in public consultations.

InDialogue's Response to Procedural Failures

In the following paragraphs, I will link the problems that were diagnosed in the organization of public consultations to the model of intervention that we have developed. In 2014 a model for the inDialogue software was prepared in regard to the deficiencies in institutional performance. In 2015 the first prototype of the software was ready to be tested and then improved using the feedback gathered from the institutional users. In 2016 tests of the software were carried out during public consultations in two municipalities.

The inDialogue software has been developed with the aim of contributing to the improvement of the quality of public consultations. It includes tools that amend or replace old procedures and practices, not only for the better delivery of community services, but also for more socially inclusive, transparent, reflexive, and legitimate decision-making. This directs us towards a model of deliberative democracy, and in particular to the model of deliberative consultations that informs our project.

As face-to-face public consultations in Poland still have more public recognition than their online counterparts, the inDialogue software has been designed to plan public consultations, which are then conducted in the traditional way (face-to-face meetings, paper questionnaires) or on the internet (text and voice group debates, plenary meetings with experts, electronic questionnaires). Moreover, the democratizing potential of ICT is used not only to apply deliberative standards in online communication between citizens and public officials, but also to provide the transparency of procedures, processes, and their results.

The inDialogue software has two interfaces: one for the organizer (clerk) of public consultations, and another for the participants in the public consultations (citizen). The organizer of public consultations' interface allows the goals of public consultations to be presented, briefing materials for participants to be prepared, experts from a database to be chosen, tools for data collection to be selected (a survey questionnaire, tools for group moderated text or voice debates), consultations to be conducted using these tools, and finally, the results to be summarized in a report. The participant's interface allows for comments to be made on briefing materials that are proposed as an input to deliberations, questions to be posed to experts, the form of a debate in which to contribute to be chosen, a survey questionnaire or vote to be filled in, and if applicable, comments to be made on a working version of the report.

The software helps to transmit knowledge about the methodology of public consultations through a system of forms and the instructions linked to these forms, which can contribute to a better quality and validity of results. It supports team work through the mechanism of distributing tasks among public administration units and employees, using a system of commentaries on public consultation methodology as well as information materials, by the co-creation of a data base of experts, and by the archiving of consultations carried out by any unit in the city or town hall.

Each registered employee of a city or town hall, as well as each registered inhabitant, has a personalized agenda of tasks to do and a record of consultations that they are involved in. A system of reminders helps them to stay informed and involved. Figure 1 shows an example of the list of tasks for a clerk.

Figure 1. Task management.

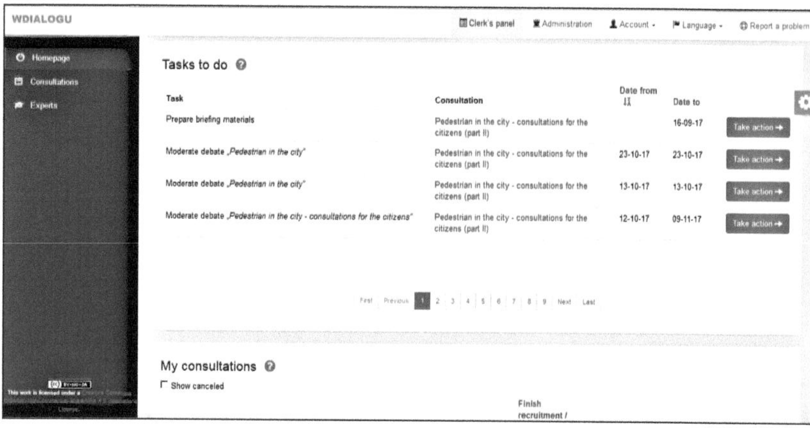

The inDialogue software supports the management of tasks in respect of time as well as to the resources of expertise used in public administration. The preparation of public consultations (methodology and information materials for participants) is divided into phases. In the first *private* phase, only the lead organizers have access to the information on a particular consultation. Once they want to make the plan and briefing materials available to their co-workers for comment, the status of the consultation is changed to *internal*. Only after the plan and accompanying materials are in their final version does the information become *public* and registration opens up.

Depending on the topic of the public consultation and the questions that guide the inquiry, the selection of participants is possible based on information regarding their place of living, or their demographics, or their responses to filtering questions. There are three levels of verifications for participants that can be implemented. First, to become a participant an inhabitant has to create an account and answer some general questions, for example, a question on place of residence. Figure 2 illustrates how a clerk introduces this criterion on the inDialogue platform. Then, in specific consultations, the organizers may allow only the participation of inhabitants that verified their account using an ID number. Some surveys would demand a still more reliable verification in the town or city hall; one-time verification of an account at a town or city hall would be sufficient.

Figure 2. Criteria for selecting participants.

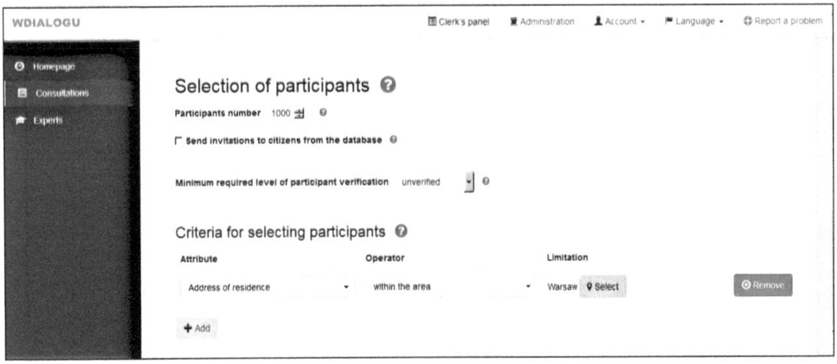

The inDialogue platform encourages clerks to reflect on the composition of deliberating groups. They can either be homogenous or heterogeneous regarding the leading characteristics of the participants. Depending on the goal of the debates and the emotional relations between the defined groups of participants, for example, in a discussion on a traffic issue, we can invite into one room only car owners, or car owners and those who do not own a car. The goal of each debate and the selection criteria of participants should be described and justified by the consultations' organizers.

Our focus on deliberation in consultations requires a more detailed explanation of the management of debates in the inDialogue platform. As has been previously mentioned, the organizers of public consultations can plan parallel online (text and voice) and face-to-face debates. The availability of different forms of debate opens them up to participants with various needs and preferences. The participants can also indicate in the online schedule which dates for a debate are convenient for them.

Briefing materials and meetings with experts (synchronous or asynchronous) are available to participants in order to stimulate fact-based conversations and to include in them legal, budgetary, or other limitations that may affect solutions to the problem. The debate settings organize communication by questions or discussion points. The tool that serves for the planning of public debates is shown in Figure 3.

Figure 3. Planning of debates.

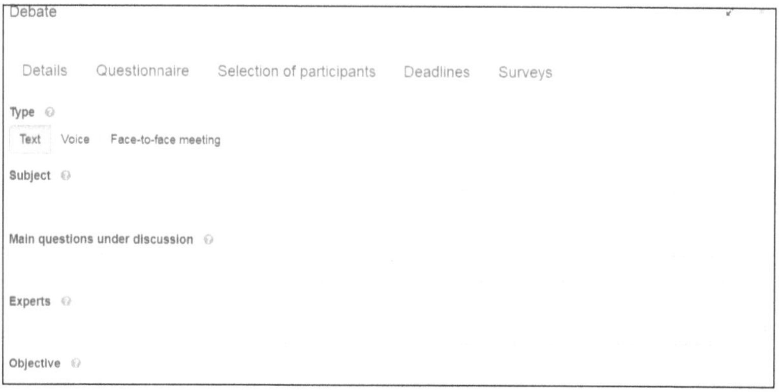

Face-to-face as well as text or voice online debates are moderated, although the actions of a moderator differ between their specific forms. The questions for group debates are present in the text forum right at the start of a debate and participants are asked to respond to them. Moderators can withdraw a post that either is disrespectful or does not correspond to the discussion topic. They can also move a post from one part of the discussion to another whenever the answer does not match the question under which it was posted. In each case the action of a moderator has to be justified. The posts that have been removed remain available to everyone, but not on the front panel. They can be read together with an accompanying comment by the moderator. Figure 4 shows the view of a text debate available to a moderator. On the right, there are buttons that can be used by a moderator to edit and manage the communication.

Figure 4. Text forum.

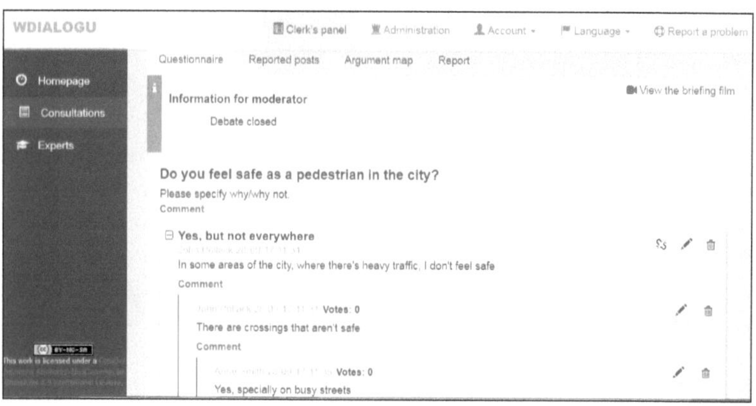

To publish a proposal or a comment in the text forum participants have to fill in a form where they are asked to provide their arguments. Due to the fact that their input is transmitted via the form with specific sections for either a proposal, or an argument, or a question, it can be shown as a diagram without any additional effort from the moderator. The map of arguments, which the text forum can easily be transformed into, helps to revise all proposals and arguments before supporting some of them or rejecting others. It is shown in Figure 5.

Figure 5. Map of arguments.

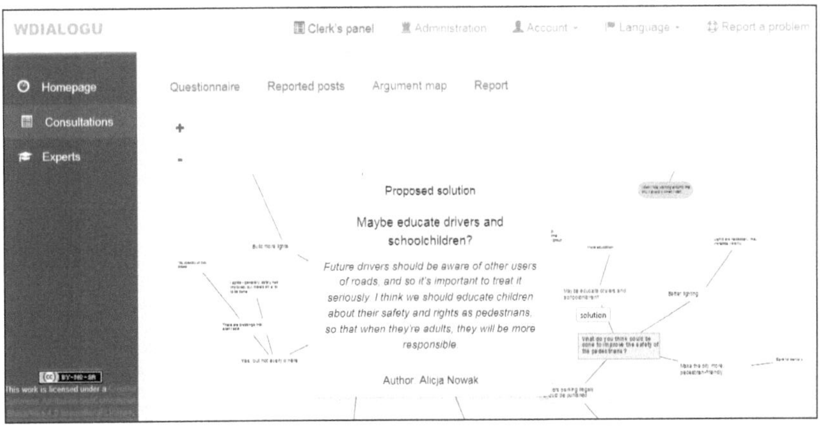

Voice discussions are organized using the TeamTalk open software package, slightly modified to meet the goals of our project and integrate with the inDialogue software. Moderators have at their disposal several tools to manage the debate. They can use a board to show the agenda or to gather together questions for experts. They can, but do not have to, control the voice distribution by switching on and off a microphone. We have also added a feature that automates the indication of the speaking order; this is established after the speaker signals that they intend to speak. A time counter for each speaker has been designed to measure the length of speech. These features should allow moderators to be more efficient when supporting the equal inclusion of participants in debates. Figure 6 shows a discussion room.

Figure 6. Voice debate.

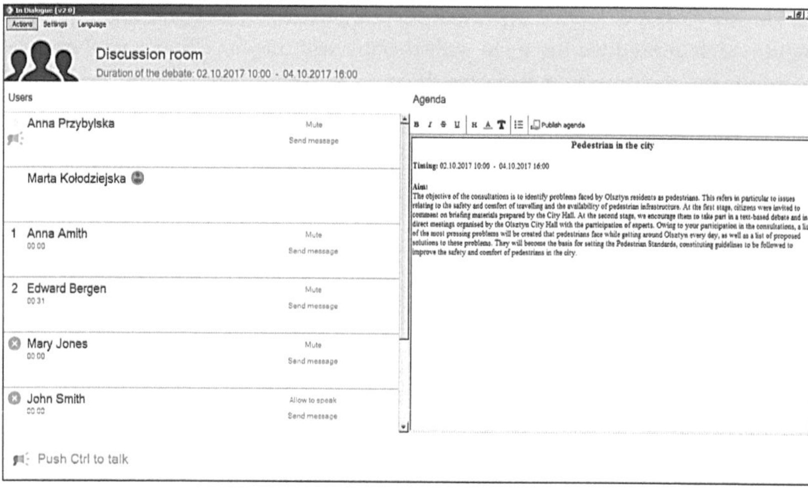

From the point of view of the management of tasks that a clerk has to complete, as well as from the point of view of transparency of the processes to the general public, the automation of some actions like the transfer of information on the methodology to the report, is an additional advantage. The report is prepared in the text editor and uploaded to allow participants to introduce comments. To embrace the rules of public consultations as a social research process, the inDialogue software supports the integration of data coming from groups debating both online and offline. Figure 7 presents a view of the clerk's panel at the moment of a report's publication.

Figure 7. Report.

Commenting on the report is available only to persons who participated in the discussions, as the aim is not to open up the discussion anew, but rather to check if all the arguments have been adequately reported. Publishing a report, as well as publishing the information materials earlier in the process, is mandatory for the city or town hall.

Conclusions

Public consultations can be a functional and effective connection between representative and participatory democracy. This requires meeting conditions beyond those defined under the law. An attempt to codify the rules of public consultations in an act of national law failed, but soft tools for monitoring and education have been developed in the form of codes of good practice, workshops, and case studies. The inDialogue software has been prepared as a middle-solution between hard (legal) and soft (advisory) measures. It guides the users through the public consultation procedure and does not allow them to omit the crucial elements that serve transparency, good quality results, and the legitimacy of processes and results.

The inDialogue platform has been designed to amend the procedures of public consultations in reference to a set of diagnosed problems. It sensitizes the organizers of public consultations to the issues of methodology. It turns their attention to the need for planning ahead of the call for participation. It attempts to make deliberation an integral element of public consultations by facilitating the sharing of knowledge within institutions and between institutions and the society as well as by supporting moderated, information-based debates. The forms and instructions regarding not only tools but also the procedure guide these actions.

Moreover, the inDialogue software has been designed not only to plan and organize public deliberations, but also to offer citizens a venue in which to discuss public issues under good conditions as described in the model of deliberation. The software is expected to oppose social exclusion by the targeted recruitment of participants who represent different socio-economic groups, access to relevant information by persons without the knowhow to search for expert knowledge, efforts to encourage people with different preferences regarding forms of communication to join debates, and respect for the standards of Web Content Accessibility Guidelines (WCAG) 2.0.

Following the literature and the results of research on the subject, we have assumed that small group moderated debates will support inclusiveness and reflexivity in public consultations. By means of dividing the participants of synchronous discussions into small groups, we make more time available for each person to interact and express their opinions. As for the inclusiveness of online voice debates, the ability to know who has spoken and who has not yet spoken should have a positive effect on the perception of the debate as being objective and so encourage participation. Regarding reflexivity, the participants, knowing when they will have their turn to speak, should focus more on listening to other members of the group and, therefore, prepare their input in reference to what they have heard. In turn, in text debates, reflexivity can be stimulated by highlighting the role of an argument in deliberations using the forms and an argument map.

Having written the above, I acknowledge the limitations of our solutions. First, we cannot expect that the ICT tools will determine behaviors to the extent that each aspect of a procedure or, even less so, processes, will match the model. There are intervening factors that we can predict but do not yet know with what force they will interfere with the solutions until we gather a substantial amount of empirical material. Still, there is little doubt that the data collected from participants in public consultations who deliberate under, mostly, good conditions; should be a little, or considerably, better quality, depending on the circumstances.

The improved procedures for public consultations demand a greater contribution not only from public consultation organizers but also from participants. Based on empirical data we hypothesize that the transparency and the predictability of the actions planned and conducted using the inDialogue software may be an incentive to participate for those who have been dissatisfied with the procedures and practices of public consultations. But, at the same time, we may lose the input from those citizens who are unwilling to spend more time and effort taking part in public consultations than they used to. This is a well-known trade-off between the quality of input/output and the scale of involvement (Manosevitch 2014).

Governmental websites are not very popular. People have disconnected from institutional politics, choosing the forms of participation that cater to their needs and that are easy to accommodate in their lives that are marked by change requiring adaptability (Marody 2014). Thus, democratic innovations that attempt to recreate a space for public debate for all social groups certainly risk failure in terms of the almost impossible mass appeal that public officials expect. It is a real challenge that we intend to respond to in a future research and ICT development project.

References

Åström, Joachim, and Åke Grönlund. 2012. "Online Consultations in Local Government: What works, When and Why?" In *Connecting Democracy. Online Consultation and the Flow of Political Communication*, edited by Peter M. Shane, and Stephen Coleman, 75–96. Cambridge, MA: MIT Press.

Budge, Ian. 2000. "Deliberative Democracy Versus Direct Democracy – Plus Political Parties!" In *Democratic Innovation*, edited by Michael Saward, 195–212. London: Routledge.

Coleman, Stephen, Anna Przybylska, and Yves Sintomer, eds. 2015. *Deliberation and Democracy: Innovative Processes and Institutions*. Frankfurt am Main: Peter Lang GmbH.

Coleman, Stephen, and Peter Shane, eds. 2012. *Connecting Democracy: Online Consultation and the Flow of Political Communication*. Cambridge, MA: MIT Press.

Davies, Todd, and Reid Chandler. 2012. "Online Deliberation Design: Choices, Criteria, and Evidence." In *Democracy in Motion: Evaluating the Practice and Impact of Deliberative Civic Engagement*, edited by Tina Nabatchi, John Gastil, G. Michael Weiksner, and Matt Leighninger, 103–131. Oxford: Oxford University Press.

Davies, Todd, and Seeta P Gangadharan. 2009. *Online Deliberation: Design, Research and Practice*. Stanford, CA: CSLI Publications.

Edwards, Arthur. 2012. "Tensions and New Connections between Participatory and Representative Democracy in Local Governance." In *Renewal in European Local Democracies. Puzzles, Dilemmas and Options*, edited by Linze Schaap, and Harry Daemen, 55–78. Wiesbaden: Springer Publishing.

Fishkin, James S. 2009. *When the People Speak. Deliberative Democracy and Public Consultation*. Oxford: Oxford University Press.

Gastil, John. 2008. *Political Communication and Deliberation*. Los Angeles: SAGE.

Gastil, John, and Peter Levine, eds. 2005. *The Deliberative Democracy Handbook. Strategies for Effective Citizen Engagement in the 21st Century*. San Francisco: Jossey-Baas.

Gastil, John. 2016. "Building a Democracy Machine: Towards an Integrated and Empowered Form of Civic Engagement." Harvard Kennedy School for Democratic Governance and Innovation. Accessed June 18, 2017. http://ash.harvard.edu/files/ash/files/democracy_machine.pdf.

Geissel, Brigitte, and Marco Joas, eds. 2013. *Participatory Democratic Innovations in Europe. Improving the Quality of Democracy?* Opladen: Barbara Budrich Publishers.

Grönlund, Kimmo, André Bächtiger, and Maija Setälä. 2014. *Deliberative Mini-Publics. Involving Citizens in the Democratic Process*. Colchester: ECPR Press.

Held, David. 2006. *Models of Democracy*. Cambridge: Polity.

Johnson, Carolina, and John Gastil. 2015. "Variations of Institutional Design for Empowered Deliberation." *Journal of Public Deliberation* 11 (1). Accessed June 15, 2017. http://www.publicdeliberation.net/jpd/vol11/iss1/art2.

Manosevitch, Idit. 2014. "The Design of Online Deliberation: Implications for Practice, Theory and Democratic Citizenship." *Journal of Public Deliberation* 10 (1). Accessed June 15, 2017. http://www.publicdeliberation.net/cgi/viewcontent.cgi?article=1325&context=jpd.

Marody, Mirosława. 2014. *Jednostka po nowoczesności. Perspektywa socjologiczna*. Warsaw: Scholar.

Melitski, James, Marc Holzer et al. 2005. "Digital Government Worldwide: An e-Government Assessment of Municipal Web Site." *International Journal of Electronic Government Research* 1: 1–19.

Nabatchi, Tina, John Gastil, G. Michael Weiksner, and Matt Leighninger eds. 2012. *Democracy in Motion. Evaluating the Practice and Impact of Deliberative Civic Engagement*. Oxford: Oxford University Press.

Pracownia Badań i Innowacji Społecznych "Stocznia", SMG/KRC S.A. 2011. Raport końcowy z badania efektywności mechanizmów konsultacji społecznych. Accessed January 2, 2015. http://www.pozytek.gov.pl/files/Biblioteka/raport_efekt_konsult.pdf.

Raciborski, Jacek. 2011. *Obywatelstwo w perspektywie socjologicznej*. Warsaw: PWN.

Zhang, Weiyu. 2015. "The Disenfranchised and eDeliberation: Beyond Access." In *Deliberation and Democracy: Innovative Processes and Institutions*, edited by Steven Coleman, Anna Przybylska, and Yves Sintomer, 57–82. Frankfurt am Main: Peter Lang GmbH.

Maja Sawicka and Anna Przybylska

Chapter 3. The Online Anonymity Controversy: Theoretical Considerations and Practical Implications for the InDialogue Platform

Introduction

The issue of anonymity during public consultations held with the use of IT tools requires urgent theoretical study as it has significant consequences in practice. The *online anonymity controversy* arises at the intersection of, on the one hand, concerns about the excessive emotionality and low quality of computer-mediated communication due to socio-psychological conditioning of human behavior in a deindividuated state (Zimbardo 1969), socio-linguistic conditioning of interpersonal communication in an environment (almost) deprived of non-verbal cues (see, e.g., Tanis and Postmes 2007) and the socio-psychological dynamics of group processes in cyberspace (see, e.g., Christopherson 2007); and on the other, far-reaching hopes for the liberating, empowering, and equalizing impact of the internet (see, e.g., Dubrovsky et al. 1991; Teich et al. 1999).

In this chapter, we aim to map the online anonymity controversy within the scope of online public consultations. First, we discuss the practical solutions that have been already implemented by public consultation practitioners. Next, we identify key problem areas to which the designers of these solutions had to respond, and we locate these within the broader framework of theoretical considerations. Third, we present the solutions adopted for the *inDialogue* platform, linking them to the issues discussed.

Practical Solutions to the Online Anonymity Controversy: Case Studies

The dilemma of the *online anonymity controversy* on a practical level translates into a fundamental necessity for deciding on the mode and level of identification of participants in the consultations mediated by online platforms. Below, we present and discuss three case studies involving solutions to the registration problem, which have been implemented by three different entities rooted in three different sectors of public life (a private company, a non-governmental organization, and a local government) in three different countries (Canada, Iceland, and Italy).

Example 1. PlaceSpeak.com Platform (Canada, British Columbia (BC))

PlaceSpeak is a web-based platform that enables social consultations to be conducted online, but only among the residents of a specific geographic region. It was created and is managed by PlaceSpeak Inc. PlaceSpeak Inc. defines itself as "a new kind of company: a 'social enterprise,' using the power of business for social good."[1] The project is funded from fees charged to consultation organizers for making the platform available to them.

The PlaceSpeak platform offers its clients the possibility of conducting consultations addressed only to users with a verified identity, especially a verified physical location. The platform was used, for instance, by the Langley town hall to organize public consultations concerning the choice between two community center projects[2]; by the government of BC in the process of crowdsourcing information about the province's film industry[3]; and by the local government of the District of Tofino for an online survey and forum discussions concerning the effectiveness of the siren system for warning against tsunami.[4] In each of these cases exact geo-verification of the participants was an important issue: in the first case, the town hall wanted to make sure that only community members—future users of the community center—participated in the consultations; in the second case, the government of BC was interested only in information from inhabitants of the province; and in the third case, the local government of Tofino District was keen to learn about the strength of the alarm signal in exactly defined locations.

The founders of the PlaceSpeak platform consider that the verification of the platform users' identity (the potential participants of decision-making processes carried out using the platform) is the basis for its functionality and usefulness; as they state through video material posted on the project's website;

> With PlaceSpeak we want people [users of the PlaceSpeak platform] to be verified, to be who they are and to live where they say they live and where they work, in order that the information they provide, that the advice that they're giving to influence decisions and public policy is based on reality. This is not a game, it's not social media for play. This is the real deal.[5]

---

1 https://blog.placespeak.com/about/ (accessed November 16, 2017).

2 https://www.placespeak.com/static/pdf/Aldergrove_Community_CentreTM_opt.pdf (accessed March 15, 2014–April 15, 2014).

3 see: https://www.placespeak.com/static/pdf/save_bc_film_project_sheet.pdf (accessed March 15, 2014–April 15, 2014).

4 see: https://www.placespeak.com/static/pdf/tof.pdf (accessed March 15, 2014–April 15, 2014).

5 https://www.placespeak.com/media/#prettyPhoto/6/ (accessed November 11, 2017).

This claim is based on a set of assumptions about the nature of online consultation processes that can be reconstructed as follows:

- First, that dividing reality into virtual and real is false since online activities—web-mediated decision-making processes—translate into living conditions in the real world.
- Second, that using one's real identity has a positive impact on the psychological and social conditions of a web-mediated debate and, conversely, the impact of being anonymous is negative.
- Third, that consultation organizers are entitled to select participants, since some decision-making processes concern only specific categories of people (Artibise 2014).

This line of argument underlies the practical solutions implemented by PlaceSpeak platform designers concerning the process of registration and identity verification. The PlaceSpeak platform enables a geo-verification process by not only encouraging the participants in consultations to register with the platform but also by requesting they give consent for the registration data to be verified, with particular emphasis on confirming the geographical location of the residential or workplace address provided. Each user, when signing up, provides such an address, as well as an e-mail address where they receive a link that allows the account to be activated. Once the account has been activated, the user's identity is verified by,

- the geo-verification of the IP address of the computer from which they have logged on to the account (therefore, during verification they have to use a computer located at the place of residence or workplace they specified) using tools developed by Google (Google Maps API), Maxmind and Trulioo;
- optionally, the location of a mobile or home phone. This method of verifying the information provided when signing up enables a potential participant in social consultations to be ascribed to a specific geographical location;
- at the time of collecting information for this text,[6] PlaceSpeak was in the process of expanding their verification procedure, including the use of the personal identification number (PIN) assigned to British Columbia identification (BCID) cards issued by administrative authorities. This would enable the authenticity of the data provided to be verified by sending *enquiries* requesting the confirmation of, for example, a combination of the BCID PIN, and full name and residential address—which are provided during preliminary registration procedure—to databases managed by the province's administration.

---

6 That is on April 2014.

> The reply would be either positive, confirming the consistency of the data; or negative, if the data was inconsistent. Additionally, this method of verification would allow the confirmation that there is one vote per potential participant.

Such solutions are rooted in the specific legal environment of Canada and BC—that is, they comply with the federal and provincial laws regulating personal data protection. From our point of view, the most important thing is the assumption underlying both the reasoning of the registration process, and the registration and verification procedure itself, that by the design of the PlaceSpeak platform it is not obligatory to submit to verification, but it is the consultation's organizers who decide on the extent of user verification (*layers of verification*). Given the above, users who have not verified their data (residential address) might not be permitted to participate in the consultations they would like to join.

Example 2. Your Priorities Better Reykjavik (BR) and Better Neighborhoods Platforms (Iceland)

The *Citizens Foundation* (CF) is a non-profit organization operating in Iceland's non-governmental sector. Two projects carried out by the foundation are worth noting: the BR platform, which forms part of the broader Your Priorities project; and the Better Neighborhoods platform, both of which are connected to the participatory budgeting procedure.

BR is an online platform for collecting and prioritizing the ideas of citizens concerning issues such as the city's development and planning of urban space, the organization of public events etc. Proposals posted on the platform can be discussed and voted for by other platform users. Voting is an advisory activity and is not binding on the city authorities. However, the city council not only has committed to consider the most *popular* ideas but also evaluates whether the implementation of these proposals is necessary and viable. It decides whether to submit these ideas to a vote within the framework of the participatory budget project, and then informs residents through the website about its decision and the reasons for it. Better Neighborhoods is the second stage of the process; the residents of specific urban districts participate in an online vote to choose the projects to be executed by the city council.[7] The founders of Your Priorities and the Better Neighborhoods platforms believe that the greatest risk to the development of e-democracy is the lack of citizens' engagement and their reluctance to devote their time to public issues, but they also acknowledge that identity verification is crucial when an online platform hosts

7 www.citizens.is (accessed April 15, 2014).

a binding decision-making process. Therefore, the processes of registering the users of the BR platform differ from those used on the Better Neighborhoods platform.

In the first case, practical registration solutions are based on the assumption that collaborative e-democracy should be as open and possible; according to Gunnar Grímsson from the Citizens Foundation, absence and a lack of interest are "the real resistance and a real method of complaining" (e-mail correspondence, 12.04.2014) against a too complex registration procedure. Nevertheless, even in the case of non-binding collaborative e-democracy processes, registering the users of the platform may be useful in some respects, as, according to its founders,

- it contributes to the transparency of the process and, thus, helps to establish societal trust in e-democracy;
- it makes it possible to contact platform users and collect their feedback and, thus, allow them to follow and be involved in all stages of the decision-making process;
- it fosters a serious and responsible attitude towards social processes mediated by the platform. (Gunnar Grímsson, e-mail correspondence, 12.04.2014)

Registration with the BR platform is effected through an account created on the BR website, where one can also register under a nickname or via social media (Facebook, Twitter), but no identity verification is required.

The Better Neighborhoods web portal does not register users, but their identity is verified via the external web portal, Island.is, managed by a central administration authority: the Icelandic National Registry (INR). A unique identification number (IceKey) is assigned to each citizen in the INR system, which has to be used to log in to the INR website. A vote on the participatory budget was designed to be held shortly after the deadline for sending in tax forms, also with the use of the INR system; the platform's founders assumed that due to the experience gained using the INR system for submitting tax forms, users of the Better Neighborhoods portal would already be familiar with the system. This method of verifying identity has replaced a previous one where the user was requested to provide a tax identification number. Another method tried out was verification using numbers associated with debit cards, which are issued by most banks operating in Iceland, but that method has never become popular (Gunnar Grímsson, e-mail correspondence, 12.04.2014).

Example 3. Region of Sicily (Regione Siciliana) Public Consultations (Italy)

The last example we would like to present pertains to online public consultations concerning the reform of local government organizational units, which were conducted by the local government of the region of Sicily between 7 December 2013 and 15 March 2014. In the course of the consultation process, residents could comment online on two drafts of administrative bills.

Posting a comment resulted in a little comment-bubble appearing in the margin of the draft resolution, more or less at the height of the paragraph or section that was to be commented on. The comment-bubble showed the number of comments posted. By clicking on the comment-bubble, one could expand the comments and thus see the full text of the written comment, as well as the author's name and, optionally, the author's photograph.[8]

In order to voice their opinions during the consultation, the participants of the decision-making process had to register using the FormezAuth (*Sistema di Autenticazione Unica per la Pubblica Amministrazione*) authentication system. The system was created to verify the identity of people using the online platforms managed by Formez PA, an entity whose aim is to modernize public administration. To register, each new user had to fill in the registration form available on the FormezAuth website. The form contained boxes concerning basic personal data that were obligatory to fill out, and also offered an option to provide additional details to complete the profile (for example to create an automatic signature formula and to send a photograph), which users were encouraged to do. During registration, a message concerning visibility settings was displayed, informing the potential user what parts of the information provided would be visible to other users of the platforms managed by Formez PA. Private information, concealed from other users, included e-mail address, date and place of birth, and sex.

This registration procedure was time-consuming; there were approximately 20 questions in the form, and filling it in took at least 15 minutes. The structure of the registration process reveals the basic assumptions underlying it: to use any online platform run by Formez PA, the user must register via FormezAuth and provide all their personal details. Thus, it may be concluded that the designers of this system believe the following:

- each participant's identity must be established and known to the consultation's organizers (although not necessarily other participants);
- participation in online public consultation entails obligations similar to those involved in other public activities—such as the necessity of revealing one's identity, and devoting some time to the process of getting involved in public debate.

8 http://pti.regione.sicilia.it/portal/page/portal/PIR_PORTALE/PIR_Iniziative/PIR_ConsultazioneConsorziCittaMetropolitane (accessed April 20, 2014).

An analysis of the solutions to the registration and verification of data provided by consultation participants described above, and the reasons for adopting them, especially the underlying assumptions, makes it possible to identify the key problem areas that constitute the online anonymity controversy in respect to public consultations. That is, the need to balance various values: to ensure consultation users have a right to privacy on the one hand, and to oblige them to take responsibility for what they say, on the other; or to open a decision-making process and encourage as many people as possible to participate, but also to ensure its transparency.

Dimensions of the Online Anonymity Controversy: What Is There to Gain, what Is There to Lose?

The dilemmas outlined above translate into two basic issues. First, the *nature* and dimensions of online anonymity. The platform designers in all of the cases presented above had to decide on the scope of anonymity they would allow. Second, the tension between the various consequences of anonymity for public debate and group processes that the platform designers had to balance.

Being Anonymous Online: Layers and Dimensions of Online Anonymity

Anonymity is most widely defined as a state in which an individual remains unknown or nameless to others (Lapidot-Lefler and Barak 2012). However, it does not necessarily demand that he or she remains invisible to others they are interacting with, but that he or she is unidentifiable to them (Christopherson 2007), and, thus, cannot become the subject of social evaluation, criticism, judgement, or control (Zimbardo 1969). Anonymity understood in this way can be viewed from two angles—technical and social (Hayne and Rice 1997). *Technical* anonymity encompasses a situation in which information about an individual that allows them to be identified, is removed from an interaction; for example, an internet communication. *Social* anonymity encompasses the subjective perception of oneself, or others, as being unidentifiable because of the lack or the concealment of this kind of information (Hayne and Rice 1997).

In the scope of online public consultations, such a conceptualization of anonymity demands clarification of who are the *others* to whom an individual remains anonymous—are they other consultation participants, consultation organizers, or both? The identity and status of the consultations' organizers is especially important, insofar as it may arouse different attitudes and reactions in consultation participants, for example, state authorities and private companies are both viewed with distrust, albeit for different reasons (Kang, Brown and Kiesler 2013).

A case in which a consultation participant remains anonymous both to fellow participants and to the consultations' organizers is possible only where no registration or provision of personal data is required in order to voice an opinion in the consultation, or where the consultation's organizers are unable to associate personal data with the opinions voiced by a specific person. However, also in these circumstances, individuals display some personal characteristics, as shown by Gary Marx (1999), the identification of an individual can be conducted at various levels.

Marx identifies seven of these levels: *legal name*, which "involves connection to biological or social lineage, and can be a key to [a] vast amount of other information" (Marx 1999, 100); *locatability*, which allows an individual to be located in their physical place of residence; *pseudo-anonymity*, in which a person's pseudonym can be linked to other information about that person, especially their legal name or location; *real anonymity*, which encompasses "pseudonyms that cannot be linked to other forms of identity knowledge" (ibid.); *pattern knowledge*, which allows the identification of an individual based on their appearance or patterns of behavior, through which there occurs an "uncontrollable leakage of some information" (Marx 1999, 101); *social categorization*, through which an individual can be placed in one of a number of broad social categories such as gender, class, income group etc.; and *symbols of eligibility/ineligibility*, where an individual is identified through their possession of certain status markers—access codes (such as passwords), artefacts (such as badges, uniforms), or skills.

Each of these modes of identification guarantees the user of an online platform a different level of anonymity. As Kimberley M. Christopherson (2007) noted, this results in different levels of privacy; that is, control over the amount and scope of social contact and autonomy; the control over one's own actions, and the ability to freely express oneself. In the following section, we consider the socially desirable and undesirable consequences of anonymity in the scope of computer-mediated public debate.

The Online Controversy Revisited: Anonymity or Accountability?

The following arguments support the notion of climbing up a *ladder of anonymity*, that is, allowing for the broadest possible scope of anonymity during web-based public consultations.

1. *Anonymity enhances the universal nature of web-based group decision processes.* An easy registration process (or its absence) encourages potential

participants to join the decision-making process; while contrariwise, a registration process that requires the provision of a lot of personal information as well as undergoing a complicated procedure for verifying it, discourages them from becoming involved. The requirement to register and to verify identity is sometimes indicated as a being a barrier to the development of online participatory democracy; practical experience shows that a large percentage of people who would potentially be interested in participating in a decision-making process, withdraw at the identity verification stage. If the IT tools are to strengthen popular involvement in local level politics, their designers must maintain and utilize the appeal of internet communication as being viewed as open, and free of the barriers and tensions that are typical of face-to-face interactions (see also Amichai-Hamburger and McKenna 2006; Teich et al. 1999).

2. *Anonymity enables persons from various social positions to be involved in consultations and ensures that participants have equal standing.* As indicated by the available body of social research, computer-mediated interactions are characterized by a lower level of social risk, and a lower barrier to entering into an interaction, and there is a tendency to experience much less fear of embarrassment or contempt (e.g., Christopherson 2007; Tanis and Postmes 2007; Storm and Moreggi 2007; Teich et al. 1999). Furthermore, it has been proposed that "electronic interaction makes power less of an issue during discussion[,] which leads group members, regardless of status, to contribute more to the discussion" (Amichai-Hamburger and McKenna 2006, 829), and this forms a certain *net advantage.* According to *the equalization hypothesis*, computer-mediated communication allows status differences to be equalized, thanks to which, power in web-based interactions is distributed more evenly than in interactions conducted face-to-face (Dubrovsky, Kiesler and Sethna 1991). The benefits for online public consultations seem obvious: anonymous interactions empower people that belong to dominated or marginalized groups, and offer an environment in which they can speak more freely (Amichai-Hamburger and McKenna 2006), or express opinions contrary to those held by members of more powerful or dominating groups (Christopherson 2007); thus contributing to the openness and inclusiveness of public debate.

3. *Anonymity in social consultations makes it possible to conduct consultations concerning sensitive issues.* This includes those relating to medical issues or disability. The need to provide sensitive information along with exact personal data may discourage people from participating in this type of consultation, whereas anonymity allows them to feel safe. This anonymity-based feeling of social security leads to "the general tendency for individuals to engage in greater self-disclosure and more

intimate exchanges [...]. Interactions online tend to become 'more than skin-deep' and to do so quite quickly" (Amichai-Hamburger and McKenna 2006, 836).

4. *The identification of persons participating in online decision-making processes requires personal data to be collected.* This entails a number of problems. Although research on the reasons why people seek anonymity is still scarce, the existing evidence indicates that the basic motivation derives from a general feeling of distrust towards various actors who are active in cyberspace (both legal: state authorities and big companies, and illegal: hackers); as well as general insecurity and a feeling of lack of control over personal data that has been revealed on the internet (Kang, Brown, and Kiesler 2013). From the point of view of the platform's users, the risk of illegal or unintended use of their personal data constitutes the basic problem. The possible risks include the sale of data to other entities for marketing purposes or the use of information about opinions voiced during consultations against selected persons. From the point of view of the public consultation organizers, the liability for storing and archiving collected data is the basic *practical* difficulty to be faced. The consultation organizer must know the regulations concerning the collection, archiving, and storage of personal data thoroughly, as well as the rules for sharing it with other entities in order to verify it. Allowing the consultation participants to remain anonymous at least within the scope of their legal name and location may seem a safer and less problematic solution to the anonymity controversy.

However, some of the claims presented here have been criticized or invalidated by other evidence. There exist some arguments that speak against online anonymity, giving precedence to values different to those discussed above. These arguments are considered below.

1. *Anonymity has specific psychological and social consequences for the course of a web-mediated debate.* As indicated earlier, the absence of embarrassment and shame may have a positive impact resulting in greater openness and willingness to participate in web-based debates; however, it may also cause adverse consequences for the course of online interaction. According to Philip Zimbardo's deindividuation theory (1969), the deindividuated state limits the individuals tendency to conduct self-monitoring and self-evaluation; or, putting it in social psychological terms, role-taking (Mead 2015/1934). As a result it weakens internalized social controls, operating through feelings of shame and guilt (see Scheff 1988; Shott 1979), and produces outcomes such as a tendency to voice radical opinions without fear of social consequences, outbursts of social hatred, and bystander apathy (an unwillingness to take an active role in the course of events). Although these phenomena are described by social psychologists for *real* groups, such psychosocial effects are thought to be present also in the online environment (see Chris-

topherson 2007) in the form of the so-called "online disinhibition effect" (Suler 2004; Joinson 2003). This is a lowering of behavioral restraints or *brakes* that are specific to the online environment (Lapidot-Lefler and Barak 2012; Suler 2004).

Through the online disinhibition effect anonymity may contribute to antisocial and antinormative behaviors. Obviously, this impedes the flow of the computer-mediated communication process, particularly when it is not moderated or supervised (see, e.g., Coffey and Woolworth 2004). For this reason, it is advisable for online communities that want to offer high levels of anonymity to their members to support, at the same time, the development of strong social norms, and provide moderation of antinormative behavior (Kang, Brown and Kiesler 2013).

2. *Anonymity may not ensure the degree of parity claimed by the equalization hypothesis*. Some research suggests that people who engage in computer-mediated communication *give off* cues that allow them to be identified at the level of social categorization even if they use pseudonyms or nicknames (see Herring and Stoerger 2014; Bernstein et al. 2011; Postmes and Spears 2002). For this reason, it has been argued that the internet is probably not such a level playing field for inter-group interactions as it is believed to be, and status differences—although to some extent concealed—still matter.

3. *Anonymity lowers accountability*. This leads to a lack of real engagement in the course of the debate (the so-called *slactivism*), and, as indicated above, to a decreased sense of responsibility for the opinions and proposals voiced, or straightforwardly to antisocial and antinormative actions (see Herring and Stoerger 2014; Bernstein et al. 2011; Suler 2004; Kling et al. 1999). Furthermore, within the perspective of social responsibility, as Jacek Haman points out in this volume, participation in the public consultation process is a form of exercising power: the outcome influences the real world, which is shared by various interest groups, and may lead to the implementation of changes "favorable to part of the community and negative for others" (see Haman p. 30 in this volume). The quality of the debate translates both into the outcome of the decision process, and into attitudes towards e-democracy; that is, a future willingness to join in online deliberation and meaningfully contribute.

The dilemmas presented here were also considered during the design of the inDialogue platform. In the last section, we present solutions adopted for the inDialogue platform in light of practical experience, empirical evidence, and the theoretical considerations discussed above.

Solutions for the InDialogue Platform

While developing the model for the inDialogue platform, we were concerned most of all with the quality of the public consultations conducted by local governments. We intended to respond to the needs of public consultation organizers regarding methodological cues. At the same time, we were concerned by the self-exclusion of some citizens from participation in the online discussions managed by local authorities (official websites) due to the discussions' abusive character and inconclusiveness (Przybylska 2010, 2014). Thus, our primary assessment of the situation, based on data gathered over years of empirical studies, was that the introduction of participants' identification at different levels and within different scopes, is necessary and advantageous for public consultation.

The design of the inDialogue application takes into consideration the general rules of social research planning, and the verification and selection of participants is a key aspect of this (see Przybylska, Chapter 2, in this volume). In social research procedures, anonymity is understood as the anonymity of a respondent in regard to the general public and third parties, but not to researchers (see Haman, Chapter 1, in this volume). Researchers, in respecting the privacy of respondents, use the respondents' data only for analytical purposes. However, in public consultations, it is not a researcher who collects the data, but a civil servant. This fact is of importance to many participants. Some, especially those living in small communities, are afraid of an abuse of power and that the information they share during consultations may be used against them. This uncertainty is particularly evident if the issue under consultation is socially sensitive, but it is possible for this attitude to become generalized and embrace all categories of issues.

Interestingly, knowing about the reluctance of citizens to register, and their potential withdrawal from participation due to either fear (justified or not) or even insufficient motivation to go through the verification process, representatives of town and city halls that participate in the In Dialogue project are mostly either supportive of participant anonymity, or they express contradictory preferences, arguing for a lack of barriers to participation as well as for the circumscription of some of the better-organized citizens' dominant position in public debates. A separate issue is that current laws do not provide the necessary legal grounds for the use of personal data for the purpose of public consultations; something not always respected by local governments as discussed by Przybylska in Chapter 2.

Taking into consideration the results of our research and applying them to the arguments for identification and anonymity presented in this chapter, we decided that a consultation organizer using the inDialogue software should be able to choose between three modes of participant verification. Figure 1 shows how a clerk can select a mode of participant verification.

Figure 1. Level of participant verification

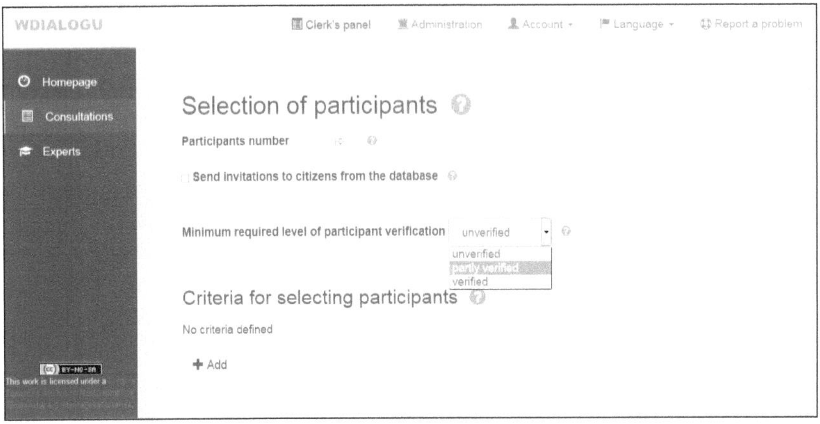

Citizens may have an unverified profile (they provide information about themselves that is unverified), partially verified (the IT platform automatically checks if a person with a given identity card number resides in the municipality), or completely verified (the system verifies the identity of a person on the basis of a given identity card number and, additionally, the person must go to the city hall to have their identity confirmed). The instructions that accompany the tools inform the public consultation organizers in what circumstances it is advisable to adopt a particular level of verification. We have taken this open approach to participant verification assuming that in the future some changes may be introduced to the law allowing the use of personal data in public consultations.

As has been pointed out in this chapter, as well as Chapter 1 by Haman and Chapter 2 by Przybylska, the importance and extent of verification depends on the subject of the public consultation and the questions being asked in the process. If a problem is being explored and ideas crowdsourced on how to solve it, organizers do not have to be very strict. This is different from a situation where opinions are counted, and every vote cast is essential. In this latter situation, it is advisable to use a mechanism for verifying participants in order to ensure that each person qualified to have an input into public consultations casts one vote only. Such a mechanism would also disable voting for anyone who is not entitled to do so. For instance, in the case of voting on a project for reconstructing district facilities, only citizens from the district concerned would be able to vote, with the possible, limited, participation of people who work in the district in respect to issues that also concern them. In such a case it would be useful to verify platform users, at least partially, for the purposes of public consultations.

In principle, if the verification of participants is automated, the consultation's organizers should not be able to make a link between particular participants and their opinions. Participants are just representatives of certain social groups with particular characteristics, for example, the owners of cars living in the city center. Only persons with particular competences (data privacy officers) would have access to personal information. We think that this rule and the mechanism supporting its implementation should be explained to all parties involved in public consultations; an explanation of procedures could ease the feeling of uncertainty, if not eliminate it altogether.

The above is particularly relevant if citizens are asked by the public consultation's organizers to add some specific information to their profiles for the purpose of particular consultations. The new criteria for participant selection can be introduced by the city or town hall's IT administrator upon request from the clerk organizing public consultations. Next to frequently used criteria like age, sex, domicile, employment, and the number of children, these could also be criteria like the car ownership or the use of public transport. Figure 2 illustrates how a clerk introduces a new criterion for participant selection.

Figure 2. Editing selection criteria

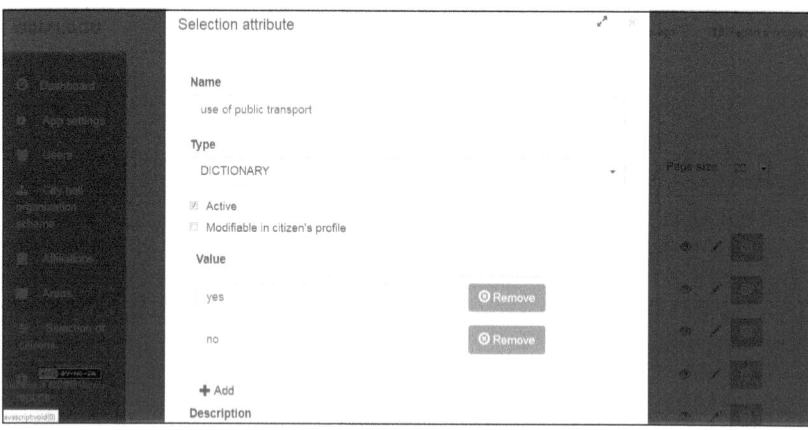

The selection of criteria by the public consultation organizer means two things: first, only persons having particular characteristics can take part in certain public consultations; and second, to take part in these public consultations, citizens have to confirm that they have these required characteristics by filling in obligatory fields in their online profile. The citizens are informed well before the beginning of public consultations what the criteria for the selection of participants are, and how they are associated with the issues raised. They can then decide if they want to provide the data that they have been asked for. Figure 3 demonstrates how citizens can edit their profiles on the inDialogue platform.

Figure 3. Citizen's profile

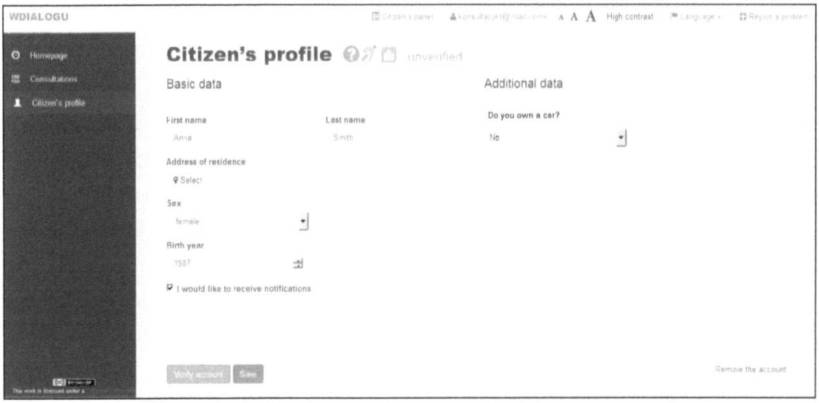

A database of citizens who have expressed their willingness to be informed about new public consultations can be used by local authorities to keep citizens engaged. The organizers of public consultations can target specific groups by knowing their characteristics, for example, the residents of a particular district, while not necessarily knowing who the participants are (i.e., identification by a legal name and exact address). It strengthens the efficacy of the process of citizen recruitment for public consultations and responds to public authorities' concerns about weak participation.

Moreover, during our research, we have documented the opinion that not only the identity of citizens willing to have input into decision-making should be verified by the city or town hall but also that their names should be publicly known. This opinion was put forward by some public consultation organizers and participants (representatives of NGOs and lay citizens alike) because—as they argued—this social control could make people more accountable for what they say or write, as well as how they express their opinions. The use of names and surnames is expected to unveil potential manipulation by institutional or party members who try to influence public opinion.

This argument for accountability has been taken into account during the design of the inDialogue platform. Some public consultations may necessitate the disclosure of names and surnames; thus, the rule of complete anonymity of participants in regards to the general public has been suspended. At the time of designing the application, we discussed this issue with experts, interested researchers, and members of NGOs. Our support for the identification of participants in public consultations by their names and surnames, in situations in which issues of particular public importance are discussed, was in accordance with the opinion of the general data protection officer in Poland at that time. As to what issues are of particular public importance is open to interpretation, but this subject could also be discussed and publicly agreed upon with the involvement of citizens at a national or local level. It relies on the decision of the organizers of public consultations and the preferences of participants in these consultations as to what can be referred to in the resolutions that regulate how public consultations are conducted in municipalities. It is important that citizens are informed about the disclosure of the names of participants in particular consultations and the justification for this at the moment the information on the public consultation is announced and registration is opened.

The inDialogue platform enables different levels of citizen identification. Our principal argument is that strong democracy requires good and transparent procedures as well as public accountability for all parties involved. However, in public consultations, the identity of participants does not always have to be verified, and additionally, it is not always advisable for participants to be known by their names. It is the public consultation's organizer, and in some instances the participants, that decide on the level and scope of anonymity. In the first case, the decision derives from the methodology of the social research and the information that the city or town hall intends to gather; the inDialogue platform facilitates choices by providing adequate examples. In the second case, it results from an understanding of the situation by the organizers of the public consultation and the participants. Accompanying instructions inform the organizers about what aspects to consider, but it is a less direct suggestion than in the case of the methodology choices.

Conclusion: to Register or Not to Register Participants in Online Consultations? The Practical Implications of the Online Anonymity Controversy

There is no straightforward answer to the question as to whether or not the participants in online social dialogue should be allowed to remain anonymous—neither the practical experience of online consultation practitioners nor the theoretical and empirical evidence provide clear-cut solutions to the online anonymity controversy. The result of this is that the choice of specific practical solutions depends, to a large extent, on the type of consultations and also their subject matter. In each case, it should be determined whether it is the *transparency of the decision-making process* or its *universality* that should be perceived as the more important value. It is worth remembering, that universality may mean that we favor those who value their personal freedom over their communal responsibilities. While those who value the latter more will be excluded due to the abusive language.

The verification of data provided during registration is important in situations where the consultation organizer wishes to subject the potential participants of the decision-making process to a selection procedure based on their characteristics. In some cases, such a selection seems necessary—it ensures that a specific decision-making process is *representative*, that is, it allows the representatives of all opinions and positions relevant to the matter in question to be heard; or the parties to or advocacy groups in a potential dispute, to have a voice. The consultation organizer must then decide on the method for registering consultation participants, the protection of their personal data, and the verification of the information provided in the course of the registration process.

Some of the practical solutions to the problem of registering and verifying, or authenticating the identity of persons participating in web-mediated social dialogue that have been implemented in other countries throughout the world require *co-operation between the organizer of the decision-making process* or the founder of a given IT platform and *other social partners*, most frequently local or central administrative authorities. In the case of the three examples described above, such co-operation consists of applying an authentication system under the auspices of central administration authorities to the participants of a mediated decision-making process, or in using information in the databases of local administration authorities. Such co-operation undoubtedly facilitates the introduction of various mechanisms for registering and verifying the identity of participants by reducing the need for personal data to be collected and stored by the consultation's organizers and online platform founders. However, it also establishes a link between consultation organizers, platform founders, and state (or local) authorities—such that attitudes towards the authorities are likely to be projected onto the consultations, and the platform itself.

The solutions designed for the inDialogue platform derive from a careful consideration of the aforementioned dilemmas. We view these solutions as our attempt to at least partially solve the online anonymity controversy by balancing concerns about the openness and accessibility of computer-mediated decision-making processes, and care for the quality of online public consultations.

References

Amichai-Hamburger, Yair, and Katelyn Y. A. McKenna. 2006. "The Contact Hypothesis Reconsidered: Interacting via the Internet." *Journal of Computer-Mediated Communication* 11:825–843. DOI: 10.1111/j.1083–6101.2006.00037.x.

Artibise, Yuri. 2014. "Why Verification." (White Paper). Accessed April 05, 2015. https://pl.scribd.com/document/85992230/White-Paper-Why-Verification.

Bernstein, Michael Scott, Andrés Monroy–Hernández, Drew Harry, Paul André, Katrina Panovich, and Greg Vargas. 2011. "An Analysis of Anonymity and Ephemerality in a Large Online Community." *Proceedings of the Fifth International Conference on Weblogs and Social Media*: 50–57. Menlo Park, CA: AAAI Press. Accessed October 21, 2017. http://projects.csail.mit.edu/chanthropology/4chan.pdf.

Christopherson, Kimberley M. 2007. "The Positive and Negative Implications of Anonymity in Internet Social Interactions: 'On the Internet, Nobody Knows You're a Dog.'" *Computers in Human Behavior* 23: 3038–3056. DOI: 10.1016/j.chb.2006.09.001.

Coffey, Brian, and Stephen Woolworth. 2004. "'Destroy the Scum, and then Neuter their Families:' the Web Forum as a Vehicle for Community Discourse?" *The Social Science Journal* 41: 1–14. DOI: 10.1016/j.soscij.2003.10.001.

Dubrovsky, Vitaly J., Sara Kiesler, and Beheruz N. Sethna. 1991. "The Equalization Phenomenon: Status Effect in Computer-mediated and Face-to-face Decision-making Groups." *Human–Computer Interaction* 6 (2): 119–146.

Hayne, Stephen C., and Ronald E. Rice. 1997. "Attribution Accuracy when Using Anonymity in Group Support Systems." *International Journal of Human–Computer Studies* 47 (3): 429–452. DOI: 10.1006/ijhc.1997.0134.

Herring, Susan C., and Sharon Stoerger. 2014. "Gender and (A)nonymity in Computer-Mediated Communication." In *Handbook of Language and Gender*, edited by Susan Ehrlich, Miriam Meyerhoff, and Janet Holmes, 567–586. Hoboken, NJ: Wiley–Blackwell Publishing.

Joinson, Adam. 2003. *Understanding the Psychology of Internet Behavior: Virtual Worlds, Real Lives*. New York: Palgrave Macmillan.

Kang, Ruogu, Stephanie Brown, and Sara Kiesler. 2013. "Why Do People Seek Anonymity on the Internet? Informing Policy and Design." In *Proceedings of the SIGCHI Conference on Human Factors in Computing Systems*, 2657–2666. New York: ACM. DOI: 10.1145/2470654.2481368.

Kling, Rob, Ya Ching-Lee, Al Teich, and Mark S. Frankel. 1999. "Assessing Anonymous Communication on the Internet: Policy Deliberations." *The Information Society: An International Journal* 15 (2): 79–90. DOI: 10.1080/019722499128547.

Lapidot-Lefler, Noam, and Azy Barak. 2012. "Effects of Anonymity, Invisibility, and Lack of Eye-contact on Toxic Online Disinhibition." *Computers in Human Behavior* 28: 434–443. DOI: 10.1016/j.chb.2011.10.014.

Marx, Gary T. 1999. "What's in a Name? Some Reflections on the Sociology of Anonymity." *The Information Society* 15 (2): 99–112. DOI: 10.1080/019722499128565.

Mead, George H. 2015 (1934). *Mind, Self, and Society*. Chicago: The University of Chicago Press.

Postmes, Tom, and Russell Spears. 2002. "Behavior Online: Does Anonymous Computer Communication Reduce Gender Inequality?" *Personal and Social Psychology Bulletin* 28 (8): 1073–1083. DOI: 10.1177/01461672022811006.

Przybylska, Anna. 2010. *Internet i komunikowanie we wspólnocie lokalnej*. Warsaw: Warsaw University Press.

Przybylska, Anna. 2014. *The Model of Deliberation and ICT Tools in the Decision-Making Processes*. Accessed June 20, 2017. http://www.wdialogu.uw.edu.pl/en/results#ModelIT.

Scheff, Thomas J. 1988. "Shame and Conformity: The Deference-Emotion System." *American Sociological Review* 53 (3): 395–406. Accessed May 15, 2012. https://www.uni-bielefeld.de/ZIF/FG/2004Emotions/members/Scheff-Shame+Conformity.pdf.

Shott, Susan. 1979. "Emotion and Social Life: A Symbolic Interactionist Analysis." *American Journal of Sociology* 84 (6): 1317–1334. DOI: 10.1086/226936.

Storm, King A., and Danielle Moreggi. 2007. "Internet Self-Help and Support Groups: The Pros and Cons of Text-Based Mutual Aid." In *Psychology and the Internet. Intrapersonal, Interpersonal, and Transpersonal Implications*, edited by Jayne Gackenbach, 221–244. London: Elsevier Academic Press.

Suler, John. 2004. "The Online Disinhibition Effect." *CyberPsychology & Behavior* 7 (3): 321–326. DOI: 10.1089/1094931041291295.

Tanis, Martin, and Tom Postmes. 2007. "Two Faces of Anonymity: Paradoxical Effects of Cues to Identity in CMC." *Computers in Human Behavior* 23 (2): 955–970. DOI: 10.1016/j.chb.2005.08.004.

Teich, Al, Mark S. Frankel, Rob Kling, and Ya-Ching Lee. 1999. "Anonymous Communication Policies for the Internet: Results and Recommendations of the AAAS Conference." *The Information Society: An International Journal* 15 (2): 71–77. DOI: 10.1080/019722499128538.

Zimbardo, Philip G. 1969. "The Human Choice: Individuation, Reason, and Oder vs. Deindividuation, Impulse, and Chaos." In *Nebraska Symposium on Motivation* edited by William J. Arnold, and David Levine, 237–307. Lincoln: University of Nebraska Press.

Bartosz Stępień and Jacek Zadrożny

Chapter 4. Where ICT Meets Disability

Introduction

This chapter aims to assess the *inDialogue* platform's compliance with disability guidelines across three dimensions: the physical, the sensory and the cognitive. First, it briefly discusses applied assistive technologies and accessibility rules; then presents some recommendations concerning accessibility rules as applied to communication software, including extending the basic requirements of the National Interoperability Framework.[1] Finally, it refers to the development and accessibility arrangements of the inDialogue platform.

People with disabilities participate in social and political life less often than other citizens (Wiszejko-Wierzbicka 2010). Among the main reasons for this are the barriers they meet and have to overcome. This requires a lot of effort and consumes a lot of energy that is often already reduced due to disability. Architectural, information, and awareness barriers, as well as others, discourage people with disabilities from being active civil citizens; however, it is the obligation of society as a whole, and the authorities elected by this society in particular, to eliminate these barriers. In an era when ICT applications are involved in every aspect of social activity, it is of the utmost importance to eliminate the barriers to information access in the electronic form, although removing physical barriers is still crucial. Information technologies and the tools being developed in the In Dialogue project is one brick pulled out from the wall that separates people with disabilities from society as a whole.

Types of Disabilities and the Barriers Linked to them

The following disability classifications have been proposed for use in this work: sensory, motor and cognitive. These classifications are quite general, and are based on a functional rather than a medical perception of disability. These divisions also prove useful as they are compatible with the structure of the *Web Content Accessibility Guidelines 2.0* (*WCAG*) (World Wide Web Consortium 2008). Later,

1 Ordinance of the Council of Ministers of 12 April 2012 on the National Interoperability Framework, minimum requirements for public registers and information-sharing in electronic formats and minimum requirements for ICT systems (*Journal of Laws*) 2012, item 526.

this will be helpful in indicating the specific guidelines for designing accessible communication tools.

Usually, it is extremely difficult to precisely assess the level of damage or disability (as will be explained later) when describing specific kinds of disability. Sensory disabilities occur when one of the five senses gets damaged (vision, hearing, smell, taste, or touch). The reason for the damage is of secondary importance here, although it is worth being aware that it can appear both at the physical level (e.g., visual impairment, a lack of physical elements necessary to be able to hear) and the neurological level (the brain damage or retardation).

Among the five senses mentioned above, the crucial ones for processing information are vision and hearing, while the other three are of an augmentative or substitutional character. Thus, a special emphasis is put on these two vital senses when designing accessibility rules, while practically no account is taken of the other senses. At this point, it is worth adding that in the case of sensory disabilities involving vision and hearing, a so-called sensory compensation occurs where the damaged sense is *replaced* with another. When the ability to see is limited, these replacement senses are hearing and touch, and when hearing is damaged—the sight and touch senses take over. Hence the extremely difficult situation for deaf-blind people, whose only accessible sense with which to communicate is the sense of touch.

Visual impairment can manifest itself in many different forms and is a multidimensional phenomenon. The medical parameters that are most frequently used to describe vision are visual field and visual acuity. The former is measured as a percentage scale or expressed as an angle, which is a rather flexible kind of measurement, while the latter is measured using a Snellen chart, which is fixed and quantified. A person with low vision is one who can only read the biggest figure on a Snellen chart from a distance of 5 meters (sometimes 6 meters). A person who is considered blind is defined as someone who can only recognize the biggest figure from half the above distance, or who cannot read it at all.

Even though some people can read much more of a Snellen chart, they are still considered to be visually impaired. This impairment can involve a lack of vision in one eye, improper accommodation, problems with seeing and distinguishing colors, night blindness, light sensitivity, or even problems with recognizing motion. This is a really wide spectrum of impairment, and each one should be taken into account when encoding information.

When it comes to hearing impairments, the variation is much smaller; but problems of a different nature appear here. The basic parameter for measuring hearing loss is a unit called the decibel. Depending on the level of this parameter, we can distinguish deaf people, hearing-impaired people and people with hearing loss. As with people with visual impairment, this disability is of a continuous nature, and very often it is not possible to clearly indicate in which subgroup a certain person should be classified. A lack or loss of hearing is compensated for by the visual sense, so communication is based on information disseminated through this channel. At first sight we may assume that information in its text form should be sufficient, however, people who are deaf from birth do not know the Polish language, or know it only at an elementary level, as their basic language of communication is Polish sign language. What is more, a lack of verbal communication during childhood impedes the development of abstract thinking and sign language cannot fill this void.

Motor disabilities exert two kinds of influence on communication. First, a problem with the hands can substantially impede using standard devices (such as a keyboard, mouse or touchscreen). Second, a problem with muscles or neurological problems can limit such people's ability to communicate their messages in a clear way. It is important to add that physical venues, for example, meeting rooms, have to be selected carefully so that a person in a wheelchair or a person with crutches can access it.

Cognitive disabilities involve all sorts of limitations in understanding information. They can result from various phenomena: lower intellectual abilities, lack of knowledge of a given language, low level of education, a lack of specialist knowledge, or dyslexia. As can be seen, the reasons are numerous, but the effects are similar—they involve problems in understanding information. Instead of indicating the kind of disability or its parameters, we should rather indicate the potential groups that have problems with processing information. For instance, these are people with intellectual disabilities, foreigners or people in Polish communities abroad, people who are deaf from birth, people with a low level of education or of a different specialty, senior citizens, or people with certain kinds of dyslexia.

Commonly Used Technologies and Assistive Technologies

Where disability and ICT meet, one can find commonly used technologies and assistive technologies. The first category comprises all devices and software developed for all users, while assistive technologies are devices and software dedicated to disabled people with the aim of catering to their special needs. However, more and more often assistive technologies are becoming an integral part of commonly used technologies, which is in line with the rules of universal design (Hersh and Johnson 2010).

Assistive technologies comprise a wide spectrum of devices and software whose aim is to enable people with various kinds of disabilities to process information. This category can also include solutions that were initially developed for common use but have become assistive technologies due to their unique functions. For example, this is the case with optical character recognition (OCR) programs, which were developed to digitize paper documents and have become a solution for blind people, as they enable people with this disability to read print. Some examples of chosen technologies are presented below.

Screen readers are a type of software that interprets the information that appears on a device's screen (a computer, smartphone etc.) and then communicates this interpretation to the blind user using a speech synthesizer or Braille display. An item of information contains the following elements: the role of the element (a text field, button, choice field, edit box, etc.), the name (label, content, etc.) and the value (checked, field content, state). All this information comes from the graphic user interface (GUI), or to be more specific, from an accessible Application Programming Interface (API) that has been implemented in a given system. Some screen readers can read information directly thanks to changing the graphic card driver and by applying OCR, but usually this solution is not reliable. This is why the key to the correct use of screen readers is to develop user interfaces according to the accessibility rules, especially so that every element of the interface can have its text interpreted and it can be accessed from the keyboard, which is the blind users' primary device.

Speech synthesizers are devices or software that can transform a text stream into artificial human speech. The text stream is usually transmitted from a screen reader, although there are also applications of a self-voicing type that do it directly. Communication between the program and the speech synthesizer relies most often on a standardized system interface, for example, Microsoft Speech Application Programming Interface (MS Speech API) or Speech Dispatcher.

Refreshable Braille displays are devices that can present text information in Braille. Six-point or eight-point modules allow a single sign to be displayed, while the number of signs in a row determines both how comfortable it is to use and the price of a device. Incorporated in each module are metal or plastic spikes that are mounted on the surface of the display and makes it possible to read with the fingertips. Piezoelectric steering elements allow the spikes to be raised and lowered very precisely, depending on the signal sent from the driving device. A Braille display can be augmented with its own keyboard or internal software and can become an independent device called a Braille note-taker.

Braille embossers can be used to print text in Braille. After the translation of the text, it can be embossed in Braille onto paper or a transparency with the use of metal needles. The same technique can be used to make tactile graphics.

Magnifying devices can take the form of optical solutions (magnifiers) or electronic solutions (TV magnifiers and electronic magnifiers), and their task is to enlarge a picture and tailor it to the perception capabilities of a specific visually impaired person. Electronic solutions have a greater range of possibilities, as the visual signal can be processed to allow the colors to be changed, the use of different filters, and other elements that improve the quality of a picture. This type of picture can also be saved for later viewing or recognition if it is text.

Magnifiers are a form of software that can transform a picture displayed on the screen of a device (computer, smartphone etc.) and adapt it to the individual needs of the user. Contrary to what the name suggests, it is not only used to enlarge a picture but can also modify colors, smooth font edges and also read information using a speech synthesizer. An enlarged picture, or a section of it, is displayed in the upper part of the screen and can be moved about with a mouse or keyboard. It can also track the mouse cursor or the keyboard focus automatically.

People with hearing disabilities, even serious ones, can enhance their hearing with hearing aids. These are devices that enhance sound then transfer them after first processing them. Such aids are usually equipped with filters that are tuned to meet the needs of a certain user. There are different solutions applied to improve their performance, both for individuals (FM systems) and groups (induction loops). Both solutions play the same role, to transfer human speech from a microphone directly to a hearing aid. Thanks to this the hearing aids do not enhance the background noises, but only the voice itself.

People that have problems with speaking can use augmentative and alternative communication technologies. These enable people with different forms of autism or people who cannot speak for other reasons, to communicate with others. These tools can also help people with intellectual disabilities. Most frequently such solutions rely on a system of icons that symbolize different concepts (actions, objects, people, etc.), which a user can choose from. In this way, he or she can convey a message, even though they are not able to write or use sign language. Currently, these applications are most often installed on tablets with touchscreens, which allow recordings or speech synthesis to be connected with icons.

People with manual disabilities can use solutions that support moving a cursor or that help to type text. The simplest solution is a keyboard with partitions between the keys that limits the chance of pressing several keys at the same time by mistake. Also available are enlarged keyboards, with keys twice as big as standard ones. Using a mouse can be facilitated by replacing it with a trackball that has a large ball, or using an enlarged mouse. If a person has an even bigger problem with their hands, they can use an indicator mounted on the head. The cursor is then steered by the movements of the head and clicking is done by breathing into a special mouthpiece. There are even solutions that control the cursor using eyeball movement with clicking done by winking. Problems with using a cursor can be additionally reduced by applying intelligent drivers that detect involuntary movement and do not take them into account when steering or moving the cursor close to a graphic item.

Switches are really important solutions, as they are devices or applications that offer only two states: on or off. Most commonly they are large buttons, although, increasingly, there are more software orientated solutions that use touch screens, cameras or other standard peripheral device. A switch activates a single function, for example, pressing a key. Special software automatically moves the focus in adjustable intervals and waits for the next use of the switch. This method even allows a person with very limited motor possibilities to enter data.

Content and Interface Accessibility

Assistive technologies can be applied when content and interfaces are designed according to accessibility rules. Many documents on this topic have been developed, but the most recognized are the *WCAG 2.0* (World Wide Web Consortium 2008). They have also been incorporated in the ISO 40500/2012 standard and are recognized in Polish law thanks to the Polish cabinet's ordinance on the *National Interoperability Framework*. Therefore, only these guidelines will be discussed below.

At the highest level of the specification there are four principles that correspond perfectly with the three kinds of disabilities discussed at the beginning of this chapter:

- Principle 1: Perceivable. Information and the user interface components must be presented to users in ways they can perceive them.
- Principle 2: Operable. The user interface components and navigation must be operable.
- Principle 3: Understandable. The information and the operation of user interface must be understandable.
- Principle 4: Robust. The content must be robust enough to be interpreted reliably by a wide variety of *user agents*, including assistive technologies.

As can be seen, the first principle refers to sensory disabilities, the second to motor disabilities, the third to cognitive disabilities and the fourth to assistive technologies.

Under these four principles, there are twelve recommended guidelines that make the principles operational. The guidelines have success criteria, and these can be measured; therefore it can be determined whether the criteria have been met or not. These success criteria are linked to one of three levels of accessibility: A (elementary), AA (expanded) and AAA (full). To meet the recommended AA level, *all* the success criteria from levels A and AA must be met. It is also worth indicating the areas where there is a need to go above AA level to ensure the platform is widely accessible. The specificity of open debates, in their different forms, shows that some areas of information can be crucial; these are, above all, accessible documents, accessible multimedia and the appropriate language of communication. The platform for open debates has to fully meet the *WCAG 2.0* requirements at the AA level; however, it also has to meet some criteria at the AAA level, which is beyond *WCAG 2.0*.

Debates involve analyzing different documents, among them, ones that are not text. Thus the basic accessibility problem is in using the right format and the right level of accessibility for electronic documents. The following are the principles for the developing and publishing of such documents:

- Text documents cannot be replaced by a scanned image. This is especially difficult when the circulation of documents within a given office is in a paper, not electronic form. Documents should be digitized and then proofread to eliminate mistakes.
- If this technique is applied, then the widest possible range of semantic labelling of information should be used in documents, especially if it refers to tables, section titles, notes and quotes as well as commentaries.
- Crucial information cannot be distinguished in only one way, for example, with a color, as it may be inaccessible to some users. This refers to the elements that are deleted, changed, commented on, important, etc.
- Graphic information should always be accompanied by text information that fully describes the picture. This sort of alternative description requires a lot of work and knowledge about the object being described. Maps, diagrams, architectural designs, infographics and charts are of the highest level of difficulty.
- The visual presentation of text, and images of text must have a contrast ratio of at least 7:1 and have the possibility for font size and colors adjustment.
- Sign language interpretation must be provided for all important texts.

Additionally:

- Information should be conveyed in an understandable way. The language should be simple, contain no jargon, and acronyms should be defined when they are first used. A mechanism for defining specific words and phrases that are used in an unusual or specific way, including idioms, jargon, abbreviations and acronyms would be useful.
- When a text requires a reading ability more advanced than the lower secondary education level, a simplified version should be made available.

Multimedia used in open debates consists mainly of transmissions and recordings, but the requirements apply to live meetings as well. The following are principles for multimedia use:

- The use of subtitles is necessary in material where voice transmission is crucial. This refers to recordings (closed captions), transmissions (live captions), as well as meetings.
- Without sign language interpretation a substantial portion of deaf people who do not read would be excluded. Thus, synchronized media containing pre-recorded or live audio content should be available in sign language. It should also be made possible for deaf people to interact in this language.
- Having low or no background sounds in pre-recorded or live media is important for hard of hearing people.

Finally, it is worth noting the following:

- Information about a user's location within a set of web pages should be available. This is very important for users who are not experienced in using modern internet sites.
- Context-sensitive help should also be accessible (Rutter, Lauke et al. 2006; Paskiewicz and Dębski 2013; Zadrożny 2014).

InDialogue Platform Compliance Testing

In this part of the chapter, we report on the results of the inDialogue platform's compliance test; dividing the analysis into four parts so that each part refers to one of the aforementioned principles of accessibility: *perceivability, operability, understandability* and *robustness.*

Both the citizens and clerks' panels were tested (including the TeamTalk voice communication tool). Full compliance with the WCAG 2.0 guidelines means that the platform is accessible to people with various disabilities (sensory, motor, and intellectual).

Evaluation According to Principle 1: Perception

When checking accessibility in the area of perception, the first thing to do is test the *non-text elements* such as bitmaps, multimedia, maps, form fields, and security mechanisms like CAPTCHA, etc. According to the guidelines, all non-textual content must have a textual equivalent. This means, for example, the need to include alternative text for graphic elements that will allow blind people to read the content presented in the graphic. The graphics on the page are primarily icons used as a link to open the help window, or graphics in the debates' information materials. The help icons in the inDialogue platform have been described properly, so blind people receive the right information about their functions. Graphics (photos) placed in the information material have no alternative text.

The inDialogue platform is equipped with the ability to add alternate text for graphical elements (images, etc.), which is available to the editors (officials) that embed the content. To make it practical the WCAG 2.0 guidelines, and techniques for implementing these guidelines should be included in the manual for the public officials who publish the content online.

The next item to be tested is *time-based media*, that is, movies and audio recordings. According to the WCAG 2.0 guidelines, time-based media should be provided with alternative content that can be read by users who have minimal vision or are blind. In the case of movies without audio, it is necessary to make a transcript or audio clip that shares the same content as the video. Transcripts should be provided for all audio recordings. For movies with audio, it is necessary to provide captions and an audio description. Captions include a dialogue list and a description of the sounds appearing in the video that are relevant for the proper understanding of the content. Audio description is a verbal description of the content presented in the film (e.g., the look of the rooms, clothing, actors, objects, etc.) that enables blind people to access more content from the film. The audio description is prepared as an additional audio track. The above requirements do not apply to live streaming, or to audio and video as an alternative to texts.

The type of multimedia used in the inDialogue platform is video content with sign language as an alternative to text content. Transcripts or audio descriptions of these materials are not necessary, however, as the audio recordings of the discussions will be published, the organizers of public consultations should be aware that they will need to be transcribed. The training of inDialogue users (content editors, clerks) needs to include a dedicated section on the preparation of alternative content for time-based media. It is particularly important to be able to distinguish between media types over time and to match alternate content to the type; it is important for consultants to acquire the practical knowledge and skills to enable them to create the above components. The training must include the technical issues related to the handling of programs and platforms that support alternative content creation (audio-video editing programs, captioning software, online captioning platforms, captioning for YouTube, Facebook, Vimeo etc.). As for the use of live discussions (TeamTalk), voice-debate software has been simplified (compared to the original version) so that the version provided to users of the platform only has the features needed to conduct voice debates. This makes the software easy to use even for low skilled users. TeamTalk is fully accessible to screen reading software; all the buttons have labels and all functions are accessible through the keyboard.

The proper *use of semantic tags* has a significant impact, not only on the screen reader's ability to read content but primarily on the user's ability to understand the structure of a web page.

The use of semantic tags for the text objects on the page (headings, lists, form field labels, titles, and table headers) was validated. There were no errors in this area, as the semantic tags are automatically assigned by the platform software, so the user cannot make a mistake in this area. Also, in the use of sensory properties as operating instructions no obstacles were found. The page does not use the color, shape, or location of the item as part of the instruction (for example, "press the blue button").

A screen reader reads aloud what is on the screen in lines from top to bottom. In order for the people using screen readers to understand the content of a web page, the elements must be arranged in a logical order. A possible obstacle was found in the order of these elements and, therefore, in the associated ability to properly understand the contents of the page. On the tested page, the keyboard selection (enter key) for the tabs title, displays the tab content but does not move the keyboard focus. Thus, the person using the screen reader must go through all the other tabs and the information materials button to read the contents of the selected tab. This distorts the logical order of the information and may cause some difficulty in understanding it. It is recommended that the logical order for reading the tabs' contents be preserved by the reading program, for example, by replacing the tabs layout with a so-called accordion module layout. Figure 1 illustrates bookmarks (details, debates, surveys, schedule) that organize consultation information.

Figure 1. Bookmarks view with consultation information on the inDialogue platform

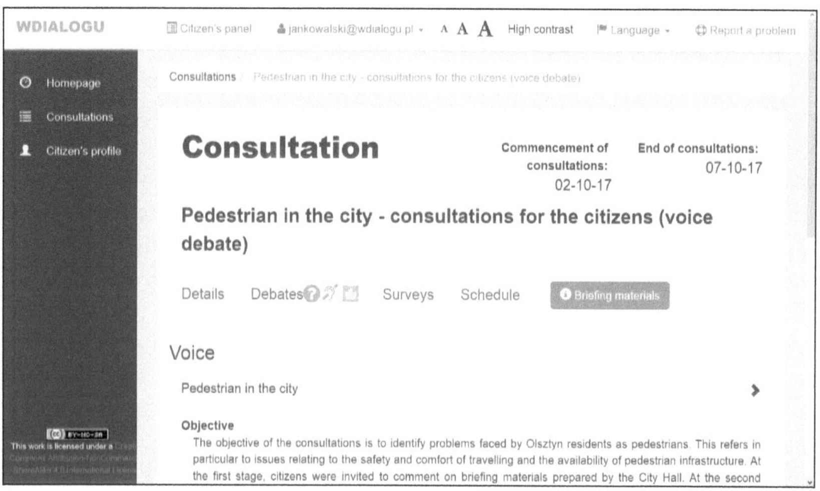

According to WCAG 2.0, the color contrast between text and background should be 4.5:1 (with minor exceptions). The tests of the inDialogue software revealed a problem with too little color contrast between text and background in both the regular and high contrast color layouts of the website. The links and features found in the upper bar of the page (Citizen Panel, Log Off, Language Change) had a contrast ratio of 4.48:1 or lower, the grey fonts in the breadcrumbs module (Consultation Name, Timeline, etc.) had a contrast ratio 2.61:1, and the remaining information shown in a grey color (a contrast ratio 2.85:1) were too low contrast in relation to the background on which they were placed. It is recommended that the contrast between the above elements and the background color *be* increased (i.e., apply a darker grey or black color to fonts). The screenshot below shows elements with a too low contrast ratio.

Figure 2. Elements with too low contrast ratio

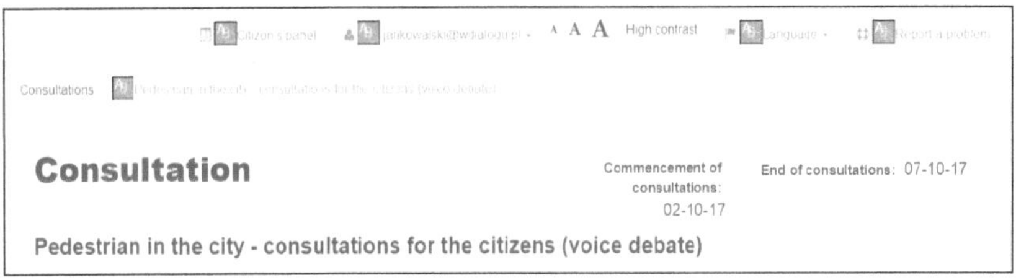

It is worth noting that a high-contrast color scheme, despite maintaining the right contrast ratio, can still be difficult for visually impaired people because of the large number of different colors used to present the information (light green, light blue, violet, yellow, white); thus, it is also recommended that the number of colors used in the high-contrast version of the page be limited. A good practice is to use a two-color page layout, for example: black fonts/white background, white fonts/black background, black fonts/yellow background, yellow fonts/black background. Figure 3 illustrates the dislplay of too many colors in high contrast mode.

Figure 3. Too many colors in high contrast mode

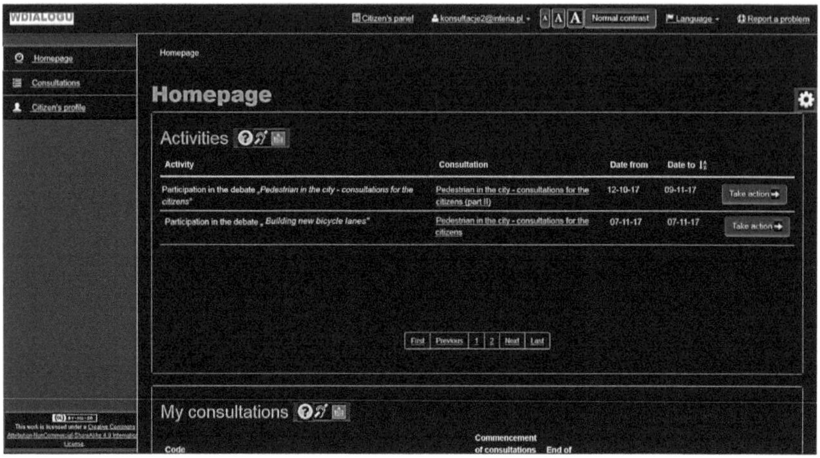

For visually impaired people, the web page offers the correct font enlargement function, thus making it possible to change the size of the text. At the same time, the site is responsive and reacts very well when zoomed in and out using the browser's zoom function. Using the platform on mobile devices does not cause any hindrances.

It is also an advantage that the inDialogue platform does not comprise any text content in the form of graphics, bitmaps or scans. Nevertheless, the platform's user training program must include a unit dedicated to the proper preparation of information materials to be published by the organizers of public consultations. A common mistake made by content editors is to place scanned documents on web pages. The bitmap is completely inaccessible to the screen reader software, so if such a document is published there should be a guaranteed alternative version to its content that is accessible. The training must include guidance on the desired formats for published documents and a section on techniques for preparing alternative content for text images.

Evaluation According to Principle 2: Operability

As far as rule 2 is concerned, the *keyboard-only operation* of the website was tested. This aspect is particularly important for users who don't use a mouse (blind people, people with neurological disorders, the elderly, people with spinal cord injuries).

During the tests, a problem with the Delete Account link/button in the citizen's profile was identified. The link could not be accessed using the tab key (the link was skipped). This restriction also applies to the Google Places option available in the Citizen's Profile tab; it is impossible to choose a residential address using the keyboard. It is recommended that the possibility of reading/operating all components of the platform using the keyboard be provided.

The lack of a visible focus indicator when navigating the page with the keyboard also raises objections. Each website element should be clearly marked with a frame when it takes the keyboard's focus. It is good practice to use Cascading Style Sheets (CSS) pseudo-class to determine the appearance of the focus element. An acceptable (though not recommended) solution is to leave the appearance of the focus to the default browser settings.

The other elements tested in the area of functionality were correct and do not interfere with the use of the inDialogue platform. These concern:

- navigation order. When navigating the page using the keyboard (tab key), the focus elements are arranged in logical order so that the content of the page is understandable;
- no keyboard trap. People who use the platform using only the keyboard must be able to handle all of its functions without the risk of locking the focus anywhere on the page (keyboard trap). This is quite a common mistake, which completely prevents the use of web pages;
- time adaptability. There is no mechanism for adjusting time in the inDialogue platform because the use of the platform (session time) is not limited. Such mechanisms are used for security purposes, for example, in electronic banking systems;
- occurrence of flashing elements that can cause epileptic seizures. If the site uses animations/multimedia, a check should be made that the content does not flash more than three times per second. This rule applies to all the video/animated elements of the website. Elements that flash too fast can cause epileptic seizures;
- page titles. This is the first information read by the screen reader after loading a web page. Poorly designed page titles stop blind people from navigating properly between pages on a website;
- link targets. The reading program recognizes the links placed on the page. When reading a page, the program notifies blind users that the text being read is a link. The construction of these links is important for users of screen reading software as the purpose of the link has to be clear;
- headers and labels. This is one of the key elements in the logical structure of a website and allows reading programs to browse web pages by *headings*. When the headings structure is correct, a blind person can find the beginning of an article, the next chapter, or the important sections of a web page more easily.

Labels are used to describe form fields, and if they are correct it makes it possible to properly fill in forms on websites;

- the ability to reach the same place on different pages. This is a feature of well-designed websites. This makes it easier to navigate the site and reduces the time it takes to find information.

Evaluation According to Principle 3: Understandability

The first aspect of the software's functioning that was tested here was the *language tag*. This concerns the webpage or its elements. Having the correct language tag for a webpage, or for part of a webpage, is important because screen readers match the pronunciation (including accent) using this tag. A Polish language website with a badly defined language tag will be completely incomprehensible to a blind person. The tests showed that the language tags for the inDialogue platform are correct.

The *adoption of the focus* by any element of the page was also tested to make sure it did not change the context, and whether data entry did not result in any changes to the webpage (e.g., when filling in a form). The results of the test did not indicate any problems in this area.

The *consistency of layout* and *marking of navigation elements* (menus, etc.) was also analyzed. This is an important feature of good websites, and not only for people with disabilities. Placing navigation elements (menus) in the same place on all pages of the website makes it easy for all users to navigate the website. It is also important that the same menus are identically labeled on each page. In the inDialogue platform, this rule is implemented very well. The side and top menus do not vary and are always in the same place. The content layout is also identical for each consultation.

A detailed analysis was performed regarding the *forms* users fill in with information. The error reporting mechanism and suggestion mechanism that operate when data is entered into a form were checked. The error message or suggested correction must be displayed and must be readable by the screen reader. All fields of the form must be properly marked in the page code. In none of the aforementioned areas were problems found.

Evaluation According to Principle 4: Robustness

In this area, the reliability (robustness) of the page code (html and CSS) was tested. The tests concerned semantic correctness and the existence of errors such as open tags or obsolete elements and attributes. The test was carried out using automatic tools, i.e., html and CSS validators. These automatic tests showed errors in both html and CSS code. It should be noted that the user test (performed by a blind person using the screen-reading software) did not show any problems in accessing the website that resulted from the errors in the html or CSS code layer.

Conclusion

In this chapter, we discussed the standards and conditions of ICT accessibility for people with disabilities (WCAG 2.0), and applied them to an analysis of the accessibility of the inDialogue platform. The main conclusions are that the site's structure and information layout are well designed. The use of WAI-ARIA[2] to designate roles and properties facilitates the use of the website by users with disabilities. The site is simple, easy to navigate and to understand. Although the inDialogue platform does not meet all of the WCAG 2.0 guidelines' requirements, it can be considered to be a relatively accessible website. Although the errors diagnosed do not have a major impact on the accessibility of the site, rectification of these errors will be performed in order to achieve the required level of compliance with WCAG 2.0.

References

Books and articles

Hersh, Marion, and Michael Johnson, eds. 2010. *Assistive technology for the hearing-impaired, deaf and deafblind.* London: Springer Science & Business Media.

Paszkiewicz, Dominik, and Jakub Dębski. 2013. *Dostępność serwisów Internetowych: dobre praktyki w projektowaniu serwisów Internetowych dostępnych dla osób z różnymi rodzajami niepełnosprawności.* Warsaw: Stowarzyszenie Przyjaciół Integracji.

Rutter, Richard, Patrick H. Lauke et al. 2006. *Web accessibility: Web standards and regulatory compliance.* Berkeley, CA: Apress.

Wiszejko-Wierzbicka, Dorota. 2010. *Niewykorzystana sfera. Partycypacja społeczna i obywatelska osób z ograniczeniami sprawności.* Warsaw: Scholar.

2 *Web Accessibility Initiative – Accessible Rich Internet Applications* (WAI-ARIA) is a technical specification published by the World Wide Web Consortium (W3C) that specifies how to increase the accessibility of web pages, in particular, dynamic content, and user interface components developed with Ajax, HTML, JavaScript, and related technologies (see https://en.wikipedia.org/wiki/WAI-ARIA, accessed October 10, 2017).

Zadrożny, Jacek. 2014. "Web Content Accessibility Guidelines (WCAG) 2.0 – zasady i wytyczne do tworzenia dostępnych serwisów Internetowych". *Niepełnosprawność-zagadnienia, problemy, rozwiązania* 12 (3): 17–23.

Legal source

The Ordinance of the Council of Ministers of 12 April 2012 on the National Interoperability Framework, minimum requirements for public registers and information-sharing in electronic formats and minimum requirements for ICT systems (*Journal of Laws*) 2012, item 526.

Other

World Wide Web Consortium. 2008. *Web content accessibility guidelines* (WCAG) 2.0. Accessed August 2015. https://www.w3.org/WAI/intro/wcag.php.

Robert Bembenik, Anna Przybylska, Aneta Świercz and Jacek Zadrożny

Chapter 5. ICT Solutions for Voice Moderated Debates

Introduction

InDialogue is a multi-functional platform that consists of several integrated tools that make deliberative public consultations practical. This includes, among other applications, the tools for text and voice-based debates. The text-based discussion forum, which is specific because of its formal structure based on questions and proposals, and the pros and cons arguments put forward by participants, was built by the In Dialogue team, along with the deliberation criteria that we had operationalized and implemented using ICT. As far as the tools for voice debates are concerned, we wanted to explore existing solutions to see if they would fit the model of communication that we had envisaged and if so, to what extent. We did not predefine whether we would use the already existing tools and try to integrate them with the inDialogue platform, or to adapt them where advisable and possible, and if so, to what degree.

This chapter aims to present the criteria that we used to assess the ICT platforms that support voice communication as well as demonstrate the results of this analysis. We have taken into consideration three broad categories of evaluation criteria: cost; technical aspects that have consequences for the accessibility of the ICT tools, especially for people with disabilities; and features that may strengthen the deliberativeness of online meetings. We conclude the chapter with information on the tools we chose for voice communication and on their development for the purpose of the In Dialogue project.

Voice Communication Technologies

ICT tools that support voice communication are known by various names: online meeting software, web conferencing software, webinar, online meeting, or video/voice conferencing. They encompass technology that allows for online synchronous communication (Web conferencing 2015; Farkas 2013). The terminology related to these technologies is imprecise, and no standards organization exists to provide an established usage reference.

Online meeting software can be implemented as follows: (i) a shared hosted service, (ii) a local installation, or (iii) a hybrid installation. The shared hosted service is a solution in which an online meeting-software service is offered by a provider. Usually, no local hardware/software infrastructure is required on the part of the client; in most cases, the software is accessible via a web browser. The local installation solution requires dedicated hardware/software infrastructure, ample bandwidth, and a support team who is responsible for the smooth operation of the system. The reason for using a hybrid solution is to combine the best features of these two systems (the local installation and a shared hosted service), i.e., cost-effective internal (within the organization) online meetings and a high performance for meetings including external participants (Web Conferencing Evaluation Guide 2015).

The features of online meeting software include voice communication and text chat (Scales and Cummings 2009). It is also usually possible to make video calls using users' webcams; video transmission, however, requires good bandwidth. Typically, online meeting software allows for the sharing and displaying of files and offers collaborative whiteboards. Most software allows for online meeting sessions to be recorded and accessed at a later time.

Using online meeting software has both advantages and disadvantages when compared to face-to-face meetings. The main advantage is that the interaction and user experience is similar to face-to-face meetings but offers the user the convenience of not having to travel to the meeting place, thus saving time and money on a journey that one would otherwise have to make. The problems related to online meeting software include the potential difficulties that participants may have in running and operating the software (Bower 2011; Farkas 2013; Kear et al. 2012; Morrison 2011). These problems may be related to low computer literacy, old computers, or unreliable internet connections. In addition to this, problems related to the system's configuration and fine-tuning may come into play. These problems typically concern the audio configuration (microphone not working correctly or not activated, echo, etc.) and trouble displaying the images projected by the speaker during the meeting. We have also been challenged by these problems while conducting experimental projects during 2011–2012.

Rankings of online meeting software can be found on the internet. Various winners emerge from these rankings, although there is a group of tools that appear in many of the lists. Reviews of online meeting software are presented in the Gartner report, who analyzes commercial communication solutions (Elliot et al. 2017). The internet service, toptenreviews.com, presents the current ranking of the best services for voice and video collaboration (Web Conferencing Reviews

2015). For comparison, the following criteria have been taken into consideration: presenter tools, participant tools, web conference features, and help and support. The leaders in the rankings were Onstream Meetings, InterCall, GlobalMeet, Adobe Connect Pro, ClickMeeting, ReadyTalk, WebEx, GoToMeeting, FUZE Meeting, and iLinc. The top ten web conferencing tools are also presented in a dedicated report by the service, business-software.com, which specializes in software comparisons and rankings. The software presented in the report were compared according to key features: SaaS platform, SaaS & on-premise, HD video/audio, screen sharing, recording, mobile app, one-click meetings, surveys & polls, collaboration tools, and reporting. The winners included in the report were as follows: ReadyTalk, Citrix GoToMeeting, GlobalMeet, Cisco WebEx, Skype, Adobe Connect, Microsoft Office Lync Office, ClickMeeting, and Personify Live. These rankings focused on software quality and the availability of functions for business users, and did not take into account that the platform may be used by disabled people; so accessibility functions for the disabled were not a selection criterion.

Deliberation and ICT Assessment Criteria

Decades have passed since Arterton (1987) presented his categorization of technical tools to be used in public consultations. Some of them support plebiscitary forms of two-way communication between public officials and citizens, while others are dialogue-oriented. Following on from Arterton's research numerous applied studies were undertaken on the use of various methods for running deliberative meetings, for example, deliberative polling, planning cells, and consensus conferences. This might be regarded as the first step towards the institutionalization of public deliberation (Crosby 1975; Dienel 1997; Fishkin 2009). There is no doubt that online deliberative consultations, their prerogatives and formal solutions have been the subject of scrutiny and development up until today (Dahlberg 2004; Davis and Gangadharan 2009; Coleman and Shane 2012). All these projects influenced our thinking concerning a model for ICT supported deliberative public consultations, especially that part devoted to mini-public online voice meetings.

Our work in developing tools to support voice debates has been informed by the core values of deliberation, such as openness, inclusion, reciprocity and reflectiveness, which we have operationalized and presented as formal components of the software. In Chapter 2 these values are discussed in reference to the inDialogue platform model at large; here we will be more specific. Thus, we propose to analyze openness in reference to the technology's affordability for local governments and inhabitants, due to the various license types and costs demanded by license owners. The most crucial aspect in respect to both openness and inclusion is access to multimedia for people with disabilities. Further, we demonstrate the possible consequences of some of the technical aspects of moderation for reciprocity. Finally, we consider the potential dependence of reflexivity on the technical arrangements for the availability of information and experts.

The tool for voice debates should meet a number of requirements that result from the particular needs of the project. First of all, the tool must be multichannel, i.e., be able to transmit information through different channels:

1. Voice channels for the transmission of speech.
2. Visual channels for transmitting presentations, movies and the sign language interpreter's image.
3. Textual channels for introducing information and a description or transcription of the video and audio.
4. Binary channels for the transmission of additional materials, such as documents, plans, etc.

The tools must be easy to use so that all users, even those with little digital competence, are able to operate them. This is indirectly linked to the need for a solution that should be as independent of the user's system as possible; this strongly favors web-based solutions. Simplicity of use is important so as not to create further entry barriers. During the testing of the tools, special attention was paid to whether the interface was in Polish (or easily converted to Polish) and whether it was easy to use. What made meeting these conditions of simplicity even more difficult was the fact that the tool had to support multiple functionalities, including some quite exotic ones such as toggling on a sign language interpreter.

The availability of accessibility features in ICT for people with disabilities means openness and inclusion. Users with disabilities should be able to enter a *virtual room* for discussions, which fulfills the requirement of openness. They then should also be able to use all the tools available to those participants without disabilities, which fulfills the requirements of inclusion. The accessibility of the interfaces is typically programmed at the interface implementation stage and is the developer's responsibility, while the accessibility of the content depends on all the people who publish this content on the web. The latter subject is discussed in Chapter 2.

Assistive technologies are the various technical solutions whose function it is to compensate for the limitations resulting from disabilities. In the context of the platform for voice debates, screen readers, speech synthesizers (to assist the blind), magnifying software (to assist the visually impaired) and remote sign language interpretation (to assist the deaf), are of key importance. In the wider context of social consultation, induction loops, FM systems (to assist the hard of hearing), devices to assist data entry (for people with motor disabilities), and devices to assist augmentative and alternative communication (AAC, e.g., for people with intellectual disability) should also be added. In most cases, assistive technologies are used by the people with disabilities themselves (e.g., FM systems, which are personal devices), but technical infrastructure during meetings must be provided by the organizer (e.g., remote sign language interpretation or induction loops, which are installed in meeting rooms). Bartosz Stępień and Jacek Zadrożny elaborate on this issue in the context of web content accessibility guidelines in Chapter 4.

In deliberative consultations, we aim to create an environment that is conducive to reciprocity and reflectiveness. In our analysis, we have attempted to assess existing internet platforms for voice communication according to the criteria that, in our opinion, create the conditions for these values to be implemented. The minimum condition for reciprocity is met when participants in a discussion listen to each other and are attentive to other speakers' arguments. It is difficult to create an environment in which people learn from the experience of fellow participants when many of them speak at the same time. In a face-to-face encounter, there are more elements of control, which may prevent such a situation occurring. Even so, it is the rule rather than the exception; thus, we had to think about applications that could be integrated into the tools for voice discussions that would encourage some types of group behaviors while limiting others.

First, we searched for software that would allow a closed group of participants to be invited; thus, only those who were invited could enter a discussion room. The participants would either have to register with a login and a password, or would receive a link that opened the room at a set time. Then there is the condition concerning parallel meetings. If group discussions are to be efficient, they need to have an imposed limit of participants. The more questions and the shorter the time, the smaller the number of people permitted to attend the meeting. For focus groups of 2.5 hours, this would be approximately 12 people. In our opinion, it is harder to keep a high level of attentiveness and activity during online voice discussions than it is with face-to-face discussions. Thus, having other similar conditions, we would recommend that approximately eight participants meet at a time in online voice deliberations. Parallel rooms would be a convenient solution to the problem of increasing the total number of participants. Of course, we may also hold asynchronous discussions; but it is good to have a choice, especially if, apart from group discussions, we want to organize a plenary session with experts for all participants meeting in one room. It is easier and more efficient to organize five groups of participants at the same time than organizing a plenary session with experts five times for each group or two meetings for each group—one for a discussion and one for a plenary session. It is worth noting that a room that can hold a minimum of 80 people is needed for a plenary meeting with experts.

Next, for the purposes of an orderly discussion it may be important that information on who is speaking should be visible to everyone. When a speaker who is talking is distinguished, for instance, by the sign of a microphone next to their name, it is easier to refer to them directly once they have finished their speech. This function may increase reciprocity and support group formation, irrespective of the opinions held by its members. Depending on the group and the behavior of its members, it may or may not be useful to control the discussion by switching on and off a microphone. A self-governing group respecting the rights of everyone to voice their opinions is certainly an ideal that occurs in practice, but rather rarely. When at least some of the members cannot control their emotions or are not used to deliberating, the moderator's control over the microphone is a compromise. Besides, it is useful for the moderator's profile to be distinct from the profile of other participants. The moderator is the one who initiates the debate and introduces the rules, follows the schedule and proposes questions, as well as keeps track of the time. They react to any abuse of the rules and can exclude from the discussion any participants who fail to obey them. It might be practical for all groups, including self-governing groups, to be able to follow the list of people who are requesting the floor, which can be displayed on the screen in real time. Each participant can *virtually* raise their hand, which indicates a willingness to speak and enables them to take a turn when they are listed first without any intervention by the moderator. They can also withdraw from a line, giving up their turn to someone else if they decide that their opinion has already been presented by another person. This transparent turn taking procedure strengthens the impartiality of the process of deliberation and may support the building of trust. It allows people to focus on talk rather than on speculation regarding whose opinion is favored by the moderator.

Undeniably, the open and reciprocal exchange of information and arguments among participants contribute to reflection on the subject of consultations. It is a well-known fact that people tend to assemble with others who hold similar opinions to their own (Mutz 2008). Thus, public consultations in which people from different socio-economic statuses can meet in one room is a unique opportunity to get acquainted with points of view that they would otherwise not have known about. This may lead to a change in established and often unchallenged opinions. Software allowing parallel meetings of small heterogeneous groups facilitates this. An additional factor that may strengthen reflectiveness is the presence of a *virtual board* on which the moderator may show relevant information from the briefing materials prepared for the purpose of consultations, or make notes summarizing each point of the debate. The technical possibility of being able to record the conversation and make it available to participants may also help them to better reflect on the subject before the next round of discussions or before they express their preferences.

Research Methodology and the Results of a Comparative Analysis

We have prepared a ranking of the platforms based on a system where points are awarded for meeting the standards of the adopted model.

Our analysis started with an overview of 89 platforms according to the following criteria:

- cost (the ICT tools' commercial or non-commercial status)
- the installation location (online or on the user's computer)
- technology (e.g., presence of *Java* or *Flash* not accessible to blind people)

At this stage, the analysis was based on the information published in the documentation provided by the producers. When information on the issues that interested us was lacking we contacted the producers; however, in many cases, we were unable to obtain the data that we were searching for. For this reason, in the table that presents the results of the preliminary analysis, we do not claim that some of the software concerned did not, for example, have accessibility features; instead, we indicate that it was not possible to determine whether it had them.

In the later phase of our analysis, we compared several platforms (including commercial platforms and tools without accessibility features) to find out if they supported deliberation (moderation and access to information), and if so, how. The accessibility of tools for people with disabilities was non-negotiable. In turn, the features that may strengthen or weaken the deliberativeness of debates were optional, with one exception: the possibility of inviting a defined group of people to a debate. But, it is the number of points attributed in total that decides which platform is the most functional; vis-à-vis the model that we adopted.

Openness and Inclusion

The overview of the voice communication software covers both open source as well as commercial tools. The existing online meeting software is compared in Table 1 together with the following information:

- *License type.* Generally one can divide existing software licenses into open-source or commercial. Choosing open-source software entails installation, configuration and maintenance of the software. Choosing commercial software involves direct monthly/yearly licensing payments.

- *Accessibility* features according to the documentation. An essential aspect of the In Dialogue project is to make the deliberative platform accessible for people with disabilities.
- *Use of Flash technology.* In our preliminary tests of the communication tools, we learned that the screen readers used by blind people cannot interpret/ operate with software developed using Flash technology.
- *Use of Java technology.* This had similar issues to Flash technology, but after installing the appropriate libraries in the reader, it was possible to access such software. We decided such software was worth considering.
- *Implementation method.* Online meeting software can be implemented as a shared hosted service, a local installation, or a hybrid installation.

A comparison of the 89 software packages for online meetings is presented in Table 1. The primary source of information concerning existing online meeting software was Wikipedia.[1] Our comparison covers most of the tools listed there, plus some additional software. As there were a large number of online meeting software packages considered for use in the project, we did not test for accessibility features of every piece of software ourselves. At this stage, we filtered the available software based on the accessibility information found in the documentation and obtained from the manufacturers via e-mail or telephone. The actual testing, in this respect, was carried out in stage two of the selection process on software that mentioned accessibility features. The usage of Flash or Java technology was an additional means helpful in determining accessibility.

Table 1. Juxtaposition of commercial and open-source online meeting software

No	Online meeting software	Licence type	Accessibility	Flash-based?	Java-based?	Implementation method
1.	4Webcom	comm.	NDA	NDA	NDA	shs
2.	AccuConference	comm.	NDA	NDA	NDA	shs
3.	Adobe Connect	comm.	NDA	y	n	shs
4.	AnyMeeting	comm.	NDA	y	NDA	shs
5.	AT&Y Connect	comm.	NDA	NDA	NDA	shs
6.	AVIDO Web Conference	comm.	NDA	NDA	NDA	shs

1 Comparison of web conferencing software, https://en.wikipedia.org/wiki/Comparison_of_web_conferencing_software, accessed January 15, 2015.

No	Online meeting software	Licence type	Accessibility	Flash-based?	Java-based?	Implementation method
7.	Banckle Online Meeting	comm.	NDA	NDA	NDA	shs
8.	BigBlueButton	LGPL, GPL (Mozilla)	NDA	y	n	shs
9.	BigMarker	comm.	NDA	NDA	NDA	shs
10.	Blackboard Collaborate	comm.	NDA	NDA	NDA	shs
11.	Cisco WebEx	comm.	NDA	NDA	NDA	shs
12.	Citrix GotoMeeting	comm.	NDA	NDA	NDA	shs
13.	ClickMeeting	comm.	NDA	y	NDA	shs
14.	Cliqmeet	comm.	NDA	y	NDA	shs
15.	CUMeeting	comm.	NDA	NDA	NDA	shs
16.	eLecta Live	comm.	NDA	NDA	NDA	shs
17.	FaceMe Web Conference	comm.	NDA	y	NDA	shs
18.	FastViewer	comm.	NDA	NDA	NDA	NDA
19.	FreeConference	comm.	NDA	NDA	NDA	shs
20.	FUZE Meeting	comm.	NDA	NDA	NDA	shs
21.	Genesys Meeting Center	comm.	NDA	NDA	NDA	shs
22.	Glance	comm.	NDA	NDA	NDA	shs
23.	GlobalMeet	comm.	NDA	y	n	shs
24.	GoMeetNow	comm.	NDA	n	n	shs
25.	Groupworld	comm.	NDA	n	n	shs
26.	Homer Conferencing (beta)	comm.	NDA	n	n	li
27.	IBM Sametime	comm.	NDA	n	NDA	li
28.	iLinc	comm.	NDA	NDA	NDA	hi
29.	iMeet	comm.	NDA	y	NDA	shs
30.	Infinite Conferencing WebInterpoint	comm.	NDA	NDA	NDA	shs
31.	inphra online	comm.	NDA	n	n	shs
32.	InterCall Unified Meeting	comm.	NDA	NDA	NDA	li
33.	Jitsi	LGPL	NDA	n	y	li
34.	join.me	comm.	NDA	NDA	NDA	shs

No	Online meeting software	Licence type	Accessibility	Flash-based?	Java-based?	Implementation method
35.	Kablink	Common Public Attribution License 1.0 (CPAL)	NDA	NDA	NDA	li
36.	Lucid Meetings	comm.	NDA	NDA	NDA	shs
37.	ManageMeet	comm.	NDA	NDA	NDA	shs
38.	Meetecho	comm.	NDA	NDA	NDA	shs
39.	MeetingBurner	comm.	NDA	NDA	NDA	shs
40.	MegaMeeting.com	comm.	NDA	NDA	NDA	shs
41.	Microsoft Lync	comm.	NDA	NDA	NDA	hi
42.	Mikogo	comm.	NDA	n	NDA	hi
43.	Momentum Meeting Solutions	comm.	NDA	NDA	NDA	shs
44.	MyOwnConfernce	comm.	NDA	NDA	NDA	shs
45.	Nefsis	comm.	NDA	NDA	NDA	shs
46.	omNovia Web Conference	comm.	NDA	NDA	NDA	shs
47.	Onstream Meetings	comm.	NDA	y	n	shs
48.	OnSync	comm.	NDA	n	NDA	shs
49.	Openmeetings	Apache License	NDA	y	n	shs
50.	Palava.tv	open source	NDA	n	n	shs
51.	Personify Live	comm.	NDA	NDA	NDA	hi
52.	PHP Video Conference	comm.	NDA	y	NDA	li
53.	PowWow365	comm.	NDA	NDA	NDA	shs
54.	PowwowNow	comm.	NDA	NDA	NDA	hi
55.	ReadyTalk	comm.	NDA	y	NDA	shs
56.	RedBack	comm.	NDA	n	NDA	shs
57.	RHUB	comm.	NDA	NDA	NDA	li
58.	SaasBoard	comm.	NDA	NDA	NDA	NDA
59.	Saba Meeting	comm.	NDA	NDA	NDA	shs
60.	Secretly Meet (beta)	comm.	NDA	NDA	NDA	shs
61.	Skype	freemium	y	n	n	li

No	Online meeting software	Licence type	Accessibility	Flash-based?	Java-based?	Implementation method
62.	Solgenia Weblive Facsys	comm.	NDA	NDA	NDA	hi
63.	Spreed	comm.	NDA	NDA	NDA	shs
64.	StartMeeting	comm.	NDA	NDA	NDA	shs
65.	TeamTalk 5	freeware/ open source	y	n	n	li
66.	TeamViewer	comm.	NDA	NDA	NDA	hi
67.	Teleskill Live	comm.	NDA	y	NDA	shs
68.	tokbox	comm.	NDA	n	n	shs
69.	TrueConf	comm.	NDA	NDA	NDA	shs
70.	Twiddla	comm.	NDA	n	NDA	shs
71.	UberConference	comm.	NDA	n	NDA	shs
72.	Ubipitch	comm.	NDA	NDA	NDA	NDA
73.	VConNDAHD	comm.	NDA	NDA	NDA	shs
74.	Veeting Rooms	comm.	NDA	NDA	NDA	shs
75.	VenueGen	comm.	NDA	NDA	NDA	NDA
76.	VideoMost	comm.	NDA	NDA	NDA	shs
77.	VisiMeet	comm.	NDA	NDA	NDA	li
78.	VisiWeb	comm.	NDA	NDA	NDA	shs
79.	vLine	comm.	NDA	NDA	NDA	shs
80.	Vyew	comm.	NDA	NDA	NDA	shs
81.	webAula Live Player	comm.	NDA	NDA	NDA	shs
82.	WebELS Meeting	comm.	NDA	NDA	NDA	NDA
83.	WebHuddle	open source	NDA	n	y	shs
84.	WizIQ	comm.	y	y	NDA	shs
85.	YouGov	comm.	NDA	NDA	NDA	NDA
86.	Yuuguu	comm.	NDA	NDA	NDA	shs
87.	Zip Conferencing	comm.	NDA	y	n	shs
88.	Zoho Meeting	comm.	NDA	NDA	NDA	shs
89.	Zoom Video Communications	comm.	NDA	NDA	NDA	shs

Source: Own analysis based on the available documentation.
Abbreviations: y – yes, n – no, NDA – no data available, shs – shared hosted service, li – local installation, hi – hybrid installation). Highlighted items fulfill criteria of the analysis at the stage one.

Among the listed platforms, 81 are commercial while 8 have an open-source license. From the In Dialogue project's perspective, it would be desirable to have open-source software, as it does not involve the payment of monthly or yearly fees, which is the case with commercial software. For city halls, the prospect of some charges might adversely affect the use of our ICT platform for deliberative consultations. But the use of open-source software entails inconveniences such as setting up hardware and software infrastructure capable of handling live voice conferences (i.e., a dedicated server machine powerful enough with respect to the number of cores, RAM and available bandwidth) and maintaining the ICT environment so that it works dependably. By choosing the commercial solution, these worries would be the responsibility of the commercial provider. Both open-source and commercial licensing have their pros and cons for the project, though we tend to favor open-source solutions rather than commercial ones as the disadvantages associated with them are less acute for the project judging from a perspective of the overall aim.

The documentation from only three software providers mentions accessibility for the blind, and 15 tools use Flash technology. It is possible that other tools also use this technology, but there was no information on the manufacturers' websites to confirm this. Based on information published about online meeting software, there are two tools in the comparison that are based on Java technology. We assumed that the remaining software does not include accessibility features for the disabled, as otherwise, being such a vital property, it would certainly have been highlighted by the manufacturer. To verify our assumptions, we contacted the 70 commercial meeting software manufacturers who had made their contact information available (e-mail, online form, or telephone number). We wanted to know if it would be possible to conduct tests on the communication software, and we also asked about the accessibility of the software for people with disabilities, particularly the blind. Most of the responses we received were primarily of a marketing nature and did not respond to the query. In phone calls, when asked about accessibility features, the consultants either did not know about such features or knew they did not exist. The conclusion reached concerning commercial tools' accessibility features for online meetings is that commercial companies do not regard accessibility as being an important feature of their communication software solutions, which were mainly aimed at mainstream business customers. Out of all responses, only one confirmed accessibility as being a feature of their tool.

The tools that had accessibility features for the disabled (according to the documentation or based on the manufacturers' responses), as well as all the open source software, met the first stage criteria and needed to be verified in the second stage. These were as follows: OpenMeetings, BigBlueButton, WebHuddle, Kablink, Jitsi, Palava.tv, Skype and TeamTalk 5. The first five in the list are completely inaccessible to people using screen readers. All that a blind user can "see" is a blank screen, which means that the screen reader cannot read anything at all; this is because the underlying technology is incompatible with screen readers. The first two instant messaging communicators, OpenMeetings and BigBlueButton, are created within a Flash environment; a blind user can connect to the server and see a web page, but all it indicates is that it was created using Flash. The persons' screen reader is not able to provide them with information about any of the elements visible on the screen, so a blind participant in a debate cannot operate this instant messaging communicator. Another tool, WebHuddle, is based on Java technology, which makes it just as inaccessible as the previous two. The next one, Kablink, creates problems even at the level of the installation: the screen reader user sees no information in the installer window, so they are not even able to install the program. In regards to the Jitsi communicator, a blind person may be able to install it without any assistance, but after launching the program, the screen reader does not provide the blind person with any information about what is displayed on the screen. The next two tools, Palava.tv and Skype, are available to screen readers, but fail to meet the other requirements of the project and so could not be used. The first one, palava.tv, is a very basic communicator but this simplicity, which may often be an advantage in some cases, has proven to be an obstacle in the case of the In Dialogue project. This communicator supports the transmission of audio and video but does not allow the transfer of text or binary data, which is necessary for inclusive voice debates. In turn, the widely used Skype software was rejected despite its accessibility features because the project required a tool that would support voice debate with more participants than is possible with this communicator.

In terms of meeting the requirements of the project and accessibility features, TeamTalk 5 proved to be the best communicator. It supports audio, video, text and binary transmission. It is accessible to users of screen readers, but only partially. The sliders and some graphic buttons visible on the home screen are not labeled, and one of these is not even accessible via the keyboard. This particular button is to signal the wish to take the floor in a moderated discussion, which means that a blind participant in the debate cannot take part in the discussion.

As it is precisely this discussion model that is used within the project, this fault effectively disqualifies the communicator as a tool that could be useful for project's purposes. In addition, labels are also missing from the icons that inform participants whether particular designations represent the names of channels or the nicknames of participants in the debate. Furthermore, some features of the communicator are theoretically accessible, yet very inconvenient to use in practice. Another disadvantage of this communicator is that it is very complicated, especially at first use. The project required a simple tool that could be quickly operated by an inexperienced user.

Reciprocity and Reflectiveness

In Table 2 we have listed all the criteria and indicated whether we consider them to be compulsory or optional. The compulsory or optional conditions were evaluated by giving them a designation of either "0" or "1." If a software program received a "0," it was rejected for not meeting the requirements, and if it received a "1," it met the requirements and was assessed against other criteria. Accessibility for the disabled has already been discussed and is a criterion the software program must meet. In the analysis that follows the only compulsory condition, apart from integration with the inDialogue platform for public consultations, is that an organizer can invite certain people to participate in the debate; other criteria, although important, are optional. Each optional criterion has an ascribed number of points. The points are allocated after a subjective comparison of criteria and their importance in attaining a debate's reciprocity and reflectiveness. A software program gaining the maximum amount of points for all criteria would represent the ideal situation. The software programs meet the criteria selectively and to varying degrees, the rankings are presented in Table 2. For informational purposes, the ranking includes software that both passed and failed the accessibility tests. The highest-ranking software package was the open source software, TeamTalk 5.

Table 2. Additional assessment criteria of the software for group voice debates

Criterion	Openmeetings	BigBlueButton	Palava.tv	WebHuddle	TeamTalk 5	Jitsi	Skype	WizIQ
Licence	(Apache License)	(LGPL, GPL) (Mozilla)	(open source) -> LGPLv3	(open source) -> GPLv2	(freeware/open source)	LGPL	freemium	comm.
Accessibility to disabled persons	n	n	y	n	y	n	y	y
Discussion limited to invited participants	y	y	y	y	y	n	n	y
Possibility of integration with the platform "In Dialogue"	y	y	y	y	c*	n	n	y
Platform address accessible to many participants of the debate	y	y	y	y	c**	c**	c**	y
Synchronous discussions in many rooms (1.5 points)	1.5	1.5	1.5	1.5	1.5	0	0	1.5
Room for plenary sessions for at least 80 people (1 point)	1	1	NDA	1	1	1	0	1
Distinguished status of a moderator (2 points)	2	2	0	2	2	0	0	2
Distinguished status of a speaker (1.5 point)	1.5	1.5	0	1.5	1.5	0	1.5	0
Switching a microfon on and off by a moderator (1 point)	1	1	1	1	1	0	0	1
Voice registering (1.5 point)	1.5	0	0	1.5	1.5	1.5	0	1.5
Board for presenting a. text (1 point) b. multimedia (1.5 points)	1.5	1.5	0	1.5	1.5	0	0	1.5
Information on who is willing to speak next a. participant "raises their hand" and a moderator gives the floor (1 point), b. participant "raises their hand" and the system shows the next speaker (1.5 points)	0	1.5	0	0	1	0	0	0
The system helps a moderator to monitor the activity of speakers by providing forms to fill in (0.5 point); The system monitors the activity of speakers e.g. how long they speak, how many of them participated (1 point)	0	0	0	0	0	0	0	0
Technical room (0.5 point)	0	0	0	0.5	0.5	0	0	0.5
Points in total	10	8.5	2.5	10.5	11.5	2.5	1.5	9

Source: Own elaboration based on tests.
n – "no", y – "yes", c – "conditional", NDA – no data available.
** Integration requires some tweaking and is possible.*
*** Usage of this meeting software requires client application installation.*

TeamTalk 5 makes it possible to hold synchronous discussions in many rooms, as well as a plenary session. It distinguishes the status of the moderator and the current speaker, it has means for activating the microphone and recording conversations. Participants in a debate can get acquainted with any briefing materials in multimedia form and make notes. Finally, members of a discussion group can inform fellow participants and the moderator about their willingness to speak. Meetings can be hosted in meeting rooms, one of which can act as a *technical room* where users can consult a technician in case they experience any difficulties with the software during a debate. As yet, it is not possible for the system to monitor participants' activity so that the moderator can react more specifically and encourage those who have withdrawn. It is also not capable of automatically giving the floor to participants in the order in which they request it. These applications may be subject to consideration, development and testing.

Conclusion

In our analysis of the existing tools for voice debates, we have applied the following group of evaluative criteria: cost and the installation location, accessibility for people with disabilities, and ICT features that influence the debate's performance. We have also demonstrated how these criteria are linked to the values of deliberation: openness, inclusiveness, reciprocity, and reflectiveness.

The accessibility of the software for people with disabilities, and the possibility for creating closed groups of participants were essential criteria for choosing software for voice debates that could be integrated with the platform supporting the planning and implementation of the deliberative consultations developed in the In Dialogue project. We have also favored open-source software over commercial software so as not to exclude from the group of potential users, inhabitants of cities where the city halls would be unable or unwilling to pay the fees for commercial software licenses. All other criteria, although important, were optional.

Nobody could deny the legitimacy of the claim that every citizen of a city or a country has a right to participate in public consultations, just as he or she is entitled to execute other civic rights. But, even though the law stipulates the equality of all citizens' rights, this does not always follow in practice. Once public consultations go online, it should be guaranteed that the software will not create barriers to participation for people with disabilities. The overview of available platforms for voice debates proved that it would be hard to find tools that have accessibility features. Of the aforementioned preferences regarding open source software, we have recommended TeamTalk 5 for further work.

As TeamTalk 5 is open source software, it allows for the development and optimization of the recommended features. We decided to simplify TeamTalk 5 and also improve its accessibility. The tool supports the basic functionalities necessary for participation in voice debates. Graphical buttons are used to request access to a moderated discussion and to send a message to the moderator or another participant within the voice debate. All these buttons are labeled and because of this, are accessible to screen readers. Also, keyboard shortcuts allow blind interlocutors to provide a quick response; a blind user can quickly respond by pressing a specific key instead of looking for a graphical button on the screen. The tool automatically adjusts the microphone volume so that the user can enjoy the conversation in good quality. This process is also available to screen readers. Additionally, applications that make the process of turn-taking more transparent were added to other applications that are conducive to knowledge-based moderated debates.

We hope that the set of simple fixes that we have proposed, based on our earlier observations and experiments, may contribute to better quality, task-oriented discussions, conducted in an atmosphere of mutual respect.

References

Arterton, F. Christopher. 1987. *Teledemocracy. Can Technology Protect Democracy?* Newbury Park: SAGE.

Bower, Matt. 2011. "Synchronous collaboration competencies in web-conferencing environments – their impact on the learning process." *Distance Education* 32 (1): 63–83.

Coleman, Stephen, and Peter M. Shane, eds. 2012. *Connecting Democracy. Online Consultations and the Flow of Political Communication*. Cambridge, MA: MIT Press.

Crosby, Ned. 1975. *In Search of the Competent Citizen*. Working Paper. Plymouth: Center for New Democratic Processes.

Dahlberg, Lincoln. 2004. "Net-Public Sphere Research: Beyond the 'First Phase.'" *Javnost/the Public* 11 (1): 27–44.

Davis, Todd, and Seeta P. Gangadharan, eds. 2009. *Online Deliberation. Design, Research, and Practice*. Stanford, CA: CSLI Publications.

Dienel, Peter C. 1997. *Die Planungszelle*. Wiesbaden: Westdeutscher Verlag.

Elliot, Bern, Megan M. Fernandez, and Steve Blood. 2017. *gartner.com*. "Magic Quadrant for Unified Communications." Accessed February 15, 2017. http://www.gartner.com/technology/reprints.do?id=1-1YWQWK0&ct=140806&st=sb.

Farkas, Meredith 2013. "Web conferencing software." *pdx.edu*. Accessed October 10, 2015. http://archives.pdx.edu/ds/psu/9364.

Fishkin, James. 2009. *When the People Speak. Deliberative Democracy and Public Consultation*. Oxford: Oxford University Press.

Kear, Karen, Frances Chetwynd, Judith Williams, and Helen Donelan. 2012. "Web conferencing for synchronous online tutorials: Perspectives of tutors using a new medium." *Computers & Education* 58 (3): 953–963.

Morrison, Kristan A. 2011. "Using web conferencing to teach constructivist discussion-rich seminars. Can it work?" *Quarterly Review of Distance Education* 12 (4): 269–274.

Mutz, Diane. 2008. "Is Deliberative Democracy a Falsifiable Theory?" *Annual Review of Political Science* 11: 521–38.

Scales, B. Jane, and Lara Cummings. 2009. "Web conferencing software." *Library Hi Tech News* 26 (9): 7–9.

Toptenreviews.com. "The Best Web Conferencing Services of 2015." Accessed February 15, 2015. http://web-conferencing-services.toptenreviews.com/.

Webconferencing-test.com. "Web Conferencing Evaluation Guide." Accessed February 15, 2015. https://www.webconferencing-test.com/en/evaluation-guide.

Wikipedia.org. "Comparison of Web Conferencing Software." Accessed February 15, 2015. https://en.wikipedia.org/wiki/Comparison_of_web_conferencing_software.

Wikipedia.org. "Web Conferencing." Accessed February 15, 2015. https://en.wikipedia.org/wiki/Web_conferencing.

Paweł Tymiński and Marta Kołodziejska

Chapter 6. Usability Testing of the InDialogue Platform

Introduction: Constructing the Usability Test

Usability testing is one of the most effective methods for verifying how real users experience a machine, a piece of software, or a website. It is usually a necessary step in the implementation process, as it helps to improve the solution, functionality, and design of the software based on how users perform certain tasks, and the observations they make in the process. The testing usually involves a machine (or software etc.), a group of producers (i.e., engineers, developers, etc.), a user, and a tester (Sullivan 1989, 256). Testing usually occurs within a designated space (i.e., in a controlled environment such as a computer lab, testing room, etc.), and within a particular timeframe. This laboratory setting involves the relationship between non-human and human actors, as well as between the various groups of human actors, some of whom may not be present personally, but whose input, in the shape of a working machine or software, is the object of the testing. Furthermore, the machine itself, i.e., its functions, format, and outcomes, become conceptualized by all participating parties. Thus, usability testing can be analyzed from a technological perspective—finding out how a new product works and locating potential problem areas—as well as a sociological one. The latter supposes a *Latourian* perspective concerning human and non-human actors (or *actants*), that is, entities that modify "another entity in a trial" (Latour 2009, 237), and involves analyzing the social construction of the participants of the trials: the producers, the machine itself, the users, and the testers. As Steven Woolgar (1990) has aptly pointed out, *the user* is, in fact, a social construct that fulfills a specific set of criteria in order for *the test* (yet another construct, i.e., a set of actions isolated in a lab-environment) to be conducted successfully. The very definition of *success* in the context of a usability test is also constructed and exists within a specific set of parameters. In fact, the tester/researcher expects the user to complete a particular set of tasks, usually in a specific order, which also have predictable, predefined outcomes. Therefore, the user cannot be just anybody: he or she must have the capabilities to be able to perform the task at hand. This could be abilities such as computer literacy and digital competence, but the user cannot be an actual expert in the field (unless expert testing is intended). The user must, in some cases, be bound by a confidentiality agreement, especially if the machine/software being tested is a prototype intended for commercial production, but as Woolgar shows, some companies choose to have particularly valuable devices tested by the company's staff as a result of security concerns (Woolgar 1990, 83). Regardless of the test's context, the recruitment process must involve some consideration of the aforementioned issues, and its purpose is to find a group of people who are *in the middle* or *neutral* in terms of their knowledge and competence, and who were not involved in the product's production.

However, in some usability trials, the user must possess a specific set of characteristics that limit the circle of potential participants. In the case of tests done on the *inDialogue* citizen panel, the most important aspect of the software was its accessibility. Thus, the group of users had to include people with disabilities. As users of various websites, software, and devices that have varying degrees of accessibility, the participants could offer insights into the functionalities of the platform and suggest improvements that would otherwise be difficult for the project team to spot or develop; thus, the user experience of people with disabilities is invaluable. In the case of the inDialogue platform's clerk/admin panel, the users had to be recruited from among representatives of participating city halls. Therefore, despite there being no explicit concept of *the user* in the course of the project, all the elements discussed above, as well as the peripheral texts (in the form of user manuals), had to be considered during the development of the inDialogue platform.

The usability trials were planned as goal-oriented tasks, which each participant had to perform on their own, but in which they could ask for help if they couldn't solve a problem by themselves. The *trial* was based on the assumption that the most typical or common sets of tasks would be performed during the test to ensure its reliability and applicability to real-life situations. Success was implicitly defined as the completion of all tasks, preferably without impediments or time-consuming difficulties. The researcher was also the developer of the inDialogue platform, which was justified by the task division within the project team and had several advantages: first of all, the tester had full knowledge of the platform's functionalities and features, and was also the most competent person to answer potential questions; and second, the tester/developer was aware of the existing shortcomings of the software and was able to tackle technical problems if they emerged during the trials; last but not least, the tester/developer could then implement the key recommendations and suggestions in order to improve the platform's functionalities.

Drawing on the aforementioned issues, this paper summarizes the methodology and results of the tests (including user observations), and also outlines the functionalities and features of the platform that have been modified as a result of the test. It ends with a discussion of the process with regards to the construction of the key actors that participated in these usability trials.

The Usability Testing Process and Outcomes

Methodology

The usability test was conducted on a group of 12 real users. The users consisted of people from two groups: representatives of six city halls (incl. Nowa Dęba, Radom, and Słupsk) and regular users (incl. users with disabilities). They were divided into two six-person groups: one tested the platform as a city council clerk, while the other tested the functionalities of the citizens' module. All tests took place in July–August 2015, and the test report (in Polish) is available at: www.wdialogu.uw.edu.pl/images/Rezultaty/Raport_z_testu_uzytecznosci.pdf.

Each test was conducted individually in the form of participatory observation (remotely, i.e., via phone or the "GoToMeeting" software; or on location, in a computer lab at Warsaw University of Technology, or The Centre For Deliberation). In the case of remote testing, the researcher and the participant used audio communication, and the user shared their browser screen with the researcher.

The aim of the test was for the user to perform a series of tasks that were selected as being the most commonly performed by a city hall clerk or a citizen during an actual consultation.

Test Results: Group 1. Clerk

The participants for this test were representatives from the various city halls (Table 1).

Table 1. The participants

City	Representative	Location of test
Dąbrowa Górnicza	Mr. Marcin Dziubek	remote test
Nowa Dęba	Mrs. Maryla Siudem	remote test
Lublin	Mrs. Kinga Jarmołowicz	remote test
Radom	Mr. Paweł Dycht	on location
Łódź	Mrs. Ewa Owczarek	remote test
Słupsk	Mrs. Iwona Chrapkowska	remote test

Each participant was presented with the same set of 10 tasks:

1. Creating a draft version of a consultation on the platform
2. Defining a debate
3. Defining a questionnaire
4. Preparation of information materials
5. Adding a comment to an existing consultation plan
6. Adding commentary to information materials
7. Publishing the consultation (externally)
8. Moderating a text debate
9. Preparing a partial report from the debate
10. Preparing a final report

The average length of each test was two hours. Participants were given instructions beforehand (during workshops) so that they could perform each task independently, using their knowledge of the platform's functionalities. All the users succeeded in performing the tasks.

There were several key issues regarding the platform's functionalities that emerged during the tests. They can be divided into three fields:

1. Comprehensibility/visibility
2. Sequence of actions
3. Purpose and applicability

In terms of comprehensibility, the primary issues were related to the unclear meaning or purpose of a particular functionality or active field. For instance, when creating the questionnaire, most of the users found the purpose of some of the options unclear. The "Priority list" and "Division" options were particularly difficult to comprehend, as the users did not know what problem these types of questions could be used for. Similar difficulties were observed during Task 1 above: the "Self-select" option (i.e., a functionality allowing citizens to sign-up for any debate on the platform without the need to verify their identity as inhabitants of a particular area or district) was unclear to half the users, as was the "Characteristics of the target group" option; in particular the fact that the characteristics of the target group that were defined for the entire consultation (such as age) were automatically pre-defined for a particular debate (which was done by the test coordinator, but would normally be done by the coordinators of a particular consultation).

Another issue connected with comprehensibility was the actual visibility of the active fields and buttons. There were some cases where several users could not locate an action button or expected it to be located elsewhere, as in the case of the consultation form being in the read-only mode. A similar problem was encountered during Task 6, where an option for commenting on a particular section of the materials (rather than commenting on the entire document) was overlooked by all the users participating in the test.

A sequence of actions that caused some problems concerned obligatory fields in the consultation form. For some users, the difference between the obligatory fields and the optional fields was not clear. Another common issue was that of the error notification within the form: if the user did not fill out a mandatory field, or chose the wrong date, etc., a notification would appear at the top of the page informing the user of the errors and disabling the "Save" action. Some users ignored the notification, and thus could not save their consultations.

When on the main page, some users would try to access the consultation by clicking on its title: this was not enabled during the tests, but was implemented later on as a useful feature. The researcher also noticed some minor navigational issues during the tests, which were solved within a few minutes.

Purpose and applicability issues were connected with the first field: in some cases, not only was the meaning of a button unclear, but also its purpose. Such was the case with some tabs in the information materials form (Limitations), and with the more advanced question types in the questionnaire forms. Some users attempted to fill in the "Consultations ID" field, which is generated automatically.

The users offered suggestions and possible solutions to the problems they encountered during the tests. Overall, over 20 suggestions were made. Those that were considered a priority included the following:

- Enabling citizens' comments for selected consultations (moderated)
- Enabling Word-format editing of information materials (this suggestion was the result of concerns that copying large sections of text into the platform's editor would result in formatting errors and that the built-in editor may be inflexible)
- Adding experts from a list
- Adding attachments to the report
- Adding moderator's comments at all levels of discussion (i.e., proposed solutions, comments, questions. This suggestion stemmed from concerns regarding the visibility of the moderator's comments.)
- Adding attachments as part of user's commentary
- Enabling the recruitment phase to continue throughout the consultations (this suggestion may be connected to the current practice of open recruitment at city halls).

As a result of the test, several improvements have been made to the platform. The layout and functionalities of the software have been altered so that they are more user-friendly, omit unnecessary steps, and are clearly visible. Attachments can be added to information materials, forum comments, and reports, so that all interested parties can then download the material to their hard drives.

No commentaries or complaints were made by the members of the first test group regarding the accessibility of the platform, that is, its adaptation to the needs of users with disabilities. This aspect of the platform, however, was put under scrutiny during the second test.

Test Results: Group 2. Citizen

The participants in the second test included representatives of several organizations, as well as users with disabilities Table 2.

Table 2. The participants of the test in Group 2

Name	Organization (if applicable)	Location	Additional information
Mr. Marian Anasz	Polish Disability Forum (PFON)	on location	—
Mr. Karol Mojkowski	—	remote test	—
Mr. Grzegorz Kozłowski	Society for the Aid of the Hearing and Visually Impaired (Towarzystwo Pomocy Głuchoniewidomym)	on location	A person with auditory and visual disabilities.
Mrs. Agnieszka Bal	—	on location	A person with kinaesthetic and visual disabilities.
Dr. Stanisław Jakubowski	Polish Society for the Blind	remote test	A person with visual disabilities.
Dr. Aneta Świercz	Politechnika Warszawska	on location	A person with visual disabilities.

All participants in the test were asked to perform three tasks that were considered to be typical, or most commonly performed, by a citizen using the inDialogue platform. These tasks were as follows:

1. Signing up for a debate
2. Participation in an online text debate
3. Voting for solutions during a text debate

As in the case of the users participating in Test 1, participants in Test 2 were given instructions on how to use the platform and received appropriate training. During the tests, the users were offered minimum help in order to simulate an everyday situation, which allowed users to look for solutions independently. Most of the participants succeeded in performing the tasks, and the average length of the test was two hours.

One of the vital aspects of the citizen's panel test was the accessibility of the platform and its functionalities. Since there were users with a range of disabilities participating, the test allowed the researcher to pinpoint those areas, functions, and features that caused problems, i.e., that were difficult to use and/or locate.

The comments and concerns that the users voiced have been grouped into two categories:

1. Comprehensibility/visibility
2. Accessibility

In terms of comprehensibility and visibility, the users would, in some cases, experience difficulties in either locating a button or understanding what actions they were supposed to undertake in a particular step. For instance, the users complained that the debate they could sign up for was not clearly visible, nor were the tables with the chosen dates for the debate. Two users thought the checkboxes were too small and that the text font in the text debate should have been larger. During Task 3, some users suggested that the buttons for putting each solution in order were too similar, and therefore caused some confusion. Regarding comprehensibility, there were some misunderstandings concerning the purpose of collapsible text blocks that contained details of the particular debate, the "Edit your preferences" button, and the need to transfer the solutions from the "Available" list to the "Chosen" list (part of Task 3). Another important observation was made regarding the information on the end dates of each step of the consultation. The users stated that there should be some form of notification that they had signed up for the debate, or that they have a certain deadline in which to decide on their participation.

There were also some misunderstandings regarding where to choose the date for the debate—some users attempted to choose the date from the table, although in order to sign up for a particular date they had to use the appropriate dialog box. Once the choice had been made, some users were not sure if their choice was saved or what date they had finally decided upon. Similarly, some users found the various consultation and debate statuses confusing, as well as the structures of the debate, that is, the division between arguments and proposed solutions.

Comments regarding accessibility were also connected with the comments regarding comprehensibility, however, they were voiced by users with various disabilities, which was a sign that the platform required improvements in terms of adjusting its functionalities to varying needs. For instance, some buttons were considered to be not clearly visible and the contrast not high enough for users with visual disabilities; in addition, the platform layout would at times be confusing, so it was not clear which tasks should be performed in what order and in which sections. Furthermore, there was one complaint that the popover screens disappeared too quickly and were thus difficult to read by people with visual disabilities.

The participants in the test made five suggestions for possible platform improvements:

- Extending the duration of a session so that users who need more time to read and write can comfortably use the platform
- Enabling more options that enhanced content visibility—such as different color schemes, high contrast, different resolutions, etc.
- The titles of each page or subpage should indicate which one is currently active
- Comments made by a user who is logged-in should be emphasized and highlighted
- Some elements of the interface could be enlarged once tracked by the cursor

The updated version of the inDialogue platform does include several modifications that enhance visibility, accessibility, and clarity. In the process of the platform's development, high contrast and font enlarging options were implemented, and the tasks that citizens must perform in order to participate in the consultations have been simplified and made clearer (e.g., through the change of field, button and tab titles). Furthermore, help windows have been equipped with sign-language as well as an easy-to-read version, with the help of PFON.

During the consultations in Olsztyn, Nowa Dęba and Warsaw, the vast majority of users did not report any major issues with using the platform's functionalities or features. The In Dialogue team received mostly positive feedback about the platform's usability, clarity and usefulness. In Olsztyn and Nowa Dęba, there were some elderly citizens who participated in the consultations using the platform, although some of them had participated in the workshops before the consultations were opened. However, in sum, it must be stated that the inDialogue platform performed well during both usability tests and actual consultations.

What could be further improved is the accessibility of the functions and content. The platform is adaptable and customizable, so new features can be added and unnecessary ones removed. For instance, during online voice debates, aid for the hearing or visually impaired could be provided by more advanced built-in functionalities such as a pop-up screen showing a sign language interpreter (live), or adjustable contrast and resolution controls could be implemented.

Conclusion

After having summarized the technical aspects of both rounds of usability testing, it is worthwhile looking at the process from a sociological perspective.

The underlying assumption behind the usability testing of the inDialogue platform is that the software being tested is supposed to act predictably when used by *real people* who are not specialists in the field of computer science and may have little knowledge about how the object of the test was created. The software is, therefore, an *actant* in the testing process, as it *responds* to human action while influencing it at the same time by imposing a certain order of operations. As the inanimate product of human actions, the machine also connects its creators with the testers and the users, although the connection may not be apparent to the participants of the trials while they are occurring. However, the machine/software is used during the test and is the object of evaluation and further actions.

The conceptualizations of human actors, as was stated at the very beginning of this paper, were formulated primarily implicitly, with the caveat that the users' special characteristics (i.e., representatives of local self-government, and people with disabilities) played an important role in the recruitment of the test's participants. In both cases the users were expected to have *expert knowledge* in a particular field, such as local governance, conducting public consultations, or using software and devices with accessibility features, and so on. It was then assumed that this knowledge would be used in the course of usability trials and would constitute the basis for criticism of the platform as well as suggestions for improvements and modifications. This merger of the different types of knowledge and competences was observed primarily in the citizen panel's testing, as the users with disabilities assessed the platform's functionalities from the point of view of accessibility features and clarity. The city hall representatives, on the other hand, did not use their expertise in conducting public consultations, but instead focused on the technical and design aspects of the platform. While this did not undermine the reliability of the testing (nor was it necessary for the completion of the trials), eliciting additional knowledge that could potentially benefit the testing and the software may be a desirable initiative.

One more aspect that, to our mind, should be emphasized more explicitly during the tests is the socio-technological environment of the usability testing and its participants. In the case of the In Dialogue trials, individual users differed in terms of their level of computer literacy—one of the participants was a doctor of computer sciences—so the *technological milieu* of urban Poland may be an important factor to take into account. The level of digitalization of public institutions, common knowledge of digital and mobile technologies, openness to new technologies and their use in education, public life, work and so on, may influence how the users approach the software being tested; what problems they will bring up regarding its use; and what aspects of the software they will see as most significant (see Aykin 2014, xvi). If the software is to be tested internationally, these traits and characteristics, although not immediately perceptible, may, in fact, result in the tests yielding very different outcomes. Even within one country, when its regions differ substantially in terms of levels of wealth, computer literacy, digitalization and so forth; such discrepancies in outcomes may be expected. In the case of the inDialogue trials, there were some differences in terms of users' familiarity with online software and digital literacy, which are also connected with the use of computers in the workplace; this was visible during the clerk panel testing. In some city halls, computers and the internet are widely used on a daily basis for various purposes, including internal and external communication, citizen service and so on. In others, the available software is used primarily for storing and browsing through data and is used for communication purposes only to a limited degree or on special occasions. Such differences shape the users' perception of the aim and importance of the software being tested and constitutes background knowledge that is used to assess the difficulty of task performance as well as the platform's functionalities. However, when analyzed carefully, this diversity may, in fact, help create software that is comprehensible to the widest audience possible and adaptable to changing conditions.

References

Aykin, Nuray, ed. 2014. *Usability and Internationalization of Information Technology*. London: Laurence Erlbaum Associates, Publishers.

Latour, Bruno. 2009. *Politics of Nature. How to Bring the Sciences into Democracy*. Cambridge, London: Harvard University Press.

Sullivan, Patricia. 1989. "Beyond a narrow conception of usability testing". *IEEE Transactions on Professional Communication* 32 (4): 256–264.

Woolgar, Steve. 1990. "Configuring the user: the case of usability trials". *The Sociological Review* 38: 58–99.

Tomasz Kulisiewicz

Chapter 7. Integrating the InDialogue Platform into the Local Administration ICT Environment

Introduction

As described in Chapter 2, the *inDialogue* platform may be used as an autonomous, separate ICT solution supporting local administration in conveying public consultations. In such an approach the data and information needed for the consultation are loaded into the inDialogue platform manually (typed in or imported) and the results are published independently of other ICT systems used in the municipality's office. Links to the inDialogue platform and the results (reports) from consultations may be published on the municipality's general website as the functionality of the inDialogue platform supports this. In this context, *manually* means that feeding data into the inDialogue platform and exporting results needs to be done directly (typing the data) or by manually initiating imports and exports to word processors, spreadsheets, or website content management tools.

In this chapter the possibility of a more integrated approach is presented, that is, using the inDialogue application as part of a model that anticipates integration or automated data exchange with the ICT systems used by municipal administrations. The main aspects of the interoperability between the inDialogue software and the ICT systems used in public administrations, are discussed—in particular *document management systems* (DMS). The advantages and obstacles of an integrated approach are also briefly presented.

The Aim and Basic Aspects of Using DMS

DMS are ICT systems that are developed and used for the electronic handling and archiving of documents in commercial organizations and public institutions. The basic rule in the deployment of DMS is that all the documents within the organization are processed in electronic form. Incoming paper documents are converted into electronic form, while native electronic documents are converted into formats that are required (accepted) by the organization, or accepted straight away if their original formats are already compatible with these formats. At the end of the procedure, outgoing documents are issued in electronic or paper form depending on the needs of customers and external organizations.

The most important part of the DMS is the electronic filing system. The DMS can support automated document creation according to the laws, procedures, design, and development of web-based form applications.

DMS are not only used for handling and archiving documents; equipped with additional tools for monitoring the progress of procedures and the execution of tasks, a DMS may also provide work-process (workflow) management. These tools help to achieve the efficient management of procedures and the optimization of resource use. When compared to the traditional handling of paper documents, a DMS offers far more options for gathering, categorizing and searching information within the documents processed in the organization, or stored in its electronic repository. A DMS enables the efficient distribution of documents and tracking of their circulation, managing access to information according to rules and procedures. The processed documents are traceable and safe from manipulation.

A DMS is usually integrated or connected, by various means, to other systems used within an organization: financial and resource management, that is, Enterprise Resource Planning/Management Systems (ERP/EMS), Human Resources (HR), Customer Relations Management (CRM), Supply Chain Management (SCM), transaction systems, distribution and sales management, and so on. In public administration DMS are integrated with CRM systems, HR and financial (budget planning and management) systems, web-services and e-government websites. The advanced use of DMS by public administration consists of integration or data exchange with Geographical Information Systems (GIS) to be used in the planning and management of various spatial processes and procedures. DMS may be equipped with interfaces for e-payment and e-procurement systems.

DMS in Polish Local Administration

The legal foundation for the use of DMS in Poland's administration is the regulation concerning office procedure instructions, classification, circulation and the archiving of documents. Other legal acts concerning the handling and archiving of electronic documents include the law on electronic signatures,[1] the regulation for the national interoperability framework, the law for the computerization of

1 This was superseded in 2016 by a new national law on trust services that implements Regulation (EU) N°910/2014 on electronic identification and trust services for electronic transactions in the internal market (so-called eIDAS Regulation).

entities performing public tasks, the regulation on creating and handling electronic documents, and the law on national archives.[2]

The EZD PUW System

The EZD PUW is the most popular DMS system used in Poland's local administration. The system was developed in-house by the ICT department of the Office of Podlasie Voivodship (north-eastern Poland)[3] in 2011. Since 2012, after pilot deployment projects in Białystok (the capital of Podlasie and the ICT department's base), Kraków and Opole, it has been used by voivodship offices and other units of the Polish central administration. In 2015 an agreement was signed between the voivode of Podlasie, the then Minister of Administration and Digitization (now Minister of Digital Affairs) and the Union of Polish Metropolises to begin cooperation on the deployment of a DMS for the whole public administration—both central and local. The first deployments in cities took place in Łódź (the third biggest city in Poland, population 700 thousand) and Gdańsk (population 460 thousand). The software and licenses for the EZD PUW are supplied free of charge by the Office of Podlasie Voivodship; the deploying authorities are considered to be partners and receive support from the ICT Department of Podlasie as well as from other partners.

Between October 2014 and December 2015 the development of the EZD PUW was supported by the Operational Program of Innovative Economy, which was co-financed by the European Regional Development Fund (ERDF) during the 2007–2013 funding period. The budget for the project was approximately PLN 7.8 million (EUR 1.9 million) (Podlaski Urząd Wojewódzki w Białymstoku 2016).

By July 2016, the EZD PUW system had 540 installations (production, pilot, test and training installations combined) in public institutions out of which, 248 had the official status of partners who cooperated in the development, deployment and maintenance of the system. Since 2015 the ICT department of the Office of Podlasie Voivodship, together with its partners, has worked on proposals for a new version of the system, which will be named EZD PUW 4.0.[4]

---

2 Legal acts mentioned in the text are listed separately in the References.

3 The name of the system (EZD PUW) is not an official acronym but it reffers to the Polish term for the DMS (EZD - Elektroniczne Zarządzanie Dokumentami) and to the name of the Office of Poldasie Voivodship (PUW - Podlaski Urząd Wojewódzki)

4 *Op.cit.*

Other DMS Used in Poland's Public Administration

The document management system that is widely used in Poland's central administration is eDOK, which was developed by the Centre for Informatics Technology (COI), a government ICT organization established by the Ministry of the Interior, but now reporting to the Minister of Digital Affairs. By 2015, the eDOK system has been used by approximately 60 central administrative units, including the Chancellery of the Prime Minister (Ryciak 2015).

Local administrations and other public institutions are using a wide range of DMS, either developed in-house or procured from ICT vendors, and range from simple secretarial support (e.g., Kancelaria.NET, Madar) through office document management and archiving suits (e.g., DMS Studio, ProgMate DOCs, iSoft DMS, AtSoftware DMS) to complex DMS solutions (e.g., mDOK, OfficeObjects Document Manager). Most of these systems are customized according to needs of the organization. A common phenomenon in local administration, especially at the level of municipalities, is the parallel use of a DMS and a traditional, paper document management system. A survey done in 2011 showed that such parallel use was common in approximately 86% of the offices at municipality level throughout all 16 Polish voivodships (see Figure 1). Since 2011 the situation has not improved dramatically; according to data from the Ministry of Digital Affairs' annual report,[5] only in 5% of the 2,095 offices of public administration units surveyed (out of which 1,690 were municipal offices) used a DMS as a basic tool for documenting their official procedures (AMC/Ministry of Digital Affairs 2016). In 65% of the units surveyed, document management was reported as paper-oriented but supported by ICT tools,[6] and in 30% of the units document management was done solely using the traditional paper-oriented system. Even in the case of the central administration and its local units (offices of voivodships) the share of units using a fully electronic system was only 32%, while 58% of units used mixed systems and 10% of units managed their documents in paper form only. At municipality level the percentage of offices using only a DMS was 4%, the paper-centric ICT supported system was used by 63% of offices, and the traditional paper-document system supported 33% of the offices of local administration (Figure 2).

5 The survey took place between October 12th and November 3rd of 2015.

6 Experts are even using separate terminology for the two ways of managing the documents: the full DMS is designated by the EZD abbreviation (*Elektroniczne Zarządzanie Dokumentami*: Electronic Document Management), the traditional IT supported systems are called EOD (*Elektroniczny Obieg Dokumentów*: Electronic Circulation of Documents), see Niemczyk 2015.

Figure 1. The rate of parallel use of DMS and paper-based documentation in the municipality's offices

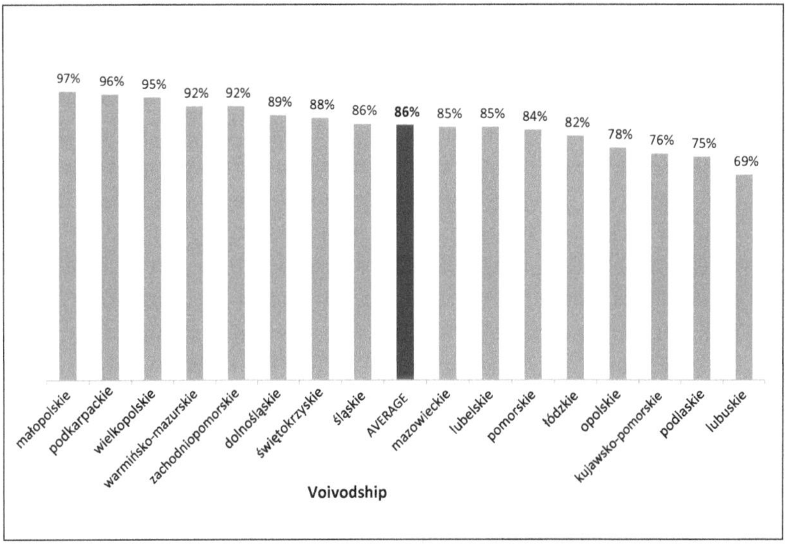

Source: Batorski, Peszat and Płoszaj (2012)

Figure 2. The use of document management in public administration

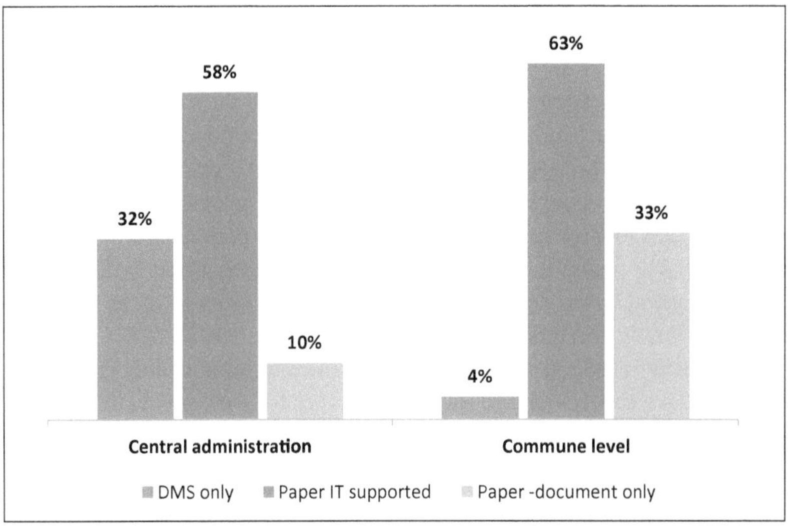

Source: (AMC/Ministry of Digital Affairs 2016)

The Standardized DMS for Public Administration

According to representatives of the local administration, the main problem concerning the use of DMS in local administration is the lack of standardization, despite the fact that the main rules for the use of DMS by public administration are defined in the aforementioned regulations concerning office procedures. Local administrations have, on various occasions, repeatedly called for standards to be set centrally, and expecting such action from the ministry responsible for the deployment of ICT in public administration (now Ministry of Digital Affairs).

In June 2016, after an analysis of the main DMS being used in public administration, the Ministry of Digital Affairs announced the start of the development of an official DMS. The project is running under the name EZD RP. The new DMS will combine the main functionalities that were planned for the EZD PUW 4.0 with those of the new version of COI's eDOK. The new system will be cloud-based, with multiplatform local clients. The planned functionalities will include full interoperability with the ePUAP main e-government platform and with the financial systems used by public administration (see § *The Basic Models of Integration and Interoperability* in this chapter). The EZD RP is expected to constitute unified standards for documents, formats and other characteristics. There was also a declaration from official circles concerning the introduction of corresponding changes in office procedure instructions and other regulations (Ministerstwo Cyfryzacji 2016).

ICT Support for Public Consultations

Most of the public consultation procedures launched at the lower levels of Polish public administration (municipalities and towns) are supported by ICT tools in one way or another, but this support usually does not extend beyond the municipality's official website. The most frequent support consists of publishing the announcement of consultations on the Public Information Bulletin page, an official, obligatory website by public institutions and units of the public administration that contains basic information on the structure, contacts and official activities of the institution.

As the analysis described in Chapter 2 has shown, only 65 out of 912 towns analyzed had a website or webpage dedicated to consultation. Only the presence of a dedicated website/webpage was analyzed (i.e., for announcing the consultations; publishing the briefing materials, and announcing debates, meetings, the publishing of reports, etc.), thus it does not mean that 65 towns used the on-line consultation web-services. In some cases, the presence of electronic forms, i.e., for consultation of participatory budgets, was noted.

In the fifth annual survey, "Impact of Digitization on the Operation of Public Administration Offices in Poland," conducted in November 2014 by the then Ministry of Administration and Digitization, there was information that open online consultations with the community "in matters within the office's scope of competency" were conducted in 30% of the 1,644 units of the administration surveyed (out of which 1,565 were municipality offices) (PBS/Ministry of Administration and Digitization 2015). The result of the survey neither included a description of the consultation's procedures, nor the extent to which online ICT tools were used. In a report from 2011 on the effectiveness of the mechanisms used in public consultation, there were some data on the use of on-line tools in 340 district offices, 124 town halls and 250 municipality offices. The possibility of collecting opinions during consultations by email was used in approximately 62% of the units surveyed (the sum of the answers "often" and "always"), while the collection of opinions using social media, forums, chat and other forms of electronic communications was mentioned in only in 24% of the units. There was no information on the use of the dedicated consultation platform (Pracownia Badań i Innowacji Społecznych Stocznia/SMG/KRC Poland Media 2011).

Two of the participation tools mentioned in Chapter 2 have been used by public administration in Poland at the central level; the first one described below has also been extended with a module for local consultations:

- *mamzdanie.org.pl.* Deployed in 2010 as the first web service supporting open public consultations on a country-wide basis. The platform was developed jointly by the Stocznia NGO (The Unit for Social Innovation and Research "Shipyard") and the Pretius company, and was deployed as an open solution at no charge. The platform was used by the former Ministry of Administration and Digitization for consultations on legislation and other documents setting up public policies. It has been developed using open source solutions: Liferay enterprise portal software, PostgreSQL database and Apache Lucene information retrieval library (Pracownia Badań i Innowacji Społecznych STOCZNIA/Pretius 2016).
  In the new version, a module for local consultations has been added. Details of the consultation (topic, attached documents, issuer's data) are available on the portal and in the form of an Application Programming Interface (API) described on the support webpage. The registered organizations and issuers of the consultation may obtain an API key for their calls on the API. Mamzdanie.org.pl portal is now offered in two versions: basic (free of charge) and extended (with subscription fee).
- *konsultacje.gov.pl.* A portal for public consultations launched by the central administration in order to support consultations for the proposal of legal acts. The portal was developed in-house by the ICT department of the then Ministry of Economy, using the Drupal open source Content Management System (CMS)

and content management framework. The portal is the front-end part of the system, while the back-office part is the ministry's application for supporting its legislative activities. According to information published at the beginning of the project, the communication between the portal application and the back-office application is done by a separate communication server. No specification for the API has been published.

For each process of consultation, the konsultacje.gov.pl portal provides a description of the topic, the latest comments and opinions expressed on the consultation forum by registered participants, links to attached documents, links to similar projects/consultations, and various other links. The first version of the portal was launched in 2013 and during its pilot phase was used for consulting about the proposals for legislation initiated by the then Ministry of Economy. Since its official launch, the platform has been marked as a "beta version," and there is no information on further development activities, nor on the availability or description of its APIs. Since the reorganization of the central administration at the end of 2015, the konsultation.gov.pl portal has been operated by the Ministry of Economic Development. Since November 2015, use of the platform has been sporadic, for instance, between February and May 2016 only one proposal for legislation had been presented on the platform (Obywatelskie Forum Legislacji 2016). The proposals are not presented with links nor references to similar proposals.[7]

There is no information on the use of APIs by the local administrative units in their ICT systems (and in particular, in their DMS) for either of the main platforms described above. This should come as no surprise as the basic versions of both these portals have not been used in consultations at the local level. There is also no information on such use for the mamzdanie.org.pl platform.

Integration and Interoperability of DMS and the InDialogue Platform

The need for the integration or interoperability between the inDialogue platform and the DMS used in a given unit of public administration, depends on various factors, that is, the frequency of consultations, the volume of input, the briefing materials and reports, the presence or absence of a dedicated consultation unit, and the extent of use of the DMS, and so forth.

7 An example is the strategy document by the Ministry of Digital Affairs mentioned in 0. It was published in January 2016 on konsultacje.gov.pl as a plain document only, with no links, references, etc.

Obviously, consultations are initiated *manually*. The initiation is based on the decision of the town's authorities (mayor, city council) or those officially authorized to initiate the consultation. All of the consultation procedures' activities can be executed manually (i.e., announcing the departments involved, sending requests for contributing information, publications of schedules, etc.), which means announcing the schedules using phone, internal mail, paper notices; preparing and sending the lists of experts, and sending reports and other materials. The inDialogue platform can be used as a tool for supporting and organizing these activities.

Some of the activities may be automated to various extents using APIs available in the platform or the DMS. For example, setting the schedules of consultations within the inDialogue platform may result in it being sent automatically to a groupware calendar or to an appropriate module in the extended document management system, which informs the departments and officials involved. The approval for publication of a document or report may result from the automated transfer of a given document through the DMS to the content management system used for the municipality's website or dedicated webpage for consultations.

Such automation needs a certain level of integration or interoperability between the inDialogue platform and the DMS.

The Basic Models of Integration and Interoperability

Interoperability between the inDialogue platform and the DMS used in public administration may be considered to be an approach for deploying an electronic consultation platform as part of the e-government solution used by local administration. The model for document management in e-government systems was presented in a paper by Kunis, Rünger, and Schwind (2007). Presenting their model of document management, which was tailored to the execution of administrative (government) processes, the authors emphasized the role of the DMS in e-government solutions. This role is decisive because one of the main prerequisites of an efficient e-government system is the deployment of paperless office procedures.

Generally speaking the basic models for integration or interoperability of the functionalities of ICT systems are as follows:

- *Deep integration*. A given set of functionalities is a subset of the general functionalities of the ICT system. Usually, such integration is deployed at the developmental stage of the main system. The given set of functionalities are deployed as a functional module of the application or ICT system.
- *Software bus*. The communication between software modules or the program is served by the software channel. This is a concept similar to the system bus used in computer hardware for interconnecting hardware units within the

machine (Central Processing Unit (CPU)) or between the CPU and other hardware modules and peripherals. The software bus architecture is common in bigger ICT systems consisting of several programs.

- *Data exchange platforms.* These are complex software solutions used by enterprises and governmental institutions, especially for the secure interchange of documents and data among trusted partners (enterprises, organizations, regions, countries, intergovernmental organizations). Such data exchange platforms support the definition of document templates, data structures and the generation of web forms. The processes for creating, managing, revising and exchanging documents and forms are automated, following the validation rules and operational procedures defined by the organizations. The latest data exchange platforms are built using cloud-based architectures.
- *API.* This is a set of routine definitions, protocols and tools used for building applications. It is a software component that is used for communications between modules and applications independent of the programming language. A very popular use for APIs are Web APIs, which are used in web development. Web APIs are usually defined as a set of Hypertext Transfer Protocol (HTTP) request messages together with a definition of the structure of response messages. The most common response message format is Extensible Markup Language (XML) or the JavaScript Object Notation (JSON) format. Today, the most popular one in use is the Representational State Transfer (REST) style web resources. In REST services an API can be considered to be a specification for remote calls to the application. Data access APIs describe commands in order to retrieve and modify data from a generic data source.

In the case of the public consultation platform, the choice between the models described above is limited.

The deep integration model needs the deployment of inDialogue functionalities at the developmental stage or during an upgrade of the DMS. In practice the public administration unit will not rewrite nor upgrade its DMS in order to extend its functionalities with functions supporting the consultations process, as consultations, despite the legal obligations, are generally regarded as second-range or subservient to the main activities and procedures of public administration.

Almost the same thing applies to the software bus and data exchange platforms (and generally the middleware) class of solutions. As the DMS itself is considered to be a tool for the back-office of the administrative unit, there is a very low probability that the local administration will procure or develop an integrated, complex back-office system to run all its activities and procedures, in which the DMS and the platform for public consultations will be implemented as separate applications communicating by the means of software bus or data exchange platform.

The most obvious and viable way for functional integration and interoperability between the inDialogue platform and the document management system used by the public administration is the API model. This model has been implemented by the public administration as a tool for the interoperability of various applications used in administrative units and departments, but there is no information on integration (API) with the basic consultation tools used by local administration.

In the case of ZRODLO, an official application supporting access to the Central Registry System—the system of applications servicing the referential public registries such as PESEL (registry of Personal Identification Numbers), ID cards registry, acts of civil status et cetera—there is already an official path available for obtaining the full specifications of its API. The independent developers of applications (suppliers of ICT solutions for Polish administration) may enter the application certification procedure in order to exchange data with ZRODLO.

As users and developers of the inDialogue platform do not need a direct connection between the inDialogue platform and the ZRODLO application, there are no plans to apply for such a certification in the foreseeable future—especially in view of the uncertain future of this application, which has been heavily criticized by local administration users.

According to plans published in March 2016 by the Ministry of Digital Affairs, the whole integrated infrastructure system of reference registers, including the Central Registry System, the Central Register of Vehicles and Drivers (CEPiK), the Central Register of Personal IDs (RDO), and the Central Register of Issued and Lost Travel Documents (CEWiUDP), will be redesigned as the part of strategic actions by the Ministry of Digital Affairs (Ministry of Digital Affairs 2016). In June 2016, Mariusz Madejczyk, plenipotentiary of the Ministry of Digital Affairs on Cooperation with Public Administration (and former head of the EZD PUW development team) declared the publication of API specifications for the Central Registry System in order to facilitate access to the data through trusted services and the EZD RP document management system mentioned earlier (see § *The Standardized DMS for Public Administration* in this chapter). According to this declaration, APIs will be the way of integrating (data exchange), the new EZD RP, and the various dedicated ICT systems used in public administration (Orłowski 2016).

Areas of Interoperability of the InDialogue Platform with DMS

From the point of view of its users, the inDialogue platform can be regarded as a highly configurable and flexible CMS. The application running the platform has been developed in Java 8. It uses the PostgreSQL open source object-relational database with PostGIS spatial database extender, which adds support for geographic objects allowing location queries. The application is licensed under an open-source software license.[8]

The main and most common areas of integration, interoperability and data exchange[9] between the inDialogue platform and the document management system used by local municipalities may consist of the following:

1. Setting up the logistics of the consultation: initiation; selection of the internal units that will be involved; planning the schedules; issuing notices, reminders, and messages; and sending them to the internal communication infrastructure of the office of the municipality (email system, groupware software or DMS);
2. Selection of participants, internal and external experts, observers, etc., from the databases, list, and registers available from the ICT infrastructure of the office;
3. Supplying the participants in consultations with background documents (briefing materials) generated by other applications used in the office;
4. Collecting the results of consultations (opinions, proposals, data on the number of proposals, number of participants, and the excerpts from final reports) in order to include them in the workflow of the administrative unit and in the procedures that initiated the public consultation;
5. Publishing reports about the consultation on the municipality's website (Public Information Bulletin).

In the case of smaller administrative units, using basic level, simple DMS—common office productivity suits (word editors, spreadsheet etc.), client applications for access to the Central Registry System and inDialogue (i.e., as a cloud service)—in the consultation process, there may be no need to exchange data between the inDialogue platform and the office's ICT infrastructure. This could be considered as a separate (free-standing) model of the inDialogue platform. In such a model the messages from the inDialogue system (Point 1 above), selection of the participants and experts (Point 2), loading the briefing documents (Point 3), and collecting and publishing the results (Points 3 & 4) may be done using manual procedures (re-typing, manually initiating the export and import of data from external sources and to the external systems, i.e., the website CMS). In the case of bigger units, using an integrated DSM solution, dedicated GIS systems, groupware

8 The open source tools used in development consisted of: Java 8, Spring Framework, PostgreSQL/postGIS (backend), AngularJS 1.4 (frontend) and TeamTalk 5 SDK (debates, chat-rooms, messaging).

9 The terms *integration, interoperability* and *data exchange* are used in this point in the common use of these words, not in the formal meaning described in 0.

software etc., along with the processing of big volumes of data, automated data exchange is vital, not only from the point of view of labor and time consumption but in order to avoid the possible mistakes and errors occurring from manual procedures (especially from re-typing). The most frequently quoted examples of such errors are the erroneous street names, typed in manually instead of importing them automatically from TERYT (the official register of addresses, including streets, municipalities, etc.).

In general, it can be said that specific areas of interoperability between the inDialogue consultation platform and the DMS used in the unit should be selected and designed according to the model of consultation deployed by the municipality. Thus the specific setup of interoperability and data exchange between the inDialogue platform and the ICT systems may be determined on a case-by-case basis according to needs of the unit initiating the consultation, the roles played in the consultation by clerks, and the method used for the consultation (surveys, meetings, on-line debates, forums etc.)

APIs for InDialogue and DMS

During the preparations for the EZD PUW 4.0 mentioned above (see § *The EZD PUW System* in this chapter), the plans for interoperability with other systems were declared (in the form of an API). As the new EZD RP project is in the very early stages of planning (full deployment of the EZD RP system is planned for 2019) (Ministerstwo Cyfryzacji 2016), there are no details on interoperability, especially on interoperability with public consultation platforms. The other DMS used by local administrations usually support API calls in one way or another.

As the inDialogue platform offers the whole set of API functions following the REST model, it is interoperable with any ICT system able to use such APIs. The inDialogue APIs cover the following categories:

- Description of the structure of the given municipality office (administrative unit)
- Description of the consultation procedure
- Briefing materials
- Selection and enrolment of participants
- Surveys (questionnaires and forms)
- Details of debates (type, participants, dates, proposals)
- Consultations reports (versioning, comments)
- Tasks of participants and clerks
- Contact forms

- Users and participants
- Users and participants' accounts
- Help and guides

In total 75 APIs are defined with standard GET, POST, DELETE and PUT calls. An example of definitions is shown in Figure 3.

Figure 3. An example of the inDialogue platform's APIs

		GET (Pobranie)	POST (Zapisanie/edycja)	DELETE (Usunięcie/anulowanie)	PUT
Afiliacje	app/rest/affiliations/:id				
Ustawienia aplikacji	app/rest/settings/:id				
Obszary (predefiniowane obszary, które można wykorzystać np.	app/rest/area/:id				
Kategorie obszarów	app/rest/area-category/:id				
Wydziały urzędu	app/rest/departments/:id				
Słowniki	app/rest/dictionary/item/type/systemType/:systemType				
Ekspert	app/rest/experts/:id				

Source: Internal documentation of inDialogue platform

Advantages of Integrated Use

The separate approach usually demands time-consuming activities for the manual transfer of data and information from the inDialogue system to the DMS, or other applications used in the office. Manual transfer usually means reading the information from a screen or from printouts and re-typing it into another computer—which is not the most sensible procedure in an administrative ICT environment (but unfortunately common enough). The integrated approach saves time and effort, increases the quality of information (as it helps avoid mistyping and allows for the use of proofing tools) and increases the efficiency of the processes. In general all the advantages that are listed concerning the various aspects of e-government, are also valid in the case of interoperability or data exchange between the inDialogue platform and DMS used by municipalities: reduced costs, high operational efficiency, easy and quick implementation, and a high level of security (eMunicipality, Kratos Technology 2014).

Obstacles

For an integrated approach consisting of using the inDialogue platform together with a document management system, the main obstacle is the already established practice of dealing with all the tasks and duties of administration separately. This practice may be derived from the nineteenth-century paper-document oriented, traditional model of administration (bureaucracy) in which information was processed in isolated units dealing separately with each issue and matter. The obvious cause for such an operational model was the lack of adequate, powerful information processing technologies that could support the growing volume of official matters. The whole structure of public administration has been built accordingly, resulting in isolated silo-type structures dealing with separate matters and using separate procedures. Such an approach may influence the use of the inDialogue platform, resulting in a tendency to use it as a separate, stand-alone ICT tool and prohibiting the use of the consultation platform as an element of the integrated ICT environment (and DMS) of the municipality.

An additional obstacle, which originates from this traditional model and approach, is the high rate of non-machine-readable documents used in public administration. An example of the percentage is shown in Figure 4.

Figure 4. The structure of the formats of documents in the City Hall of Warsaw and its units

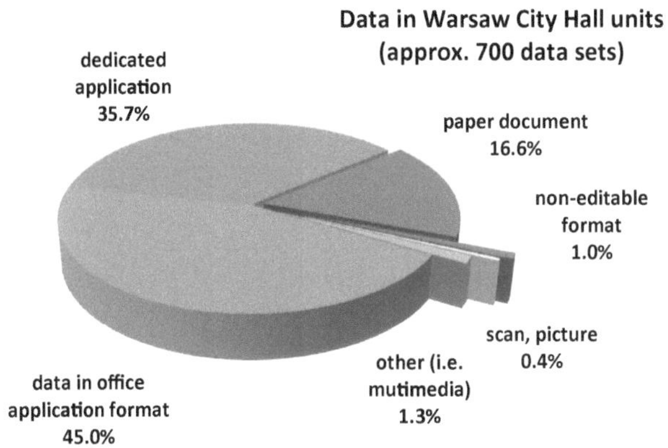

Source: Work report of project "Data po warszawsku (Warsaw Data)," Warsaw, 2015 (unpublished)

A typical example of publishing documents in non-machine-readable formats (not to speak of an appropriate level of data openness as defined in the 5-star Open Data deployment scheme proposed by Tim Berners-Lee)[10] is presented in Figure 5. The document shown is a proposal for a regulation by the Minister of Agriculture and Rural Development published on the official web service of the Chancellery of the Prime Minister concerning legislative process. As can be seen, it is a picture (scan) of a paper document with hand-written signatures and the stamps of the officials of the Ministry of Agriculture and Rural Development. If

10 http://5stardata.info/en/ (accessed July 15, 2016)

one needs to use the information included in the proposal (i.e., in another ICT system), the content of the document would have to be read and re-typed manually[11] into the other system, despite the fact that the document has been prepared using office software, so it also exists in a machine-readable format with the issuing ministry.

Figure 5. Example of public document in non-machine-readable format

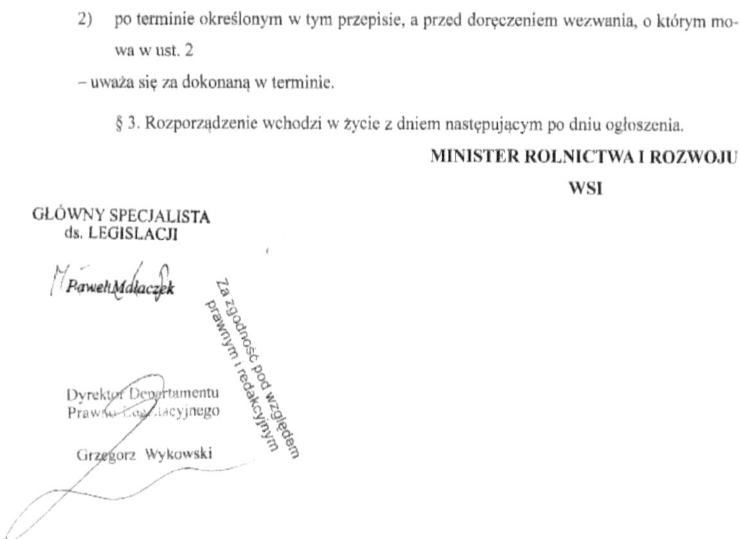
2) po terminie określonym w tym przepisie, a przed doręczeniem wezwania, o którym mowa w ust. 2

– uważa się za dokonaną w terminie.

§ 3. Rozporządzenie wchodzi w życie z dniem następującym po dniu ogłoszenia.

MINISTER ROLNICTWA I ROZWOJU WSI

GŁÓWNY SPECJALISTA ds. LEGISLACJI

Paweł Małaczek

Za zgodność pod względem prawnym i redakcyjnym

Dyrektor Departamentu Prawno-Legislacyjnego

Grzegorz Wykowski

Source: http://legislacja.rcl.gov.pl/projekt/12287105/katalog/12362084#12362084

Amongst the of legislative projects mentioned in the report on public consultations by ministries (Grzeszak, Sadło and Stokłuska 2015) the majority (30 out of 49, that is 61%) were published in non-machine-readable formats, so the data and information included in these document were non-searchable. None of these 49 documents were published in the open data format.

The approach shown in Figure 5 creates an obstacle for on-line consultations and thus the integrated use of on-line platforms and electronic DMS in the offices

11 A more advanced option is to use OCR (Optical Character Recognition) software in order to convert the picture of the document into machine-readable format. Such an option assumes that the one who needs the information from the document involved: (1) has the OCR software at hand, (2) can use it, and (3) the quality of the document is sufficient.

of local administration, as it hinders the possibility of automated data exchange between systems. This approach can be observed even in the biggest cities, including Warsaw, the capital of Poland. On the website dedicated to the Department of Public Consultation and Participation of the Centre for Public Communication of Warsaw's city hall (konsultacje.um.warszawa.pl) the process for consultations is described and forms supplied for supporting motions and proposals—all based on the Ordinance of the Town Council of Warsaw of 2013.[12] Despite the binding regulations concerning electronic signatures and e-government services, it states that both the motion and the list of supporters, along with their names, addresses, and Personal Identification Numbers, have to be signed by hand by the person supplying the motion, and all the supporters and then supplied in paper or sent by fax (this means in the form of a picture). The vast majority of the documents published on the konsultacje.um.warszawa.pl website are in non-machine-readable formats (even the map annexes for consultations) despite the fact that Warsaw City Hall has a relatively strong ICT department.

Conclusion

The level of use of DMS in the offices of municipalities varies according to the scale of their, and the functionalities of the DMS. The areas covered by DMS vary from simple secretarial support to complex DMS solutions, fulfilling not only tasks prescribed by official regulations (office document management and archiving) but also playing the role of a workflow and process management system for the whole office.

The extent of the integration of the inDialogue platform into the document management system used by a given office of local administration depends on two main factors:

- the extent to which the document management system is used
- and the frequency and extent of use of the inDialogue platform

The inDialogue platform (its core application) uses the standard REST mechanism of APIs, so a deep of integration with the structure of the office and the model of data exchange with its ICT environment depends on the needs and competences of its users.

The presence of a dedicated consultation unit in the municipality raises the chances of the integration or interoperability of the inDialogue with the DMS. This

12 "Uchwała nr LXI/1691/2013 Rady Miasta Stołecznego Warszawy z dnia 11 lipca 2013 r." http://konsultacje.um.warszawa.pl/kompendium_wiedzy/uchwala-rady-mst-warszawy-z-dnia-11-lipca-2013-konsultacje-z-mieszkancami (accessed May 10, 2016).

dedicated unit, or department of the office, may be more determined to use the integrated approach than other units that conduct consultations less frequently; it may better see the advantages of an integrated approach, or the shortcomings of dealing with each consultation separately, i.e., repeating manually the same preparatory steps in each case.

Such manual preparation is simplified by the fact that the information needed may be retrieved internally within the inDialogue platform from other consultations that have used the platform before. Such basic information (e.g., the organizational structure of the municipality, database of experts, etc.) may be considered to be internal elements of the organizational (information) system of consultations supported by the inDialogue platform.

Even in the case where an integrated approach is needed it does not necessarily mean that the determination and will of the separate unit mentioned above will be enough to follow an integrated approach using data exchange and interoperability between the inDialogue platform and the DMS.

On the one hand this depends on the position of such a separate consultation unit in the hierarchy of a given municipality, while on the other hand, it depends on the level of knowledge of such possibilities (functionalities), as the integration requires appropriate customization of the DSM or the initiative to use the tools already included in the document management system.

The category of dedicated systems that are used by administration, i.e., various geo-localized applications for spatial planning, environment protection, agricultural monitoring and so on, represents an exemption for the integrated use of inDialogue and DMS. The obvious way for data exchange between the inDialogue system and dedicated application is to use the inDialogue's APIs and/or GIS-based applications directly, as there is no need to use the document management system (in its basic role of electronic document management) as an intermediate step. The inDialogue platform uses PostgreSQL open source object-relational database with PostGIS spatial database extender; thus direct data exchange with GIS-based applications is supported using inDialogue's APIs or the GIS application. The situation may be different in the case of advanced DMS solutions, where the DMS is acting in the role of an ERP-class system for the whole office of the municipality, managing not only documents but all the activities of the office. In such a setup all the applications used in the office—including the GIS-based dedicated applications and the inDialogue online consultation platform—are exchanging data with the DMS solution, usually by the means of APIs and common data platforms.

References

Books and articles

AMC/Ministry of Digital Affairs. "Raport Wpływ cyfryzacji na działanie urzędów administracji publicznej w Polsce w 2015 r." *Ministerstwo Cyfryzacji.* 2016. Accessed July 18, 2016. http://mc.bip.gov.pl/fobjects/details/97393/raport-wplyw-cyfryzacji-na-dzialanie-urzedow-administracji-publicznej-w-polsce-w-2015-r-pdf.html.

Batorski, Dominik, Klaudia Peszat, and Adam Płoszaj. 2012. *Technologie informacyjno-komunikacyjne a samorząd lokalny i rozwój lokalny w województwie mazowieckim.* Warsaw: MGG Conferences.

eMunicipality, Kratos Technology. 2014. "4 Major e-Government Advantages for City Mayors." *eMunicipality.* Accessed June 5, 2016. http://www.emunicipality.com/4-major-e-government-advantages-mayors/.

Grzeszak, Jacek, Katarzyna Sadło, and Ewa Stokłuska. 2015. *Konsultacje publiczne w ministerstwach.* Accessed May 20, 2016. http://partycypacjaobywatelska.pl/wp-content/uploads/2015/08/RAPORT-nt.-KONSULTACJI-PUBLICZNYCH-W-MINISTERSTWACH_wersja-finalna.pdf.

Kunis, Rafael, Gudula Rünger, and Michael Schwind. 2007. "A Model for Document Management in e-Government Systems." *Electronic Journal of e-Government.* Accessed May 20, 2016. www.ejeg.com/issue/download.html?idArticle=101.

Niemczyk, Dagmara. 2015. "Dlaczego i jak należy oderwać się od papieru." *ICT w Administracji*, 05 2015: 38.

Obywatelskie Forum Legislacji. 2016. *VII Komunikat Obywatelskiego Forum Legislacji.* Accessed May 30, 2016. http://www.batory.org.pl/upload/files/Programy%20operacyjne/Odpowiedzialne%20Panstwo/Komunikat%20z%20VII%20obserwacji.pdf.

Orłowski, Jacek. 2016. "Ogólnopolski Konwent Informatyków." *ICT w Administracji* 07 2016: 11.

PBS/Ministry of Administration and Digitization. 2015. The Impact of Digitization on the Operation of Public Administration Offices in Poland in 2014. Accessed July 14, 2016. http://m.mac.gov.pl/files/pbs_mac_cyfryzacja_short_eng_fin_2014.pdf.

Podlaski Urząd Wojewódzki w Białymstoku. 2016. "O EZD PUW, Statystyki." Accessed July 5, 2016. https://ezd.gov.pl/www/ezd/partnerzy.

Pracownia Badań i Innowacji Społecznych STOCZNIA/Pretius. 2016. "O czym jest Mam Zdanie." Accessed June 12, 2016. https://mamzdanie.org.pl/apex/f?p=600:CZYM_JEST_MAMZDANIE:::NO:RP::.

Ryciak, Igor. 2015. "eDOK w KPRM." Accessed June 24, 2016. https://www.coi.gov.pl/artykul/edok-w-kprm-cyfrowy-standard-zarzadzania-panstwem.html.

Legal and public administration sources

Ministerstwo Cyfryzacji. 2016. "Komunikat Ministerstwa Cyfryzacji w sprawie Programu EZD RP." *Ministerstwo Cyfryzacji, Aktualności.* Accessed July 29, 2016. http://m.mc.gov.pl/aktualnosci/komunikat-ministerstwa-cyfryzacji-w-sprawie-programu-ezd-rp.

Ministry of Digital Affairs. 2016. "Strategic Action Priorities of the Ministry of Digital Affairs in computerization of public services." Accessed March 11, 2016. https://mc.gov.pl/files/mdas_strategic_action_priorities_in_public_services_-_final.pdf.

The regulation on office procedure instructions, classifications, circulation and archiving of documents: *Rozporządzenie Prezesa Rady Ministrów z dnia 18 stycznia 2011 r. w sprawie instrukcji kancelaryjnej, jednolitych rzeczowych wykazów akt oraz instrukcji w sprawie organizacji i zakresu działania archiwów zakładowych* (Journal of Laws of 2011, 14, item 67).

The law on electronic signature: "Ustawa z dnia 18 września 2001 r. o podpisie elektronicznym." *Journal of Laws* of 2001, 130, item 1450.

The regulation on national interoperability framework: "Rozporządzenie Rady Ministrów z dnia 12 kwietnia 2012 r. w sprawie Krajowych Ram Interoperacyjności, minimalnych wymagań dla rejestrów publicznych i wymiany informacji w postaci elektronicznej oraz minimalnych wymagań dla systemów teleinformatycznych." *Journal of Laws* of 2012, item 526.

The law on computerization of entities performing public tasks: "Ustawa z dnia 17 lutego 2005 r. o informatyzacji działalności podmiotów realizujących zadania publiczne." *Journal of Laws* of 2005, 64, item 565.

The regulation on creating and handling electronic documents: "Rozporządzenie Prezesa Rady Ministrów z dnia 14 września 2011 r. w sprawie sporządzania pism w formie dokumentów elektronicznych, doręczania dokumentów elektronicznych oraz udostępniania formularzy, wzorów i kopii dokumentów." *Journal of Laws* of 2011, 206, item 1216.

The law on national archives: "Ustawa z dnia 14 lipca 1983 r. o narodowym zasobie archiwalnym i archiwach." *Journal of Laws* of 1983, 38, item 173.

Radosław Sierocki

Chapter 8. How ICT Tools Intervene in Public Consultations

Introduction

The goal of this chapter is to sketch a short history of the public consultations implemented in Olsztyn in the context of the use of online platforms for consultation. Following the introduction concerning the issues, initiatives and modes of public consultation, two case studies are presented; the first one concerns using the Platform of Public Consultation, and the second the *inDialogue* platform. Although there are regulations concerning public consultations in which there are some paragraphs about using internet platforms, in practice, the modes and goals of using the ICT (Information and Communication Technology) seem to be problematic. The Platform of Public Consultation (Platforma Konsultacji Społecznych—PPC), which includes an internet forum as part of the PPC, is the main platform used in Olsztyn, while the inDialogue (W Dialogu) platform was tested by authorities during a consultation about pedestrian traffic during spring and summer 2016.

The inDialogue platform was part of the project "New Perspectives for Dialogue: ICT and Inclusive Decision-Making" conducted by a consortium led by the Centre for Deliberation (Warsaw University). One of its goals was "to project and prepare the ICT tools that would support the planning, conduct and reporting of the public consultation results held by city halls" (Przybylska 2015, 1).

The development of online platforms for public consultation is connected with an increasing interest in public consultation, deliberative democracy and, on the other hand, the crisis of traditional "electoral democracy" (Długosz and Wygnański 2005, 7; Przybylska 2014, 121). Political alienation, a decrease in social trust and low social capital are indicated as being reasons for this crisis (Wnuk-Lipiński 2008, 175–177). These new mechanisms of civic participation have been proposed as a remedy. Civic participation takes a variety of forms including the following: searching for information about decisions, the authorities' projects and plans, public consultations, and social negotiations. Citizens have different possibilities, depending on the form, for taking part in the decision-making process. By taking part in the process, citizens should gain, along with specific outcomes, an awareness of a real influence on politics at the central and local levels (Makowski 2014, 2; Przybylska 2014). In 2005 Dagmir Długosz and Jan Jakub Wygnański observed a paradox: they wrote, that in Poland there is the whole range of legal regulations and institutions that should support communication between citizens and administration, but that they are rarely used. The problem, they claimed, is a lack of habits and skills (Długosz and Wygnański 2005, 10). Since 2005 the situation has changed a little. Grzegorz Makowski points out that this is the effect of, firstly, the influence of EU politics, which forces the involvement of citizens in the works of administration and the decisions of authorities; secondly, the increasing role of non-governmental organizations; and thirdly, changes in the mentality of politicians, who find more and more advantages in informing citizens, consulting, and negotiating solutions with citizens (Makowski 2014, 1; Przybylska 2014).

The activities of authorities are also criticized by citizens. Citizens are learning how to effectively control those who are in charge; for example, the modes and quality of public consultation held by city halls. Olsztyn's public consultations can be used as an example. The quality of public consultations held during the period 2011–2016 was the subject of a report prepared by one of the local NGOs (Suchowiecki and Szczur 2016). The conclusions of the report were not positive, and among the weaknesses pointed out were problems with the information materials, the low number of meetings, the lack of conclusions, and the lack of outcomes resulting from the further activities of authorities. From the other side, the city hall has tried to improve the quality of public consultation, and therefore, new models and tools have been used and tested.

Some indications concerning the mechanisms of public consulting are in the Constitution of the Republic of Poland, which speaks both about representative democracy and about direct democracy. Besides the constitution and the regulations made in the acts of law,[1] there are local acts passed by local governments. In the Statue of the City of Olsztyn (Statut Miasta Olsztyn)[2] public consultations are mentioned twice in the chapter about municipal auxiliary units (jednostki pomocnicze miasta—MAU). According to the document, the city estates (osiedla) are auxiliary units, and any project for the formation, consolidation or division, appending names, or drawing borders of these estates are within the competences of the city council (Rada Miasta), after conducting a public consultation with the citizens (§12, point 1–3, Statue of the City of Olsztyn). Two forms of consultations are provided for: a meeting of citizens, or a meeting between councilors and

1 "The Act on Municipal Government of 8 March 1990" ("Ustawa o samorządzie gminnym"); "the Act on County Government of 5 June 1998" ("Ustawa o samorządzie powiatowym").

2 "The Statute of the City of Olsztyn" was introduced by a "Resolution of the City Council of Olsztyn VIII/65/11" of 29 March, 2011.

citizens.[3] The rules, principles, and procedures for public consultations in Olsztyn were regulated in detail in the city council's resolutions as follows:

- resolution LXVIII/842/06, passed on 27 September 2006;[4]
- resolution IV/15/11, passed on 26 January 2011;[5]
- and the current resolution XXXIV/605/13, passed on 27 March 2013.[6]

The Issues, Initiative and Modes of Public Consultations

In the aforementioned resolutions, the scope of the questions that could be given under consultations with citizens was broadened successively with each later resolution. The splitting of compulsory and optional consultation appeared in the last document. The first resolution mentioned (2006), repeated the notations of the statute: what should be consulted upon are questions regarding the MAUs. Moreover, changing the municipality's (city) borders should be done under consultation, as should the method of organization, the range of the MAU's activities, and changes in the official name of the city.

The greatest changes were made by the resolution passed in 2011. The arrangements given in the statute were not mentioned directly (it was said, that public consultations are necessary in issues that are, (1) pointed out in the acts of law, and (2) important for citizens), but a set of other questions were proposed. The questions were mainly connected with investments and strategies to do with city development. What should be done under public consultations particularly, were written as follows:

3 A similar notation about public consultations was in an earlier version of the Statue of the City from 2003 (The Statue of the City of Olsztyn, introduced by a Resolution of the City Council of Olsztyn VI/67/03, of 26th February 2003) in §12, point 1–4.

4 Resolution LXVIII/842/06 of the City Council of Olsztyn, of 27th September 2006, concerning the rules and procedures of public consultations with inhabitants of the city of Olsztyn (Uchwała Rady Miasta w sprawie zasad i trybu konsultacji z mieszkańcami Miasta Olsztyn).

5 Resolution IV/15/11 of the City Council of Olsztyn, of 26th January 2011, on establishing the rules and procedure for conducting public consultations with the inhabitants of the Olsztyn Commune (Uchwała Rady Miasta Olsztyn w sprawie określenia zasad i trybu przeprowadzania konsultacji społecznych z mieszkańcami Gminy Olsztyn).

6 Resolution XXXIV/605/13 of the City Council of Olsztyn, of 27th March 2013, on establishing the rules and procedure for conducting public consultations with the inhabitants of the Olsztyn Commune (Uchwała Rady Miasta Olsztyn w sprawie określenia zasad i trybu przeprowadzania konsultacji społecznych z mieszkańcami Gminy Olsztyn).

- Strategies for the development of the city's community,
- Long-term investments plans,
- Construction investment by the city,
- The organization of public transport,
- The waste management plan,
- A program of cooperation with non-governmental organizations,
- Local law acts,
- Strategies for solving social problems,
- Other strategies and trade programs within the fields of community tasks.

The adoption of the last of the resolutions concerning public consultations (passed in 2013) was preceded by public consultations with citizens, local NGOs and the Municipal Council of the Public Benefit Organization (Gminna Rada Działalności Pożytku Publicznego—MCPBO) for which the topic was a project concerning the resolution on public consultations. The resolution says that public consultation should proceed in regard to the following:

- The strategy of the city community's development,
- A program of cooperation with NGOs,
- Acts of local law regarding NGOs,
- Questions that must be asked under consultation in accordance with other acts of law (Statute of the City),
- Questions that should be consulted as requested by citizens, i.e., if there are at least 500 signatures on the application.

There are also some other issues that could be given under consultation (optional):

- Investments planned by the community,
- Organization of public communication,
- Waste management plans,
- Other strategies and trade programs in the field of community tasks,
- Issues important for citizens (if there are less than 500 signatures).

According to the resolutions passed in 2006, a consultation could be initiated by the city's president or the city council. Citizens also had the right to initiate a consultation if the application was signed by at least 5% of the city's population, in the case of consultations concerning the municipality; or 10% of the MUA, if the case concerned an estate. The next resolution widened the range of groups who could initiate a consultation; the Council of the Estate (MUA), the Municipal Council of Public Benefit Organization, and local NGOs were added. In 2013 the city's Youth Council was also taken into account. Moreover, as was mentioned earlier, it was obligatory to start a consultation in cases where an application was signed by at least 500 citizens, and could also be started, but was not obligatory, in cases where an application was signed by at least 50 citizens. Regardless of the initiating group, the consultations had to be ordered by the president of Olsztyn (with an actual order).

As the data available from the electronic Platform for Public Consultations (www.konsultacje.olsztyn.eu)[7] and the website of the Bulletin of Public Information (Biuro Informacji Publicznej) show, from the beginning of 2011 the president of Olsztyn ordered public consultations 58 times (excluding some additional orders that extended the terms of consultations), and it was a very rare situation in which subjects other than the president initiated the debate. The two exceptions concerned a consultation regarding citizens' opinions about the development of a playground in Zatorze (one of the estates in Olsztyn); and a consultation dedicated to the naming of a new street in the central part of the city. The first of these two consultations was an initiative by citizens, the second was the initiative of the council of the MUA where the new street runs. Pursuant to the resolution of 2011, 28 public consultations were passed, and another 30 after the resolution of 2013.

The resolutions also differentiated the modes and forms of participation for running the consultations. The broadening of the forms allowed them to be adapted more accurately to both the problems and the participants in the consultations. According to the 2006 resolution, there were only two forms of public consultations:

- A meeting with all citizens or with the citizens of specific a MUA (if the issue was concerned only with the given MUA),
- An opinion poll (with a closed or open question).

The 2011 resolution gave more options. Besides the forms introduced in 2006 there were also the following:

- Meetings with the representatives of local NGOs,
- Sending a proposal for changes or solutions to MCPBO with a request for an opinion,
- Sending (via email) a proposal for changes or solutions to local NGOs with a request for an opinion.

7 Accessed August 10, 2016.

Opinion polls also included publishing consultation issues on the consultations' electronic platform or on the city hall's website, and then collecting opinions via electronic mail or a non-electronic form, which was available at the buildings of the city hall.

Additionally, the unit that was responsible for the public consultation was obliged to conduct social research in which two methods of social research were available: focus groups or a representative survey of public opinion.

The rules were changed a little in the 2013 resolution. The unit responsible for consultations had to choose three forms of participation out of the given list:

- At least one open meeting with the citizens (citizens should have the chance to express their opinions and their statements should be written down in the official record),
- At least one workshop involving citizens that provides information about the issue being consulted and aiming towards a solution,
- Collecting opinions or proposals for solutions in writing (including electronic mail),
- Publishing the issue that is the subject of the consultations on the Platform for Public Consultations (users were able to submit their comments to the forum connected with the platform),
- Meeting with members of the local NGOs,
- Sending the proposal of changes or solutions to MCPBO for an opinion,
- Sending (via email) the proposal of changes or solutions to local NGOs with a request for an opinion,
- Qualitative or quantitative social research.

An analysis of the aforementioned resolutions leads to a conclusion about the increasing role of tools that are dependent on the internet: the Platform for Public Consultations has appeared as a specific space dedicated to public debates, sending proposals for changes and solutions through electronic mail, collecting the opinions of NGOs and citizens through email, communicating with citizens via the internet forum (part of PPC), and collecting the surveys online. In 2016, a new platform for public consultation, inDialogue (W Dialogu), was tested; and also the Citizen's Panel, an internet tool for conducting survey research, started working. These are only a small part of a whole spectrum of possibilities for using internet tools in broadening the democracy toolbox (Tomkova 2009, 2).

Platform of Public Consultations and the Internet Forum

The website specifically dedicated to local public consultations in Olsztyn is the Platform for Public Consultations (Platforma Konsultacji Społecznych, PPC).[8] An internet forum is part of the PPC and is one of the most important tools for communicating with citizens and for collecting their opinions and ideas, but also criticism. The regulations for the PPC were established by order of the president in June 2011,[9] with some changes made in October 2011. According to the regulations, the PPC is a site for discussion, the exchange of views, and opinions concerning investments and municipal projects in the city that are under public consultation, but it is also a tool for providing information about the goals and proposals of the city hall. Taking part in the electronic discussions is possible after registering and logging in. Although there is an obligation to provide a real name on the registration form, participation in the discussion under a nickname is possible, and most users seize the opportunity. Less than 20% of the 135 active forum members (those, who wrote at least one post) used their full name.

At first, the possibility for opening a new topic or for putting pictures on the forum was reserved for the administrators and moderators who lead the discussions. But other users demanded the same rights; they wanted to have the opportunity to open new topics concerned with, what was from their point of view, important problems. Pictures (photos, maps, diagrams) were also seen as important forms of expression. Despite the standard rules that are characteristic of all of internet forums (for example, concerning inappropriate content), there were the rules about the city hall's right to use the whole or part of any messages in other city hall publications. There was also an obligation to answer citizens' questions within a period of no longer than three working days (with the exception of problems that required deeper consideration for which there was a maximum of 21 working days).

According to the order of the president,[10] the forum worked in two modes: (1) in an *information mode*, and (2) in a *consultation mode*. The second mode is initiated after the publication of the president's order concerning the opening of

8 The Platform of Public Consultation is available at the website: www.konsultacje.olsztyn.eu. In some documents and in the texts on the website, the Platform of Public Consultations is also called the Platform of Public Communication. Accesed August 10, 2016.

9 Order of the President of Olsztyn concerning the Regulations for the Forum of Platform for Public Consultations in the city hall of Olsztyn, 30 June 2011, 187/2011 (Zarządzenie w sprawie wprowadzenia Regulaminu Forum Platformy Konsultacji Społecznych Urzędu Miasta Olsztyn).

10 Ibidem.

a public consultation. In this situation, either a new topic is started in the forum, or a post with information about the consultation is published in the topic that is already running. One of the *greatest* discussions (with sixty-five users publishing posts and over one thousand replies), which was concerned with trams in Olsztyn, can serve as an example of the functioning of the forum. At first, the thread "Tramwaje w Olsztynie" (Trams in Olsztyn) was used in the information mode. The topic was started on 22 February 2010 with information about a special website dedicated to the tramways, which was published by one of the administrators. As can be read in the posts, local government officials were waiting for opinions about Olsztyn's trams and tramway, while the users were mainly asking about the beginning of public consultations; it seemed that the citizens were expecting the debate about trams to become a public consultation. The president's order concerning a public consultation on this matter was signed over a year later—on 20 August 2011—and was concerned with the location of tram stops. The public consultations lasted two weeks (from 14 to 30 September 2011) and during this time there were 33 posts (out of 1,068 published for the whole thread). The topic concerning the trams is still open, however, in the regulation, there is a notation that states that the topic will be closed when the public consultation ends.

The internet forum is recognized as a tool for public consultations that is equal to other forms. The practice of using the forum has changed, even though there has been no change in the official regulations; users who are not administrators or moderators are now able to start a new topic, as well as to add some pictures.

The Platform of Public Consultations and the forum were the forms most often used for collecting opinions from citizens in consultations (Graph 1). In 48 out of the 58 presidential orders concerning public consultations, there was an obligation to publish the information on the PPC. In 10 cases there was no such a requirement (i.e., order 235/2016, which concerned modes of work and appointing members of the MCPBO, read that the consultations are to proceed using the following forms: sending the proposal document to local NGOs via e-mail with a request for opinions, a meeting of the Council of NGO's for Olsztyn, and receiving opinions from the Council of NGO's for Olsztyn).

Graph prepared by author.

Graph 1. Forms of communication used in public consultations in Olsztyn in years 2011-2016

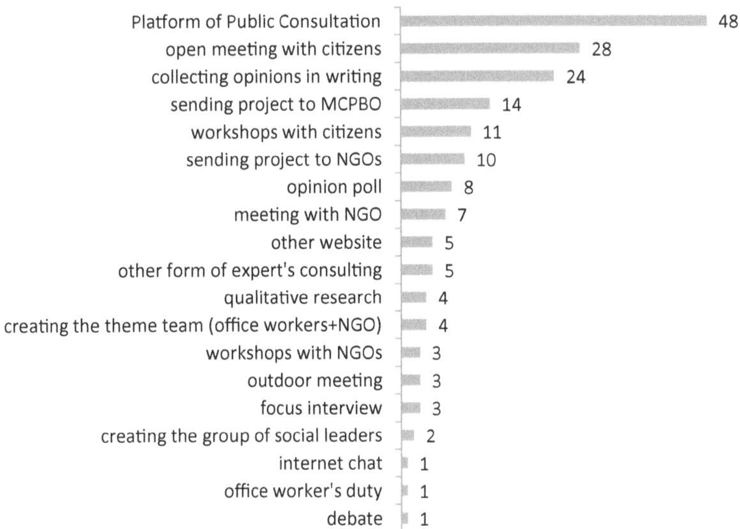

Among the other important and often used forms of public consultation indicated in the official acts (orders) were also open meetings with citizens, collecting citizens' opinions in writing (by email or by a form available at the city hall), sending the project to MCPBO and local NGOs, and workshops with citizens.

Although public consultations reports should be published on the website, only 25 reports were available on the Platform of Public Consultations and the forum. There is no specific format for reports, therefore the reports vary in form, number of pages, and conclusions. The report about public consultations in Olsztyn (2011–2016), which was prepared by members of the Forum of Development of Olsztyn (Forum Rozwoju Olsztyna), said that out of 40 public consultations,[11] there were 17 reports published on the PPC and 5 published on the city hall's website; some of the reports were, in fact, protocols from the meetings (Suchowiecki and Szczur 2016, 17).

11 There was a different methodology for counting the consultations in the report than in this chapter.

Most often public consultations were concerned with infrastructure (building, rebuilding and the modernization of streets. 17 cases), non-governmental organizations (8 cases), revitalization (6 cases), municipal economy (heating system for Olsztyn, waste management, low emission economy plan. five cases) and social problems (5 cases). There were also some consultations about public transport (trams in Olsztyn), the image and cultural marketing of the city (official souvenir and symbol for Olsztyn), and historical politics (the contents of the information board for a monument dedicated to the soldiers of the Red Army, by Xawery Dunikowski).

There were 39 forum threads dedicated to public consultations that were ordered by the president, therefore, it is possible to make a quantitative summary about the forum users. As mentioned above, not all of the topics were opened and closed under the strict terms of public consultations, and the official consultation period was usually only a part of a longer discussion (for example, the discussion regarding the trams in Olsztyn during the public consultation was approximately 3% of all the posts published on the thread). In all of the discussion topics that were in part or in whole for public consultations, 135 people (including administrators and moderators) published at least one post. Of the total, 3 took part in 17 discussions and 78 people published posts in only one topic. The median and the mode were 1, and the average was 2.18.[12]

What is also worth mentioning is the duration of the consultations: the shortest period between the opening and closing of consultations was 14 days (a consultation about the naming of a new street), and the longest was 324 days (a consultation about the program for the spatial development of the city's downtown area, which went from 11 February to 30 December, 2012). The average time was 59.31 days, and the median was 31 days. There was also a consultation concerning the *Civil Participatory Budget for 2017* (Olsztyński Budżet Obywatelski), although the order stated there were 601 days allocated for public consultation, from 10 May 2016 to 31 December 2017, in fact, this period should have been allocated to *all* of the activities connected with the participatory budget: from the appointment of the Coordination Team and Participatory Council; through receiving applications with ideas promoting activities, and voting; to carrying out the chosen projects and project evaluation. The whole participatory budget was treated as the public consultation.

According to the conclusions of the civil report concerning Olsztyn's public consultations, the PPC (with the internet forum) was one of the most often used form of public consultation, but it was also one of the easiest forms of consultation.

12 Statistics for August 2016.

In 19 out of 40 consultations there was no open meeting with citizens, and only in 8 cases was there more than one meeting. It was very rare that more engaging forms of public consultation (i.e., workshops involving particular groups of citizens) were used. It was also rare that the conclusions and proposals from the online debates were presented in a report resulting from the consultation.

In spring and summer of 2016, a new tool for public consultation was tested. Olsztyn's authorities took part in the In Dialogue (W Dialogu) project conducted by a consortium made up of the Warsaw University (Centre of Deliberation), the Warsaw University of Technology, the Association of Polish Cities, the Polish Forum of Disabled Persons, MIT (an ICT training company), "Cities on the Internet" Association, and the Foundation for Free and Open Software. The aim of the project is "to develop, in cooperation with social partners, a model of social dialogue with inhabitants and an ICT platform for public consultations to be implemented by local government" (Activities 2016).

The inDialogue platform with the deliberative model of public consultation was used in a consultation about pedestrian traffic in the city. The inhabitants of Olsztyn were encouraged to take part in the consultation by registering on the platform. Some articles about the project appeared in local press, for example, an interview with the director of the city hall's Office of Social Communication and Civil Dialogue (Skrzat 2016). Information was an important part of the consultation model, therefore, preparing the information materials about the pedestrian traffic was the first step in the consultation. The materials were published on the platform and everyone was able to read and comment on them.

Case Studies on the Use of ICT in Public Consultation

In this section, the case studies of two of Olsztyn's public consultations are presented. The first one was one of the *biggest* consultations—taking into account the number of forum users—and concerned the modernization of one of the most important and most rundown streets in the city—Partyzantów Street. The second concerns one of the latest consultations and was regarding the situation and problems for pedestrians in the city. In the first consultation mentioned, the Platform for Public Consultation was used, while in the second, the inDialogue platform. It has to be stressed, that the first of the consultations was ordered by the president, but in the case of the second consultation there was no order; it was not a *real* pubic consultation, but rather a *test* public consultation.

Case Study 1. Public Consultation Concerning Partyzantów Street Using the Platform of Public Consultation

Public consultations about Partyzantów Street were ordered by the president on 10 June 2013[13] and the time period given was from 18 June 2013 to 30 September 2013 (later extended to 30 October 2013). As mentioned above, the consultation concerning this infrastructure project (especially building, rebuilding and the modernization of the street) was the most commonly discussed topic amongst Olsztyn's consultations. According to the president's order, the participants in the discussion would be the citizens, and the forms to be taken by the consultation were as indicated below:

- Publishing basic information on the PPC,
- A meeting with the representative of the institutions that were located on the street,
- An outdoor meeting with the Council of Estate (MUA) members and local NGOs,
- Workshops with the inhabitants of Partyzantów Street,
- An open meeting with citizens.[14]

The goal of the consultation was to get an answer to the following question: what are the citizens' opinions about the planned rebuilding of Partyzantów street? Although the question was open, i.e., there were no proposals for a rebuilding project, it was reinterpreted; and in further announcements from the city hall, for example in the information published on the PCC website, it was said, that the authorities had asked "to what extent and how the street should be modernized?" (Kamiński 2013) (my translation).

The information about the consultation that was published on the PCC website was rather short: it mentioned the goal, the questions, the cooperation with the University of Warmia and Mazury, and about the intention of asking as many citizens as possible. It also indicated that the workshops with citizens would be the main form of consultation, however, in the president's order, workshops were one of many forms. In order to get more information about the public consultation,

13 Order of the President of Olsztyn of June 10, 2013, 177/2011, concerning the holding of a public consultation about the modernization of Partyzantów Street. (Zarządzenie o przeprowadzeniu konsultacji społecznych w sprawie "Modernizacji ulicy Partyzantów").

14 Ibidem.

or to take part in the online discussion, people had to use the PCC forum, where the online discussion had started on 18 June.[15]

Besides the online discussion there were other forms of consultation: meetings with representatives of the institutions located on Partyzantów Street (17 July 2013), a meeting with the Council of the Estate (18 September 2013), a meeting with authors of the civil concept for the rebuilding of the street (22 October 2013), and an open meeting with citizens (25 October 2013). Before the consultation started, a social survey was held on the 7–8 June 2013 (therefore, the social survey was not part of the public consultation). The survey was prepared by Krzysztof Szulburski from the Faculty of Social Sciences of the University of Warmia and Mazury and conducted by students of the faculty. The survey's questionnaire was short and consisted mainly of open questions; for example, "How would you characterize people living in Partyzantów Street?", "What do like in Partyzantów Street?", "What don't you like about Partyzantów Street?", "What should be changed in Partyzantów Street?", "What are the most urgent changes?" (my translations). Answers were collected from 112 respondents who were met on the street and who were both inhabitants of the street and people who were only passing by.[16]

Although there is not enough space for a more specific qualitative analysis of the discussions, some important remarks can be made about (1) the discussion on the PCC forum, and (2) other forms of public consultation.

There were 21 people (including one administrator), who published at least one post on the internet forum and a total of 137 posts in the topic (94 posts within the period of the consultation). The thread was administrated by an employee of the city hall's Office of Social Communication (later named the Office of Communication and Social Dialogue). The main goal of the discussion was to gather opinions about the future of the street in the city's downtown area. There was some doubt as to whether the forum discussion was part of the public consultation, but the administrator assured the participants that the "posts of forum users are the part of public consultation."[17]

---

15 The thread dedicated to the consultation was "Modernization of Partyzantów Street" ("Modernizacja ulicy Partyzantów"), http://www.konsultacje.olsztyn.eu/forum/transport-i-czno-f18/modernizacja-ulicy-partyzantow-t5272.html. Accesed August 10, 2016.

16 The questionnaire and the report from the survey are available on the forum: http://www.konsultacje.olsztyn.eu/forum/transport-i-czno-f18/modernizacja-ulicy-partyzantow-t5272-15.html. Accesed August 10, 2016.

17 Post by user *kaminski.bartosz* during the forum topic "Modernizacja ulicy Partyzantów", on July 2, 2013. Published on the *Platform of Public Consultation*. Accessed August 10, 2016. http://www.konsultacje.olsztyn.eu/forum.

It has to be stressed that the discussion that was held in summer 2013, was not the first discussion (nor the last) about that particular street; there was a public discussion in 2010 and also later, in 2015. As written by the administrator in the post that opened the forum discussion—"we are asking again, in what range and to what extent should the Partyzantów Street be modernized. The previous concept prepared by Municipal Management of Roads and Bridges (Miejski Zarząd Dróg i Mostów) was discussed widely and for a long time even after the consultation finished" (my translation).[18] When one of the users asked what had happened with the previous concept, the administrator answered that the "project previously presented for rebuilding the street is not an issue for these consultations" (my translation).[19] In further discussion the expression "consultation in Olsztyn style" (konsultacje w stylu olsztyńskim) was used, which was a sarcastic remark regarding the situation, and meaning that a consultation is ordered, citizens take part in the discussion, a report is published, but it does not have any particular consequences.

From the beginning of the online discussion two sides of the debate emerged: advocates for widening the street to four lanes (a minority on the forum), and supporters of the *alley style* concept, according to which the street should be a space dedicated mainly to pedestrians and bikers, and with only two lanes for car traffic. In the second concept, a new planting of trees was expected. Both concepts expected there to be changes; Partyzantów Street was (at the time of the consultation) a two-way road with pavements on both sides. The road and pavements were in bad condition, and there were not many trees.[20]

The main problem with the Partyzantów Street was that it was one of the main streets in the northern part of Olsztyn's downtown area. There were some historic tenements, which were a little neglected. According to the arguments of one side of the discussion, it should be an elegant part of Olsztyn, mainly for citizens and tourists. But on the other hand, Partyzantów Street connects two main broad avenues in this part of the city, which are very important for transit traffic; therefore, as other side claimed, it should be a wide street that allows the movement of a large number of cars. It was important to the discussion that Olsztyn has no bypass, which results in huge traffic jams in Partyzantów Street.

---

18 Post by user *kaminski* during the topic "Modernizacja ulicy Paryzantów", on June 18, 2013. Published on the *Platform of Public Consultation*. Accessed August 10, 2016. http://www.konsultacje.olsztyn.eu/forum.

19 Post by user *kaminski.bartosz* during the forum topic "Modernizacja ulicy Partyzantów", on June 20, 2013. Published on the *Platform of Public Consultation*. Accessed August 10, 2016. http://www.konsultacje.olsztyn.eu/forum.

20 It is worth mentioning that nothing has changed since the chapter was prepared.

The discussion between the two sides became more and more aggressive. Besides of the substantive arguments, there appeared some arguments of a personal nature: both sides accusing each other of incompetence or populism. The supporters of the "alley for pedestrians and bikers" solution were mainly members of local NGOs who were specialized in infrastructure and the image of the city. The main complaint used against them was "[a] handful of NGO members wants to decide for all of the citizens" (my translation).[21] Advocates of the four-lane street proposed an internet survey (for example on the website of a local newspaper) for all citizens, but the other side claimed that such a solution was not a good idea because of the risk of manipulation, and the number of *haters* and *internet trolls* who would write their posts and comments under the articles published in the electronic versions of the local daily press. Members of local NGOs accused the supporters who wanted a four-lane street of not using their real names, and of being "in real life" office workers of city hall. They also called them "automotive lobbyists," who only cared about cars and drivers, not about the citizens and those who lived on the street. On the other hand, the NGO members were accused of having no support among the *ordinary inhabitants*. Their opponents wrote that the NGO members were thinking that every citizen wanted to ride a bike and that they were promoting a return to the Middle Ages when there were only horse-drawn carriages in the roads of the town. One of them wrote that the NGO members who had participated in the forum discussion were "talking others into believing that biking the whole city and retarding what could be retarded is the only correct solution,"[22] and later, "We don't want you to make us happy by force, we want a four-lane street in Olsztyn, and we would bike on weekend in the forest, out of town, not in the downtown area!" (my translation).[23]

The supporters of the alley-street version accused users from the other side of lacking substantive arguments. Their only argument was that there should be

---

21 Post by user *Krzysztof Olsztyniak* during the forum topic "Modernizacja ulicy Partyzantów", on October 10, 2013. Published on the *Platform of Public Consultation.* Accessed August 10, 2016. http://www.konsultacje.olsztyn.eu/forum.

22 Post by user *Przepustowość przede wszystkim* during the forum topic "Modernizacja ulicy Partyzantów", on November 6, 2013. Published on the *Platform of Public Consultation.* Accessed August 10, 2016. http://www.konsultacje.olsztyn.eu/forum.

23 Post by user *Przepustowość przede wszystkim* during the forum topic "Modernizacja ulicy Partyzantów", on November 6, 2013. Published on the *Platform of Public Consultation.* Accessed August 10, 2016. http://www.konsultacje.olsztyn.eu/forum.

more lanes, because of the large volume of traffic, but the other side claimed, that "the more lanes, the more cars" (my translation).[24]

Conclusions from the survey, which was conducted by researchers from the University of Warmia and Mazury, became available; but it seemed that users were not interested in them as they did not make any references to them. The main conclusions of the survey were, in short, that in the opinion of the respondents: (1) the inhabitants of the street were mainly poor and old people; (2) the strengths of the street were architecture and green spaces; (3) the weak point of the street was the bad condition of the road and pavements; and (4) the most urgent changes needed were connected with the roads and pavements (Szulborski 2013).

The complex concept for rebuilding the street was published on the forum and aroused a lot of interest. The *Civil Concept for Rebuilding Partyzantów Street* was the result of the work of a few of the local NGOs (i.e., The Citizens of Olsztyn and the Forum of the Development of Olsztyn). The concept was based on the opinions of the members of local NGOs, inhabitants and housing associations (in fact "Civil Conception…" was the result of a consultation held by the NGOs).[25] It was presented at several meetings and workshops (for the first time at a meeting on 18 June 2013) and published on the forum (26 September 2013). The concept was supported by approximately 600 people who signed the document.

By the middle of the discussion, posts became more offensive and insulting and did not end with the end of consultation; users wrote, for example, "The problem is not the infrastructure, but the plebeian mentality and the thinking, that kilometers of fresh asphalt would solve the problems of Olsztyn;"[26] "Olsztyn is not your property, and as a citizen who pays not so small amount of taxes, I have the right to take part in any discussion. With no regards!" (my translation).[27] Even though the forum had become a boxing ring for the two groups, the administrator

---

24 Post by user *bartek_b* during the forum topic "Modernizacja ulicy Partyzantów", on October 1, 2013. Published on the *Platform of Public Consultation.* Accessed August 10, 2016. http://www.konsultacje.olsztyn.eu/forum

25 The *Civil Conception of Rebuilding the Partyzantów Street* is available on the website Obywatelski Olsztyn, http://obywatelskiolsztyn.org/1647/obywatelska-koncepcja-przebudowy-ul-partyzantow#Zalozenia. Accessed: August 10, 2016.

26 Post by user *Suchar* during the forum topic "Modernizacja ulicy Partyzantów", on November 5, 2013. Published on the *Platform of Public Consultation.* Accessed August 10, 2016. http://www.konsultacje.olsztyn.eu/forum.

27 Post by user *Przepustowość przede wszystkim* during the forum topic "Modernizacja ulicy Partyzantów", on November 6, 2013. Published on the *Platform of Public Consultation.* Accessed August 10, 2016. http://www.konsultacje.olsztyn.eu/forum.

did not try to discipline the users, and the only attempts to moderate the discussion were observed when the debaters departed from the topic (i.e., when they were talking about rebuilding other streets in Olsztyn). The lack of moderation was noticed; one of the users wrote "Once again—in public this time—I demand the intervention of a moderator on this topic. This forum soon will look like an internet 'discussion' on the website of the local newspaper. Unless you, administrators, are going to add all of the emotional expressions and sentences to the official protocol of consultations" (my translation).[28] There was no reaction. The administrator did answer questions when asked directly; for example, when forum users asked about the city hall's works, in which they demanded to know the schedule of the consultation and information about what had been done; and also when they informed the administrator that according to law, the city hall had only a few days to publish the information about the meeting; and so on. The forum was also used by the administrator to publish announcements, for example, about the meeting of authorities with citizens, or about an extension of the terms of the consultation. Local authorities did not take part in the online discussion (however, as has been mentioned, there were accusations that some of the forum users were, in fact, city hall workers).

Because there was no moderation of the forum discussion, some of the users tried to organize an exchange of opinions. For example, one of the users noticed that the discussion was off topic, "I have read once again our posts, and I think, that we are not making the task of city hall any easier. We keep on talking about solutions instead of talking about needs and problems. Discussion about the solutions is important, but it is not the subject or aim of consultation" (my translation).[29] In the president's order, there was no information saying that the goal of the consultation was to obtain knowledge about the needs and problems rather than about the solutions. Users made assumptions about what the authority's expectations were, but even when those assumptions were false, the administrator did not try to correct them.

In summary, the discussion on the PPC forum was an illustration of the emergence of two polarized groups. The substantive arguments were interspersed with personal and offensive comments. It is hard to draw any conclusion, and there was

---

28 Post by user *robac* during the forum topic "Modernizacja ulicy Partyzantów", on November 6, 2013. Published on the *Platform of Public Consultation.* Accessed August 10, 2016. http://www.konsultacje.olsztyn.eu/forum.

29 Post by user *BorOl* during the forum topic "Modernizacja ulicy Partyzantów", on July 4, 2013. Published on the *Platform of Public Consultation.* Accessed August 10, 2016. http://www.konsultacje.olsztyn.eu/forum.

no conclusion from the online exchange of opinions that was worth mentioning in the public consultation's final report; however, the report about the consultation appeared on the forum at the beginning of December 2013 (one month and a week after the end of consultation). The report was prepared by the same person, from the city hall's Office of Social Communication, who was the administrator on the PCC forum. The report, which concerned not only the internet discussion but the whole consultation, stated that the most important result of the consultations was the *Civil Concept for Rebuilding Partyzantów Street.* As was mentioned at one of the meetings, the proposal by the NGOs was not a *ready to use* project but only a concept.

At a meeting with representatives of the city hall, the people who were working on Partyzantów Street (17 July 2013), as well as members of the Council of the Estate supported the majority of ideas in the *Civil Concept for Rebuilding Partyzantów Street.* After the public consultation, there was a meeting of the president and some the office personnel with the authors of the concept. The participants were informed that the *Civil Concept for Rebuilding Partyzantów Street* had been given to the Gdańsk University of Technology for expert analysis. It is hard to find any information on the PPC as to what the results of the analysis were.

The only reference to the online discussion in the final report was that during the public consultation there were 94 posts published on the PPC. To summarize the almost one hundred posts, the author of the report wrote, "posts consisted of opinions, polemics, and conclusions. After the end of consultation discussion, the thread was continued, and 41 more posts were published" (Kamiński 2013, 3) (my translation).

Another public consultation on this topic was started in August 2015.

Case Study 2. Consultation on Pedestrian Traffic Using the InDialogue Platform

The public consultation regarding pedestrian issues in Olsztyn had, from the point of view of the city hall, two goals: first, it was to acquire knowledge about citizens' opinions regarding pedestrian traffic; and second, to test the new inDialogue public consultation platform. This was not an official public consultation, as there was no order by the president. The whole consultation was treated as a test public consultation. The director of the Office of Communication and Social Dialogue at city hall, Aneta Szpaderska, said in an interview with the local press that the topic (pedestrian traffic) was used in order to encourage inhabitants to take part in a test of the platform. This is not only for finding out if inhabitants liked or disliked the platform, but also to give them the opportunity to check the practical functionality of the platform. She said,

> We had to think of some important topic for the discussion. I guess we could have thought of a lot of other topics, but we thought about the question 'how pedestrians find living in Olsztyn', because each of us has been a pedestrian every day. Information collected in this way would be the basis for preparing a document, that concerns standards for pedestrian traffic. This is not an actual consultation because a public consultation needs to be ordered, and we are just testing this new platform and tool for consultations. Nevertheless, opinions will be taken into account and will be the basis for future activities (Skrzat 2016) (my translation).

The consultation had several steps, and the schedule contained the following:

- Pre-consultation about information materials (19 April–8 May 2016)
- Analysis and correction of the information materials by city hall workers; publishing materials on the inDialogue internet platform (9 May–7 June 2016)
- Recruitment of citizens for the consultation (10 June–24 June 2016)
- Text debate on the inDialogue platform (25 June–2 July 2016)
- Meeting of citizens, with the participation of experts (between 25 June and 2 July 2016)
- Preparing the consultation report on the platform and the city hall's website (by 16 July 2016) (Kołodziejska 2016a)

The city hall added one more item: a walk by authorities and citizens that was to help identify pedestrians' problems *in the field.*

One of the assumptions made about the online and offline debates was that every participant would get a transcription of the debate, and be able to verify it, as well as the report from the discussion and the report from the consultation with the possibility of adding comments.

As was written above, the main substantive goal of the consultation was to acquire knowledge about problems concerning pedestrian traffic. There were three methods of data gathering: online text debate, online voice debate, and open direct debate. The inDialogue platform was used in the online text debate.

The consultation in Olsztyn was one of the test locations for ICT as well as for the whole consultation model. As was stated on the project's website:

In Olsztyn, the platform was used to conduct pre-consultations of information materials in preparation of the "Pedestrian in the City" ('Pieszy w Mieście') public consultations. The participants of the project [pre-consultation. Author's note] included the staff of the Communications and Civic Dialogue Office (part of the city hall), and twelve recruited social Ambassadors (among whom were the presidents of Housing Estate Councils, representatives of NGOs, local public institutions and councils). The project had two main phases: preparation phase and execution phase. In the former, the Project team together with the city hall discussed the subject and theme of consultations, established preliminary time-frames, and conducted three workshops for the city hall members and social Ambassadors. The In Dialogue team recruited the majority of Ambassadors, and helped prepare the information materials to be discussed by the citizens. Monitoring of the preparation phase was conducted with the aid of other team members. Contacts with the press were also established in order to disseminate information on the consultations. The execution phase started on the 19 of April and included uploading the information materials, monitoring registration on the platform and answering potential queries. Overall, 11 comments were collected from citizens. After two weeks, once the comments were closed, they were collected by the city hall representatives in order to update the information materials. Once the materials have been updated and uploaded, the online debate was opened: the citizens could voice their opinions and answer the questions between 25 of June and the 3 of July. On 28 and 29 of June, two meetings were held at the city hall, and there was a voice debate held online on the 27 of June as well. After collecting the materials from all debates, partial reports followed by the final report have been drafted and uploaded to the platform (Summary of completed and ongoing projects 2017).

One of the goals of the consultation was to prepare the *Standards for Pedestrian Traffic*, a document that already functions in some other cities in Poland (i.e., in Lublin and Bydgoszcz). The *Standards for Pedestrian Traffic* document consists of sets of guidelines and recommendations, but not rules that are important for improving the safety and comfort of pedestrian traffic; they take into account the needs of handicapped people, elderly people and parents with baby carriages.

The consultation had to give answers to three main questions:

- What changes would make pedestrians feel safer?
- What changes would make walking on the city's streets more comfortable?
- What changes would lower the number of physical barriers for pedestrians?

Participants recruited for the consultation were able to access any of the necessary information about problems for pedestrians. All of the information was available on the ICT platform, as follows:

- The basic information about pedestrians and the pavements in Olsztyn, public transport and also statistics about traffic accidents involving pedestrians;
- Information about the limits imposed on changes due to, for example, costs, plans for city developments, the traffic act;

- Information about the pros and cons of some solutions;
- Part of the traffic act concerning the rules for pedestrians.

Text consultations (which were usually conducted on the PPC forum) started on 25 June and closed on 2 July. Recruitment was opened, and anyone who wanted to take part in the debate could register and get access to the ICT. There were 12 participants in text debate. The structure of text debate was built on four questions, which were connected with the questions for the whole consultation:

- What problems do you come across, as a pedestrian, every day in Olsztyn?
- How could the availability of infrastructure for all pedestrians be improved?
- What solutions would make it safer for pedestrians?
- What would you like to change with regards to pedestrians' comfort?

The structure of the questions led to the structure of the answers: one could answer the question directly or comment on someone else's answers. This made the debate clearer and more comprehensible than the exchanges of opinions on the PPC internet forum. In addition, there was a *map of arguments* put in place—a diagram showing ordered arguments and opinions.

What was important was that there were no names or nicknames for participants, therefore, there was no explicitly offensive arguments, nor attacks or arguments of *hate*. Users of the platform were able to propose their opinions and arguments and vote on opinions and arguments written by other participants. For example, the answers to the first of the questions were as follows:

- The low number of trees and lack of shade ("it is hard to walk on hot days");
- The pavements have high curbs;
- Incorrectly synchronized traffic lights;
- The bad condition of pavements;
- The lack of sewer drains (pedestrians are often splashed by cars).

The order of the questions and answers made the task of preparing the report *relatively* easy, as conclusions were precise and clear. The report from the text debate states that the debate produced the conclusion, "that inhabitants of Olsztyn rather than creating a 'Standard of Pedestrian Traffic'—an act that would confirm already existing solutions of law—are interested in making a list of recommendations to the authorities that state practical actions that should be taken in order to advantage all pedestrian groups" (Kołodziejska 2016b) (my translation). The consultation showed that "there is a need for social dialogue and also this means setting priorities for improving the safety and comfort of pedestrians together with the citizens" (Kołodziejska 2016b) (my translation).

Public consultations also covered direct meetings (28 and 29 June), and one additional outdoor meeting. There were 14 participants in the meetings (9 participants in the June 28 debate and 5 on 29 June). The structure of the direct (offline) debates was the same as for the online debate. In the first of the debates, three main topics were presented: the comfort of pedestrians, their safety, and the activities of the institutions responsible for their comfort and safety (Przybylska 2016a). In the second debate, there were two main topics: the comfort and safety of pedestrians (Przybylska 2016b).

In the report, there was information about how the conclusions would be considered by the city hall. It was said, that authorities are preparing an act called the *Standards for Pedestrian Traffic in Olsztyn* describing solutions that would have to be used in investments and the rebuilding of streets of the city. The document would be added to already existing standards for bicycle paths. As was announced, after the preparation of the document there will be another public consultation about the project concerning the list of standards.

Conclusion

Public consultations in Olsztyn are prepared and conducted on the basis of the resolutions passed in 2013 by the city council. As it is written in the act, there are a few problems and topics that must be taken under public consultation, but also a few where public consultation is optional. There is also the list of subjects to whom the initiative for starting the consultations belongs, but it is always the city's president who has the power to order the consultations.

Information and Communication Technologies became a very important part of the public consultations, but using the Platform of Public Consultations, and especially the internet forum connected with the PPC, is an area for fighting and the expression of offensive opinions and arguments, as was shown in the example of the public consultations concerning the modernization of Partyzantów Street. The case of the consultation about pedestrian's problems in the city shows that the structure and order of answers and comments depends mainly on the structure of asking the questions and the rules of ICT. The inDialogue platform gave the possibility for, almost, automatically organizing the discussion, while the order of the discussion on the internet forum depended on the work of moderators and administrators. Inhabitants rather rarely take part in any public consultation, and it is usually the group with the most interested persons who always speak in the name of the silent majority. The online discussion, in which there are not only substantive arguments, seems to be more attractive for passive users of the forum (those who only read posts). This could be the *weakness* of the inDialogue platform, but on the other hand, also its strength—it is a tool only for those who are interested in the topic of the consultation, and there is space only for substantive arguments.

References

Books, articles, and reports

Długosz, Dagmir, Jan Jakub Wygnański. 2005. *Obywatele współdecydują. Przewodnik po partycypacji obywatelskiej*. Warsaw: Stowarzyszenie na rzecz Forum Inicjatyw Pozarządowych.

Kamiński, Bartosz. 2013. Raport z konsultacji społecznych w sprawie "Modernizacja ulicy Partyzantów", *Forum Platformy Konsultacji Społecznych*, Accessed August 10, 2016. http://www.konsultacje.olsztyn.eu/forum/transport-i-czno-f18/modernizacja-ulicy-partyzantow-t5272-135.html.

Kołodziejska, Marta. 2016a. "Działania. Testy w miastach. Olsztyn." *wdialogu.uw.edu.pl*. Accessed February 20, 2017. http://wdialogu.uw.edu.pl/dzialania/testy-w-miastach/olsztyn.

Kołodziejska, Marta. 2016b. "Konsultacje 'Pieszy w Mieście'. Raport z debaty tekstowej na platformie 'W Dialogu'." *wdialogu.uw.edu.pl*. Accessed February 20, 2017. http://www.wdialogu.uw.edu.pl/images/Olsztyn/Raport_debata_tekstowa.pdf.

Makowski, Grzegorz. 2014. "Konsultacje społeczne – uregulowania prawne a praktyka." *Infos. Biuro Analiz Sejmowych* 20 (180): 1–2.

Przybylska, Anna. 2014. "Jaką przyszłość mają w Polsce deliberatywne formy konsultacji społecznych?" In *Partycypacja obywatelska. Od teorii do praktyki społecznej*, edited by Anna Przybylska, and Anna Giza, 121–137. Warsaw: Wydawnictwo Naukowe Scholar.

Przybylska, Anna. 2015. "Kontekst problemowy dyskusji. Jakość konsultacji." *wdialogu.uw.edu.pl*. Accessed August 10, 2016. http://wdialogu.uw.edu.pl/images/wdialogu_seminarium_11_2015/kontekst_problemowy_jakosc_konsultacji_publicznych_anna_przybylska.pdf.

Przybylska, Anna. 2016a. "Raport ze spotkania konsultacyjnego 28 czerwca 2016 r." *wdialogu.uw.edu.pl*. Accessed February 22, 2017. http://www.wdialogu.uw.edu.pl/images/Olsztyn/Raport_28_czerwca2016.pdf.

Przybylska, Anna. 2016b. "Raport ze spotkania konsultacyjnego 29 czerwca 2016 r." *wdialogu.uw.edu.pl*. Accessed February 22, 2017. http://www.wdialogu.uw.edu.pl/images/Olsztyn/Raport_29_czerwca2016.pdf.

Skrzat, Patryk. 2016. "Olsztyn testuje narzędzie dla samorządowców z całej Polski." *Gazeta Wyborcza. Olsztyn*, May 6. http://olsztyn.wyborcza.pl/olsz

tyn/1,48726,20029802,olsztyn-testuje-narzedzie-dla-samorzadow-z-calej-polski.html.

Suchowiecki, Krzysztof, Paweł Szczur. 2016. "Konsultacje pod lupą. Obywatelska ocena konsultacji społecznych przeprowadzonych w Olsztynie w latach 2011–2016." *Forum Rozwoju Olsztyna, fro.olsztyn.pl*. Accessed February 22, 2017 http://fro.olsztyn.pl/wp-content/uploads/2016/11/Konsultacje-pod-lup%C4%85-raport-FRO.pdf.

Szulborski, Krzysztof. 2013. "Ulica Partyzantów w Olsztynie. Opinie o ulicy wyrażone przez mieszkańców i bywalców ulicy Partyzantów. Raport podsumowujący sondę uliczną o ulicy Partyzantów." *www.konsultacje.olsztyn.eu*. Accessed August 9, 2016. http://www.konsultacje.olsztyn.eu/forum/transport-i-czno-f18/modernizacja-ulicy-partyzantow-t5272-15.html.

Tomkova, Jordanka. 2009. "E-consultations: New tools for civic engagement or facades for political correctness?" *European Journal of ePractice*, 7: 1–10.

Wnuk-Lipiński, Edmund. 2008. *Socjologia życia publicznego*. Warsaw: Scholar.

Legal sources

"Uchwała LXVIII/842/06 Rady Miasta w sprawie zasad i trybu konsultacji z mieszkańcami Miasta Olsztyn." *Dziennik Urzędowy Województwa Warmińsko-Mazurskiego*, 154, October 18, 2006: 9860–9861. Accessed September 10, 2017. http://bip.uw.olsztyn.pl/pl/bip/dziennik_urzedowy/2006_1/px_dz._u._nr_154.pdf.

"Uchwała IV/15/11 Rady Miasta Olsztyn w sprawie określenia zasad i trybu przeprowadzania konsultacji społecznych z mieszkańcami Gminy Olsztyn." *Dziennik Urzędowy Województwa Warmińsko-Mazurskiego* 25, March 10, 2011: 1392-13-95. Accessed September 10, 2017. http://edzienniki.olsztyn.uw.gov.pl/Compatible/Details?Oid=4383

"Uchwała XXXIV/605/13 Rady Miasta Olsztyn w sprawie określenia zasad i trybu przeprowadzania konsultacji społecznych z mieszkańcami Gminy Olsztyn." *Biuletyn Informacji Publicznej*. Accessed September 10, 2017. http://bip.olsztyn.eu/bip/plik/291572///&id=291572.

"Uchwała Nr VIII/65/11 Rady Miasta Olsztyn z dnia 29 marca 2011 r. w sprawie uchwalenia Statutu Miasta Olsztyna." *Dziennik Urzędowy Województwa Warmińsko-Mazurskiego*, 64, May 23, 2011: 3664–3697. Accessed December 4, 2017. http://edzienniki.olsztyn.uw.gov.pl/?#/legalact/2011/1057/.

"Uchwała Nr VI/67/03 z dnia 26 lutego 2003 w sprawie uchwalenie Statutu Miasta Olsztyn." *Dziennik Urzędowy Województwa Warmińsko-Mazurskiego*, 35, item 503, March 20, 2003. Accessed December 4, 2017. http://www.e-bip.pl/Start/47/ActDetails/1574.

"Ustawa z dnia 8 marca 1990 roku o samorządzie gminnym." *Journal of Laws* of 1990, 16, item 95.

"Ustawa z dnia 5 czerwca 1998 roku o samorządzie powiatowym." *Journal of Laws* of 1998, 91, item 578.

"Zarządzenie nr 187 Prezydenta Miasta Olsztyn z dnia 30 czerwca 2011 w sprawie wprowadzenia Regulaminu Forum Platformy Konsultacji Społecznych Urzędu Miasta Olsztyn." *Biuletyn Informacji Publicznej*. Accessed December 4, 2017. http://bip.olsztyn.eu/bip/dokument/276866/zarzadzenie_nr_187_z_dnia_30_czerwca_2011_r_w_sprawie_wprowadzenia_regulaminu_platformy_konsultacji_spolecznych_urzedu_miasta_olsztyna/.

"Zarządzenie nr 177 Prezydenta Olsztyna z dnia 10 czerwca 2013 roku o przeprowadzeniu konsultacji społecznych w sprawie 'Modernizacji ulicy Partyzantów'." *Biuletyn Informacji Publicznej*. Accessed December 4, 2017. http://bip.olsztyn.eu/bip/dokument/293424/zarzadzenie_nr_177_z_dnia_10_czerwca_2013_r_o_przeprowadzeniu_konsultacji_spolecznych_w_sprawie_modernizacji_ulicy_partyzantow_//&cspg_page=1&lob112415_page=12.

Others

"Activities." 2016. *wdialogu.uw.edu.pl*. Accessed August 10, 2017. http://wdialogu.uw.edu.pl/en/activities.

"Summary of completed and ongoing projects." 2017. *wdialogu.uw.edu.pl*. Accessed August 2, 2017. http://www.wdialogu.uw.edu.pl/en/activities/tests.

Marta Kołodziejska and Klementyna Świeżewska

Chapter 9. Public Consultations in Media Narratives: The Case of Olsztyn and Nowa Dęba

Introduction

The media play a crucial role in the democratic process as they not only enable the dissemination of information and facilitate grass-root monitoring of local and national authorities but also act as intermediaries between the authorities and citizens. The development of communication technologies has resulted in the modern media becoming inextricably tied to individuals' lives and becoming more adaptable, customizable and available.

The local media, that is, the mass media whose reach is limited to a particular area (which can be as small as one village or as large as a voivodship), is a term that refers primarily to print and broadcast media (Kowalczyk 2011, 65–66). However, it should also include digital media such as news portals and blogs; despite their reach being unlimited, their *locality* is determined by their content. If the majority of news, articles, commentaries and so forth are focused on local affairs and the name of the website is associated with a particular area, it can be assumed that the target audience is primarily the inhabitants of that area. Thus, digital media can also be classified as local as long as they meet the aforementioned criteria.

Dennis McQuail (2010) has pointed to five primary functions of the mass media: (1) information—disseminating, providing information and "indicating relations of power" (McQuail 2010, 98); (2) correlation—explaining events and their correlations, socializing, building consensus and understanding; (3) continuity—maintaining common values and culture; (4) entertainment—providing relaxation and reducing social tension; and (5) mobilization—campaigning and advocating the attainment of societal, political, and economic goals etc. (McQuail 2010, 98–99). Different types and genres of media can fulfill these functions to a varying degree and intensity. For instance, the primary function of news media is information, while civic journalists' blogs are aimed at campaigning to attain a particular political goal (mobilization). Audiences may also expect different things when reading the former compared to the latter; the news media are expected to remain objective, to cover a large variety of topics and to present different viewpoints unlike civic journalists' blogs, which are expected to be more subjective and focused on a limited range of issues. In the case of the local media selected for this study, the majority were news media (print and digital, including the municipality's official media outlets), with one media outlet being a civic journalists' blog (with multiple authors).

While there is an extensive body of literature on the relationship between the media and democratic processes, civic society and citizen engagement, there is little academic discussion on the role of the media in public consultations, particularly those conducted deliberatively; or on media representations of public consultations. This article aims to fill this gap by analyzing the role of local media discourse on public consultations in two Polish municipalities. We wish to put forward the thesis that while local media generally endorse the *concept* of public consultations, they do not engage in facilitating public dialogue and limit their role to disseminators of information.

It should be mentioned that the Acts regulating public consultations usually do not go beyond stating its general purpose and sketching a rudimentary timeline for announcing and conducting the consultation. It is therefore not uncommon for consultations to take different forms even within one municipality; there is no standardized time between the announcement and the consultation; some are promoted in local media and through information campaigns (posters, help-desks, etc.), and some are not; some end with the publication of a final report, and some are only summarized with a single note. Such inconsistencies, which create an image of consultations being volatile and often *autotelic*, influence the way in which consultations are commonly perceived. This article argues that this inconsistency and vagueness also results from the fact that consultations are not conceptualized and represented in the media as a process, but as a stage. What follows from this is the public image of public consultations: while they are usually considered a standard, if not desirable procedure, their methodologically and logistically justified stages; namely the preparation, execution and evaluation; are rarely a topic of media debate.

Another facet of this issue is the aforementioned lack of academic attention paid to media narratives and representations of the three-level consultation process. There are several works that focus on the watchdog functions of local media (see Dzur 2002, Saeed 2009), public journalism and its role in advocating for transparency in local governments (see Dzur 2002; Charles, Sokoloff, and Satullo 2005), and on how local authorities deploy various models for conducting public consultations (i.e., by outsourcing, using ICT tools, etc.) (see Monnoyer-Smith 2006, Muhlberger and Weber 2006; Wright and Street 2007, Wright 2009, Kies 2010; Åström and Grönlund 2012). There is also noteworthy literature on the connections between local media and authorities (see Barnett 2003; Coleman and Blumler 2010, Przybylska 2010), as well as on the role of media in the deliberative and democratic process. None of the above, however, address the issue of media narratives and media representations directly. We believe it is important to accentuate this marginalized topic, as it reflects on the possible implications that the aforementioned vagueness of public consultations may have for citizens, and thus makes a more in-depth exploration of the connections between local government, media, and public trust.

For the purpose of this article, two media case-studies in the towns of Olsztyn and Nowa Dęba were chosen. Both cities were part of the In Dialogue project, and both municipalities cooperated with the project team to test the ICT platform for the purpose of conducting public consultations. The municipalities also have networks of local print and digital media, although their number, volume, and scope differ due to the size of the municipalities: Olsztyn has approximately 174 thousand citizens (Urząd Statystyczny w Olsztynie 2015), while the population of Nowa Dęba is approximately 18 thousand overall (Urząd Statystyczny w Rzeszowie 2015).

In order to collect the data, in both cases using Google search engine and the built-in search engines of local media portals, we searched for combinations of such phrases as "consultations," "public consultations," "Olsztyn," "Nowa Dęba" (e.g., "consultations in Olsztyn" and "consultations in Nowa Dęba"). For Olsztyn, the timeframe selected was January 2014–May 2016 (inclusive), and for Nowa Dęba, January 2012–May 2016. The difference was justified by the fact that the Nowa Dęba search yielded few results overall, thus in order to gather more data, the timeframe had to be greater. We collected material from two types of local media: digital editions of print media and local web portals. For Olsztyn, we limited our findings to the six media outlets that yielded the most results for the keywords above: one official city web portal run by the city hall (Olsztyn.eu), one news portal (Olsztyn.com.pl), two online editions of the most popular newspapers (wyborcza.olsztyn.pl and gazetaolsztynska.pl), and two independent web portals (Debata.olsztyn.pl and Olsztynzyje.pl). For Nowa Dęba, the sample included: infonowadeba.pl (the official city hall portal), echodnia.pl/podkarpackie and rzeszow.wyborcza.pl (local portals of national newspapers), leliwa.pl (news website for the regional radio station, Leliwa), radio.rzeszow.pl (the website of a local radio station based in Rzeszów), rta24.eu (a regional website whose editorial board is based in Tarnobrzeg), and the local magazine "Nasze Sprawy."

The method of analysis used was *critical discourse analysis* (CDA) (Fairclough 1992). The main premise of CDA is that discursive practice, which itself includes texts, is an aspect of social practice and they remain mutually influenced. Discourse is considered to be a form of the social use of language that can construct aspects of social reality, transform them, or give them different meanings. Social practice, on the other hand, impacts upon the discursive process as it creates norms, values, notions and knowledge, which are then part of the individuals' *reference repositories*. CDA is, therefore, a constructivist approach, which takes into account the performative aspect of discursive practice. The method's focus is threefold; it reflects the stages of text production, distribution and interpretation. CDA looks into the formal properties of texts (by analyzing word meaning and metaphors), it investigates various aspects of discursive practice (intertextuality, interdiscursivity, coherence, discursive strategies, etc.) and social practice (social matrix). Thus, it not only analyzes the sample itself but also places it in a wider context, that is, historical, economical, institutional, etc. CDA was therefore chosen as the most appropriate tool to answer the following research problem and research questions.

The main problem dealt with in this study is how public consultations are conceptualized by the media in Olsztyn and Nowa Dęba. Our hypothesis is that the local media depict deliberative consultations as a stage instead of a process, and we wanted to verify this by analyzing what is being represented in the media regarding public consultations, with what discursive means (i.e., what metaphors and associations, phrasing, social context are being used), and for what purposes. We have formulated several sub-questions that address the research problem in a more in-depth way and so structures the narrative of this paper:

1. What public consultation topics are discussed in the media (regional/local affairs; specific themes and problems)?
2. In what context are public consultations represented in the media (positive/negative/neutral)? Are those representations informative, critical, or are they a form or praise and promotion of local authorities?
3. What elements of public consultations are emphasized in the media? For instance, are particular stages of the consultations discussed more extensively than others? Are the results of the consultations monitored? Are the organizational or formal aspects of the consultations discussed etc.?
4. Are media narratives about public consultations coherent and consistent, or fragmented? I.e., do they offer a particular perspective on deliberative consultations?

Our hypothesis was based, firstly, on our observations of the actions undertaken by municipal authorities and local media in Poland in regard to public consultations, and secondly, on the 2016 deliberative consultations conducted with the use of the *inDialogue* ICT platform in Olsztyn and Nowa Dęba, which also included media monitoring during the months of February–June 2016. It must be added that the consultative process in both cities involved contacting local media outlets (radio, press, local portals, and TV stations—when applicable), and the observation and experiences drawn from this process are also included in the conclusions of this paper.

Furthermore, it should be clarified that as a result of the project, the topic of public consultations has gained increased popularity in Nowa Dęba and became more extensively represented in the local media. In Olsztyn, it was observed that the project had the effect of making media narratives more thorough and process-focused than they were during previous public consultations.

Case Study 1: Olsztyn

Topics and Themes

All the media materials from Olsztyn were divided into categories of the themes that were undertaken (i.e., discussed topics) and scope (i.e., local or regional interest). In the period 2014–2016 there were numerous articles that mentioned or focused on public consultations in Olsztyn. Table 1 below, shows the total number of articles found, with the exclusion of repetitive content (i.e., cases in which one article was published twice under slightly different titles. This happened several times on olsztyn.wyborcza.pl and gazetaolsztynska.pl).[1]

Table 1. Total sum of articles per medium.

Title	Total number of articles
Olsztyn.eu	12
Olsztyn.com.pl	16
Gazetaolsztynska.pl	13
Olsztyn.wyborcza.pl	24
Debata.olsztyn.pl	30
Olsztynzyje.pl	4
SUM	98

1 Unless otherwise noted, all translations from Polish are our own.

The medium with the most articles in this set, debata.olsztyn.pl, is not a regular magazine, but a portal where bloggers and journalists can publish their own commentaries and articles. The content is often replicated on another website owned by an independent NGO called Forum Rozwoju Olsztyna (Olsztyn's Development Forum), which indicates their cooperation. The second most active medium in the set was a regional branch of the popular national newspaper, "Gazeta Wyborcza."

Interestingly, Olsztyn's official website, which is used by the local authorities as an informational/promotional outlet, had fewer articles published on consultations within the timeframe than four of the other media, both in print and digital. There was only one portal, olsztynzyje.pl, which yielded fewer keyword results.

As Table 2 illustrates, the vast majority of articles focused on local matters; this ranged from a single street to districts, and to the Olsztyn municipality. The number of consultations regarding the entire region was six times fewer than those focused on local matters. Gazetaolsztynska.pl was the only medium that published more regionally-focused material than locally-focused. Three out of the six media analyzed did not publish any articles regarding regional matters during the timeframe, which can be explained by their local focus.

Table 2. Scope and topics of media coverage on public consultations in Olsztyn.[2]

	Scope		Themes/topics/problems			
	Local	Regional	Dragoon barracks [Koszary Dragonów]	Tram line construction and extension	Combustion plant (low-carbon economy plan)	Other
Olsztyn.eu	12	0	0	0	1	11
Olsztyn.com.pl	15	1	3	4	1	8
Gazetaolsztynska.pl	6	7	0	0	0	13
Olsztyn.wyborcza.pl	20	4	4	7	2	12
Debata.olsztyn.pl	30	0	5	9	12	4
Olsztynzyje.pl	4	0	1	0	0	3
SUM	86	12	13	20	16	50

The overview of topics shows a large number of discrepancies between each media outlet. While the three topics listed in the table may be considered controversial, the analyzed media did not devote equal attention to debating them. These

2 Numbers may be higher than the total number of articles as one article could discuss several themes.

discrepancies cannot be attributed to timeframes or the scope of each media outlet, nor to the circulation or form (digital/print), but can be related to the focus of each medium and its perception of its target audience's interests.

For instance, the building of the combustion plant, which was a part of Olsztyn's low-carbon economy plan, was a source of great controversy for debata. olsztyn.pl, most of whose articles on public consultations were published about the plant. The official websites and city portals, on the other hand, mentioned the consultations only once. The tram line construction and the consultations about the possible routes were discussed by wyborcza.olsztyn.pl and debata.olsztyn.pl, as well as Olsztyn.com.pl; however, two out of the six media outlets did not bring up this issue at all. The category "other" included several topics; consultations using the inDialogue platform, which appeared four times, was one of these.[3]

The analysis of the media's material has also shown that the number of articles published on the topic did not determine their tone or context.

Context of Representations and Highlighted Aspects of Consultations

When analyzing the context for representations of public consultations, several aspects of text production, distribution and consumption were taken into account. First of all, it was observed that all articles were addressed to Olsztyn's citizens, without discriminating between any groups: the addressees were either directly referred to as "citizens," or "people living in Olsztyn," or were not mentioned explicitly but the topics were presented as being important for all readers. Statements such as "it is an important issue," "we are being manipulated by the authorities" and "we want public consultations…" (where "we" refers to "us citizens") indicate that the authors put themselves in the position of representatives of public interest and intermediaries between local authorities and citizens.

It was found that most articles presented public consultations in a neutral, informative manner, thus acting as *information transmitters* that shared with citizens the time and date of the consultations, their themes and the problems being discussed, or emphasizing the importance of active participation. This can be partially related to the setting and function of each medium: for instance, Olsztyn.eu, being the official city portal, is a tool for disseminating information that the city hall wishes to make public. Olsztyn.com.pl is the city's largest news portal, and as such, it also focuses on disseminating information rather than engaging

3 The topic of the consultation in Olsztyn was "The pedestrian in the city" (Pieszy w mieście).

in discussion, while Debata.olsztyn.pl, as an independent medium, has published the vast majority of all critical articles.

In some cases the articles were written in an encouraging tone: "we invite everyone," "all citizens are welcome to participate," which suggested that civic engagement is a desirable or expected reaction. Articles that included such encouragement were found six times on Debata.olsztyn.pl, three times on Gazetaolsztynska.pl and once on Olsztyn.com.pl and Olsztyn.eu. Except debata.olsztyn.pl, the analyzed media outlets fulfilled a predominantly informative function, as presented in Table 3 below.

Table 3. Context of media representations of public consultations in Olsztyn.

Medium	Information	Critique	Praise	Evaluation of consultations
Olsztyn.eu	12	0	0	0
Olsztyn.com.pl	12	4 (information of critique)	0	0
Gazetaolsztynska.pl	10	3 (information of critique)	0	0
Olsztyn.wyborcza.pl	21	3	0	0
Debata.olsztyn.pl	4	24	0	2
Olsztynzyje.pl	4	0	0	0
SUM	62	33	0	2

There are several conclusions to be drawn from this analysis. First of all, information about the consultations was provided by all media, but in the case of the city portal Olsztyn.eu, consultations appeared solely in an informative context. Olsztyn.com.pl and Gazetaolszynska.pl published few articles that could be considered critical; however, critiques were reported: phrases such as "citizens criticize," "NGOs criticize" indicated that the authors were distancing themselves from negative opinions. In this case, particular groups were indicated as those expressing critical views.

Second, debata.olsztyn.pl was the only medium whose articles were mostly critical. In this case, however, the authors clearly sympathized with the negative opinions, which was reflected by the use of such statements such as "we disagree," "we want," "we will not accept." Similarly, the authors would often use phrases with negative connotations, such as "pseudo-consultations" and "holy cows" (referring to the consultations of tram routes), "plant lobbyists manipulate…," "they will brainwash us" (referring to the planning of the combustion plant). What was also found during the analysis was that the criticism of the consultations was, in fact, a criticism of the local authorities:

> … public consultations regarding the combustion plant in Olsztyn must be prolonged so that the citizens can get acquainted with what company B is proposing and make a conscious choice. Meanwhile, the president has set the deadline of consultations for the 31st of March – the debated document which stipulates the erection of the plant, 'The Low-Carbon Economy Plan,' has over 200 pages and is known to very few people in Olsztyn (Socha 2015).

> Unfortunately, similar mistakes as those surfacing during the first 'tram project' are made. The citizens had no practical impact on the possible routes and re-organization of public transportation. They were given only marginal influence on secondary matters. … No public debate was organized. Once again, a decision of spending a lot of money was made top-down (Nie zgadzamy się 2015).

These two excerpts show that criticizing the timeframe and form of public consultations was a means of expressing disappointment with the local authorities who, according to the authors, are notorious for ignoring citizens and putting their particular interests before the public good. Poorly organized consultations are therefore depicted as yet another facet of the local authorities' incompetence.

Praise for public consultations was not observed in any publication, and only two articles could be classified as an attempt to evaluate the consultations. Debata.olsztyn.pl was the only medium that published follow-up articles once public consultations had finished. Nevertheless, the object of the evaluation was once again the local authorities, and not the consultation process itself, as in the following excerpt:

> … very few people participated in the pseudo-consultations regarding the new tram lines on March 2. … The decision of expanding the tram network had been made when the building of the first line was decided. The current … consultative farce is just a formality imposed by the EU regulations (Socha 2016).

"Pseudo-consultations" indicated that the consultations were in fact, according to the author, disregarded by the authorities who conducted the debate, as they were obliged to by "EU regulations." However, according to the author, the local government had no intention of genuinely consulting the issue with citizens, as the matter had already been decided. "Pseudo-consultations" also refers to the reported disappointment of citizens, who felt that a public debate was necessary. Let down by the authorities, the author expresses his negative attitude towards organizing consultations whose sole purpose is to fulfill a particular legal obligation. In this excerpt, negative comments were formulated as statements of facts: the author emphasized the lack of interest among citizens, which he then, implicitly, associated with the superficial nature of consultations.

Coherence and Consistency of Media Narratives about Public Consultations

The analysis of the media in Olsztyn has shown a certain paradox: while public consultations are, in general, presented as an important issue and often also as a key element in civic engagement, they are not discussed as a process but a series of separate events. None of the articles mentioned the planning of consultations. The authors of the articles sporadically remarked that the information materials provided by authorities were too long and unclear (Socha 2016), but these negative comments were used to criticize the authorities instead of starting a meta-discussion on how public consultations should be planned and conducted. Very general statements such as "they should hear us" or "they should pay more attention" (where "they" refers to local government) were not followed by an actual debate. Invitations to participate were not supported by a discussion on the meaning of consultations, and there was no elaborate discussion for evaluating the results. Therefore, the stages of preparation, execution and evaluation of consultations were not represented in any of the articles as stages in a complex process.

While the authors implied that they were aware that consultations had a strictly advisory function, they would often explicitly or implicitly convey their disappointment with how this form of communication between the authorities and citizens was perceived by the latter. What was repeatedly emphasized was the distance between the local authorities (especially the president) and the citizens. The media represented their own role as being a medium for the *unheard voices* of the citizens, and striving for public opinion to be heard by local government.

Furthermore, while the term *public consultations* may be known to the majority of citizens, its meaning is not clearly stated in the articles; as one quote above suggests, consultations are sometimes depicted as an obligation enforced upon Polish municipal authorities by the law, but their expected effects remain obscure. We will come back to this issue in the conclusion.

Case Study 2: Nowa Dęba

Topics and Themes[4]

As mentioned above, due to the small number of articles covering the topic of public consultations, the timeframe for data collection was extended back to 2012. This allowed for the inclusion of an additional 15 articles that appeared during the years 2012–2014.

---

4 The analysis does not take into account the documents published as part of the Public Information Bulletin.

In sum, a total of 35 articles were found and analyzed, as shown in Table 4 below.

Table 4. Total sum of articles per medium for Nowa Dęba.

Title	Total number of articles
nowadeba.pl	9
"Nasze Sprawy"	8
infonowadeba.pl	6
echodnia.eu/podkarpackie	5
rzeszow.wyborcza.pl	1
rta24.eu	2
leliwa.pl	3
radio.rzeszow.pl	1
SUM	35

Nearly half of the articles (17/35) were published by the Municipal Office (i.e., in nowadeba.pl and "Nasze Sprawy"). Among the external media, the topic of consultation was found most frequently in the online edition of the regional newspaper "Echo dnia" (echodnia.eu/podkarpackie) and on infonowadeba.pl, which is a website hosted by students with connections to the political opposition in Nowa Dęba. Two out of the six local media are radio stations, which also exhibit a mostly *authorial* attitude towards articles about public consultations published on their portals, as will be shown below.

The disproportion between regionally-focused and locally-focused topics in Nowa Dęba was not as significant as in Olsztyn. This is interesting when we take into account that Nowa Dęba is a municipality, which is a smaller administrative unit than Olsztyn, a city county (miasto na prawach powiatu). This would suggest that regional topics would appear in Nowa Dęba's media less often than in Olsztyn, however, the analysis has not confirmed this assumption. Among all the articles analyzed, approximately twice as many articles focused on local matters as on regional affairs, while in Olsztyn this proportion was approximately seven to one. What must be emphasized is that in Nowa Dęba, the media associated with the municipal office and the local opposition published most locally-focused articles, while other media outlets covered local and regional topics to a similar degree.

We have identified three themes that appear in several of the local media. The most popular was the consultations on the closure of Żeromskiego Street, which was conducted with the cooperation of the In Dialogue team. In this case, contact with the local media was one of the elements of the consultations' strategy. To ensure that the greatest number of citizens had access to the information about the planned consultation, a press release was sent to local media, and their editorial boards and publishers were asked to publish the material. The relatively large number of articles could be the result of the intense PR activity by our team. Another theme concentrated on the so-called "map of hazards," which was a project conducted by the police for the entire voivodship; Nowa Dęba was one of the towns in which consultations concerning the map took place. The third theme was the new division of electoral districts. The numbers presented in Table 5 do not reflect the diversity of the published content. For instance, in the case of Żeromskiego street's closure and the map of hazards, articles with the same content were published in several media, sometimes with minor modifications such as a changed title. This phenomenon was observed in as many as four out of eight articles regarding Żeromskiego street, and four out of six articles for the map of hazards. This *template circulation* is not surprising if we consider the fact that the vast majority of articles about public consultations are announcements providing information on the topic and time of debates, often created and sent out by the In Dialogue project team. As such, the announcements undergo few, if any, modifications before publication in the media.

Table 5: Scope and topics of media coverage of public consultations in Nowa Dęba.

	Scope		Themes/topics/problems			
	Local	Regional	Żeromskiego street closure [test consultation]	Map of hazards	Electoral districts	Other
nowadeba.pl	8	1	2*	1*	3	3
"Nasze Sprawy"	5	3	0	1*	2	4
infonowadeba.pl	3	3	1*	1*	1	4
echodnia.eu/ podkarpackie	4	1	1	0	0	4
rzeszow.wyborcza.pl	1	0	1*	0	0	0
leliwa.pl	2	1	2	1	0	0
rta24.eu	1	1	1*	1*	0	0
radio.rzeszow.pl	0	1	0	1	0	0
SUM	24	11	8	6	6	15

* *indicates that the article was a copy of an official press release regarding consultations.*

Context of Representations and Highlighted Aspects of Consultations

As mentioned earlier, most of the articles analyzed were consultation announcements. As such, all the articles analyzed fulfilled, primarily, an informational function: they reported that the consultations would take place or that they had ended. In some cases, the articles would include instructions on how, where and when to take part in the discussion, as well as what the subject of the consultation was. The overall depiction of public consultations was neutral, even if some articles discussed topics potentially controversial for the local community. One such topic was the collapse of oak trees as a result of the renovation of Gryczmana Square (Lipiec 2012) and changes in electoral districts (Sudoł 2013). In the latter case, consultations were conducted at the request of a councilor; this request blocked a vote on a resolution (Trwają prace 2012, 2–3). A notice by the mayor was published on nowadeba.pl as a summary of the consultations. The notice read as follows:

> The deadline for submitting motions by the citizens was the 8th of November. Two motions were submitted to the City Hall regarding the division of the town into electoral districts along with three in support of the draft resolution which I have submitted.
>
> Having analyzed the proposals submitted, in the light of the applicable regulations, I have not found a basis for their recognition, and therefore have not applied to the City Council for changes in the draft resolution (Ordon 2012).

Note that the announcement did not in any way mention or summarize the actual content of the proposals, but only clarified that they have not been recognized. The comments were an appendix to the final document. Although the announcement could have been a potential source of conflict between local authorities and citizens, the mayor's decision did not resonate with the media. During the analysis, we did not encounter an actual media debate or any polemical articles presenting the problem of consultations from different perspectives.

It should be added here that prior to cooperation between the city hall and the In Dialogue project team, public consultations in Nowa Dęba usually had the form of citizens submitting motions, queries or opinions directly to the authorities, instead of a debate or dialogue between citizens and the authorities. This conclusion was drawn on the basis of analyzing the documents and the announcements of previous consultations in Nowa Dęba. This was also reflected in the media narratives, which did not depict consultations as a discussion about a particular solution, and did not elaborate either on the course of the consultations, nor on their results and consequences. In other words, the information source was typically the authorities of Nowa Dęba, and the citizens were depicted as recipients/objects of information dissemination and decision-making.

Table 6. Context of media representations of public consultations in Nowa Dęba.

Medium	Information	Critique	Praise	Evaluation of consultations
nowadeba.pl	9	0	1*	0
"Nasze Sprawy"	8	0	0	0
infonowadeba.pl	6	0	0	0
echodnia.eu/podkarpackie	5	0	0	0
rzeszow.wyborcza.pl	1	0	1*	0
rta24.eu	2	0	1*	0
leliwa.pl	3	0	0	0
radio.rzeszow.pl	1	0	0	0
SUM	35	0	2	0

** indicates that the article was formulated both as information and as praise.*

Table 6 demostrates that only 3 out of the 35 analyzed articles stressed the importance of public consultations. As such, they not so much praised the particular consultations (such as their organization, topics, results, etc.), but either referred to this method of civic dialogue in general or emphasized the importance of letting the citizens express their opinions, as in the quotes below:

> Public consultations are essential to find out citizens' opinion... (Wojtkowiak 2016).

> There were no incidents or complaints that someone drives like mad on that street, but I know the voice of the residents is important because it is they who travel around the city and use the urban infrastructure every day. It's therefore worthwhile to find out how they envision Żeromskiego street and its surroundings (Tajs 2016).

Most of the articles preceding the consultations (17/35) had the form of announcements. Unlike in Olsztyn, in most cases, such announcements did not have a form of invitations, in that they did not explicitly encourage citizens of Nowa Dęba to participate. Phrases like "we invite all citizens" or "we encourage everyone to participate" did not appear in the analyzed articles related to public consultations in Nowa Dęba. Instead, the announcements were formulated as general and impersonal information. A similar observation was made with regards to information on consultations that had ended. Consider also the following:

> The project was the subject of public consultation, during which there were no comments from residents (Lipiec 2012).

> The project is the result of the diagnosis of needs in the process of the lake area development. To this end, consultations at each stage of the project were conducted (Tajs 2013).

None of the post-consultation articles offered a thorough evaluation. In most cases, consultations were only mentioned as a fringe topic to the main theme. Sporadically, information on the results of the consultation was provided, describing what took place and when, what the effect of the discussion was, and also in some cases who, on behalf of the municipality, participated in the debate. One of the most extensive descriptions of the results of the consultation was the following:

> During the work meeting, a draft Program (Program for the Cooperation with NGOs) was developed, which was then subject to public consultation. The citizens, members of non-governmental organizations have had the opportunity to express their opinion on whether the document defining the principles of cooperation between local governments and NGOs meets their expectations. During the consultation, the comments were received, meticulously analyzed in detail, and included in the Program (Trwają prace 2012, our emphasis).

None of the articles touched upon issues such as the emergence of opposing views or problems during the discussions, and none commented on the organization of consultations itself. Critique of the consultations was not observed in any of the media in Nowa Dęba. Similarly, no reflection on the long-term effects of consultations was shared with the public. In a few cases, the article included a brief mention of the effects of public consultations, for example, a discussion on the new timetable for local trains (Szpak 2015), which was presented in relation to Polish Railways agreeing on a changed timetable in the region due to construction works. However, this presentation did not include any reference to the discussion, disagreement or a compromise that developed during the consultations.

Coherence and Consistency of Media Narratives on Public Consultations

Media representations of public consultations in Nowa Dęba fulfilled, for the most part, an informational function: consultations were presented as an event, and the role of the media in the consultative process was limited to that of an advertising column. The citizens were not engaged with this representation, as the announcements were often impersonal and included only brief information on organizational details for collecting the citizens' opinions. Thus, in Nowa Dęba the inhabitants were represented implicitly as the recipients of information provided by the local authorities.

The majority of media outlets, despite being associated with different sides of the local political spectrum, did not use the consultations to either praise or criticize the local government, as was the case in Olsztyn; in fact, no medium mentioned any type or areas of conflict, opposing standpoints or mutually exclusive expectations regarding the consultations.

The lack of evaluation further proves our point: while citizens were informed about the consultations themselves, no analysis of long-term effects, nor any discussion on the debate itself was observed in media outlets. Thus, public consultations were represented as an event during which the citizens may, first of all, get informed about what the local authorities plan on doing, and secondly may voice their opinions. Laconic claims of "citizens' will" being important appeared in some articles, but they were not followed by any reflection on how this *will* is expressed and exercised, or how the local authorities make use of the opinions they gather.

Conclusion

In this article, we have argued that public consultations are not represented in local media narratives as a multi-level process, but rather as an event or a particular action. Planning the debates, conducting them, and evaluating their effects were at no time discussed in the media. Presenting the procedures (e.g., how, where and when to participate in debates), and even encouraging the citizens to participate in the debates, did not equal elaborating on the meaning of the consultations, or evaluating them as part of a larger process whose ultimate aim is to increase civic engagement and public dialogue. Thus, the functions of providing information to citizens (expected from news media) or mobilizing them (the function of civic journalism) were fulfilled to a limited degree. The meaning and objective of conducting public consultations were therefore obscure, regardless of the type of media (news media or civic journalist blog).

While in some cases conducting public consultations is a formal obligation (to citizens or the EU, for instance), the media did not explain the role of such obligations, nor did they discuss what the desired effects of the consultations may be. This was observed primarily in Olsztyn; authors of several critical articles would point out that the local government simply fulfills its duties towards some institution, but has no real intention of taking the citizens' voice into account. However, the alternative to this *empty duty* was only suggested implicitly, without the authors explaining the proceedings once the opinions were collected. Furthermore, criticism of consultations was, in many cases, an expression of the disapproval of the local authorities and their perceived lack of interest in the citizens' needs. Discussions on the effects of consultations were also focused on emphasizing the actions of the local government, and in many cases did not go beyond a critical appraisal of how they reacted to citizens' opinions. The consultations themselves do not undergo systematic evaluation, and the media analyses (i.e., professional news media and non-professional media outlets alike) do not monitor their effects from a long-term perspective.

Another facet of the lack of clarity regarding the purpose of consultations is the fragmented narrative: while each stage of deliberative consultations may be discussed in the media, the process in its entirety is not. In local media a "failed" consultation (i.e., one whose organization was rated as poor), which included suggestive questions or some form of neglect or manipulation (according to the authors of the article), may be extensively discussed in the media, but this criticism does not lead to a deeper reflection of what could be improved in public consultations themselves; possible solutions, albeit implicitly given, are usually limited to changing the local authorities. This shows that public consultations are, in many cases, closely associated with local politics and depicted by the media as a governance tool rather than a means of dialogue.

It must be mentioned that in several cases during the consultations in Olsztyn that were conducted as part of the In Dialogue project, once the media were informed about the consultations, members of the editorial teams explicitly demanded compensation for the publication of information, thus equating public announcements with commercial advertisements.[5] Thus, given the non-commercial nature of the project, information about consultations has been published successfully in only selected media outlets. In one case, a member of the editorial board indirectly declined to publish information about the consultations, stating that the portal publishes content "interesting for the readers" and suggesting that public consultations are not a topic that draws public attention. This confirms the aforementioned conclusions regarding the unclear function and meaning of consultations for citizens. It can be assumed that the practice of charging municipal authorities and NGOs for media announcements concerning consultations is not limited to Olsztyn, and as such, it should be investigated for limiting the public's access to information. While some municipalities have sufficient funds to pay

5 A similar process was not observed in Nowa Dęba. Among the local media contacted, some did not respond to requests, but the In Dialogue team was not asked for any form of compensation for publishing information on the consultations. Most of the editorial boards were keen to cooperate and agreed to support the information campaign free of charge.

for public announcements in local media, others may not, which could possibly inhibit the development of civic engagement.

During the consultations conducted within the In Dialogue project in Olsztyn and Nowa Dęba, it was found that disseminating information directly to the editors of local media outlets was in many cases the most effective information strategy. Once the editors received a ready-to-publish notice concerning the consultations, they were usually willing to publish the announcement. The greatest shortcoming in this practice, however, is that several media outlets may publish identical content, and thus the information on the consultations will be highly repetitive. Nevertheless, for the sake of disseminating and circulating information on how, when and where the citizens may participate; what the subject and aim of the consultations are, and why the citizens' opinions are important; this repetition may be seen as an asset. If we consider that citizens may only use a limited number of media outlets (i.e., they read one local paper and listen to one local radio station), this repetition may also help overcome the problems of limited access to information sources.

On the basis of the data collected we believe that the coherent and effective circulation of information in local media should include a systematic evaluation of the consultations' results: their short and long-term effects; as well as monitoring how citizens' opinions are collected, reported and included in reports; and the implementation of the consultations' effects.

The inDialogue platform aims to target the aforementioned issues of fragmentation in the consultative process and the lack of clarity regarding the function of the consultations. The platform aims to change the way in which all participants of the debate—the citizens, the media, and the local authorities—perceive consultations. By introducing the three-stage processual approach, the platform helps local authorities to engage in the stages of preparation, execution, and evaluation of public consultations, and aims to make this process transparent and comprehensible to citizens and the media. Thus, the goal is also to propose a set of standards and guidelines regarding the consultation process, which could easily be replicated and adjusted for future debates. The platform is also inclusive, so that all citizens, including those with disabilities, can participate in the debates. This is done by implementing various functionalities such as sign language instructions, easy-to-read versions of instructions, or high-contrast settings. These features, it is hoped, will encourage all citizens to voice their opinion in the way they feel most comfortable.

However, the development of the platform should also be followed by appropriate informational campaigns conducted by local authorities. Since there is no uniform act that clarifies the procedural framework and scope of public consultations, it is unlikely that all citizens understand the function and purpose of such forms of deliberation. The challenge for the local news media is, therefore, to offer a broader, more thorough and comprehensible scope of information about public consultations, which will help citizens become informed and educated about the purpose and procedures of the consultation. Civic journalists, whose watchdog role is of primary importance in a democratic society, should also make the effort to evaluate the effects of public consultations. By doing so, local media could raise awareness that consultations are a vital part of local politics and the democratic process, and could also empower citizens to demand their voice be heard.

References

Åström, Joachim, and Åke Grönlund. 2012. "Online consultations in local government: What works, when and how." In *Connecting Democracy: Online Consultation and the Flow of Political Communication*, edited by Stephen Coleman and Peter Shane, 75–96. Cambridge, MA: MIT Press.

Barnett, Clive. 2003. *Culture and Democracy: Media, Space and Representation*. Edinburgh: Edinburgh University Press.

Charles, Michelle, Chris Satullo, and Harris Sokoloff. 2005. "Electoral Deliberation and Public Journalism." Accessed May 30, 2016. http://repository.upenn.edu/gse_pubs/57.

Coleman, Stephen, and Jay G. Blumler. 2010. "The wisdom of which crowd? On the pathology of a listening government." *Political Quarterly* 82 (3): 355–364.

Dzur, Albert W. 2002. "Public journalism and deliberative democracy." *Polity* 34 (3): 313–336.

Fairclough, Norman. 1992. *Discourse and Social Change*. Cambridge: Polity.

Kies, Raphael. 2010. *Promises and Limits of Web-deliberation*. New York: Palgrave.

Kowalczyk, Ryszard. 2011. "Miejsce i rola mediów lokalnych we współczesnym społeczeństwie informacyjnym." *Środkowoeuropejskie Studia Polityczne* 1: 65–80.

Lipiec, Grzegorz. 2012. "Dęby ścięte w Nowej Dębie. Czy można je było oszczędzić?" Accessed: April 28, 2016. http://www.echodnia.eu/podkarpackie/wiadomosci/tarnobrzeg/art/8482904,deby-sciete-w-nowej-debie-czy-mozna-je-bylo-oszczedzic,id,t.html.

McQuail, Denis. 2010. *Denis McQuail's Mass Communication Theory*. London, New Delhi: SAGE.

Monnoyer-Smith, Laurence. 2006. "Citizen's deliberation on the Internet: An exploratory study." *International Journal of Electronic Government Research* 2 (3): 58–74.

Muhlberger, Peter, and Lori Weber. 2006. "Lessons from the Virtual Agora Project: The effects of agency, identity, information and deliberation on political knowledge." *Journal of Deliberation* 2 (1). Accessed May 30, 2016. http://www.publicdeliberation.net/jpd/vol2/iss1/art13/.

"Nie zgadzamy się na rozbudowę linii tramwajowych bez konsultacji społecznych." 2015. *Debata.olsztyn.pl.* Accessed May 17, 2016. http://www.debata.olsztyn.pl/wiadomoci/olsztyn/4403-nie-zgadzamy-sie-na-rozbudowe-linii-tramwajowych-bez-konsultacji-spolecznych.

Ordon, Wiesław. 2012. "Konsultacje w sprawie okręgów wyborczych zakończone." *nowadeba.pl.* Accessed May 30, 2016. http://archiwum.nowadeba.pl/informator/art1159.html.

Przybylska, Anna. 2010. *Internet i komunikowanie we wspólnocie lokalnej.* Warsaw: Wydawnictwa Uniwersytetu Warszawskiego.

Saeed, Saima. 2009. "Negotiating power: Community media, democracy, and the public sphere." *Development in Practice* 19 (4/5): 466–478.

Socha, Adam. 2015. "Domagamy się konsultacji społecznych w sprawie budowy spalarni." *debata.olsztyn.pl.* Accessed May 17, 2016. http://www.debata.olsztyn.pl/wiadomoci/olsztyn/4149-domagamy-sie-konsultacji-spolecznych-w-sprawie-budowy-spalarni.

Socha, Adam 2016. "Koniec tzw. konsultacji tramwajowych." *debata.olsztyn.pl.* Accessed May 17, 2016. http://www.debata.olsztyn.pl/wiadomoci/olsztyn/4931-koniec-tzw-konsultacji-tramwajowych-najnowsze-.

Sudoł, Barbara. 2013. "Nowe obwody głosowania w wyborach powszechnych w 2014 r." Nasze Sprawy 70 (1): 5. Accessed April 20, 2016. http://www.nowadeba.pl/gfx/nowadeba2012/userfiles/marek/nasze_sprawy_nr70.pdf.

Szpak, Piotr. 2015. "Po latach przerwy pociągiem z Tarnobrzega pojedziemy w świętokrzyskie." *echodnia.eu.* Accessed April 28, 2016. http://www.echodnia.eu/podkarpackie/wiadomosci/tarnobrzeg/art/8123760,po-latach-przerwy-pociagiem-z-tarnobrzega-pojedziemy-w-swietokrzyskie,id,t.html.

Tajs, Klaudia. 2013. "Teren nad zalewem w Nowej Dębie zyska nowe oblicze." echodnia.eu. Accessed April 28, 2016. http://www.echodnia.eu/podkarpackie/wiadomosci/tarnobrzeg/art/8636391,teren-nad-zalewem-w-nowej-debie-zyska-nowe-oblicze,id,t.html.

Tajs, Klaudia. 2016. "Nowa Dęba: Konsultacje w sprawie zamknięcia dla ruchu fragmentu ulicy w centrum." *echodnia.eu.* Accessed April 28, 2016. http://www.

echodnia.eu/podkarpackie/wiadomosci/tarnobrzeg/a/nowa-deba-konsultacje-w-sprawie-zamkniecia-dla-ruchu-fragmentu-ulicy-w-centrum,9875457/.

"Trwają prace nad 'Programem współpracy gminy nowa Dęba z organizacjami pozarządowymi na 2013 rok.'" 2012. *Nasze Sprawy.* UMiG. 68(3): 21. Accessed April 28, 2016. http://archiwum.nowadeba.pl/gfx/nowadeba/files/nasze_sprawy/nasze_sprawy_nr_68.pdf.

Urząd Statystyczny w Olsztynie. 2015. "Statystyczne Vademecum Samorządowca 2016. Miasto Olsztyn." *stat.gov.pl.* Accessed May 30, 2016. http://stat.gov.pl/vademecum/vademecum_warminsko-mazurskie/portrety_miast/miasto_olsztyn.pdf.

Urząd Statystyczny w Rzeszowie. 2015. "Statystyczne Vademecum Samorządowca. Gmina Miejsko-Wiejska Nowa Dęba." *rzeszow.stat.gov.pl.* Retrieved May 30, 2016. http://rzeszow.stat.gov.pl/vademecum/vademecum_podkarpackie/portrety_gmin/tarnobrzeski/nowa_deba.pdf.

Wojtkowiak, Wioletta. 2016. "Ulica Żeromskiego dla samochodów czy nie? W Nowej Dębie ruszyły zapisy na debatę mieszkańców." rta24.eu. Accessed April 28, 2016. http://rta24.eu/ulica-zeromskiego-dla-samochodow-czy-nie-w-nowej-debie-ruszyly-zapisy-na-debate-mieszkancow/.

Wright, Scott. 2009. "The role of the moderator: Problems and possibilities for government-run online discussion forums." In *Online Deliberation: Design, Research, and Practice*, edited by Todd Davis, and Seeta Peña Gangadharan, 233–242. Stanford CA: CSLI Publications.

Wright, Scott and John Street. 2007. "Democracy, deliberation and design: The case of online discussion forums." *New Media & Society* 9 (5): 849–869.

Tomasz Potkański

Chapter 10. Opportunities and Barriers to the Use of the InDialogue Platform by Local Government Administration

Introduction

This chapter is a contribution made from the perspective of a local government practitioner representing an association of cities, and complements the academic, research-based, and ICT technical perspectives presented in other chapters. It presents the *inDialogue* consultation platform as an important tool that is available to local government representatives who see their mission as being a service to their communities, and in conformance with the theoretical approach of public governance. More specifically the author sees the inDialogue consultation platform as a tool, or a form of practical implementation, of the open government (OG) concept. This chapter refers briefly to the responsibilities and competences of local governments in Poland regarding the implementation of public policies, it then discusses the use of public consultations in the different areas of public policies in order to focus on the advantages of the inDialogue platform's use in public consultations, and in the next step points to existing barriers that prevent it being used as an efficient tool in local governance. The author emphasizes the role of the platform for municipal administrators and local politicians, as well as for citizens, in bringing the municipality closer to the fulfillment of the participatory governance model in local communities. It concludes with considerations on the possibilities of the broader positive consequences of implementing the inDialogue software in Polish self-government units.

The importance of effective communication between local public administration and local community members cannot be overstated. It is as a direct consequence of the legal framework that defines municipality (a municipality, or a town) as a "local self-governing community within a given territory."[1] In Poland, being one of the most decentralized countries in Europe, municipalities deal with all local public tasks that are not reserved by law for other types of public

1 "Ustawa z dnia 8 marca 1990 roku o samorządzie gminnym." *Journal of Laws*, 16, item 95 as amended, art 1.1 and 1.2.

authorities[2] (e.g., counties, regions, state), and elected authorities implement them on behalf of citizens using existing administrative structures (municipal offices, municipal institutions); therefore, they are required to know the citizens' expectations and opinions. The range of public tasks specifically assigned to municipalities is very wide, covering 20 broad subjects[3] but still leaving space for the above mentioned "tasks not reserved for other types of public authorities." The responsibilities of county and regional self-governments are also wide but are phrased without this *open-ended clause*; which makes municipal self-government a basic element of the structure of self-governing public authorities in Poland, with its rights safeguarded directly under the constitution.[4] To enable the implementation of this broad mandate, local, sub-regional and regional self-governments have at their disposal approximately one-third of the country's public funds, and are responsible for the construction of approximately two-thirds of public infrastructure annually. The fulfillment of these duties requires that public consultations with citizens be conducted on a number of issues as indicated under the law (for a detailed list see also Chapter 1 by Jacek Haman). Municipalities that fulfill their tasks can also create subsidiary units, or consultative councils (elderly, youth), or create thematic advisory committees.[5]

The legal framework referred to gives local or regional government authorities wide competences for conducting consultations, and provides them with the freedom to use various tools. But this is only the legal dimension, which defines what the self-government authorities can do. Equally important is why they should do it in a practical sense. There are two main reasons: first of all, active citizens expect that the current space for their participation in local decision-making will be widened; and secondly, the complexity of issues involved in making technically and politically optimal decisions in municipal management is gradually growing every year, requiring the effective use of the knowledge possessed by citizens or by social and economic partners. These reasons bring us to the practical application of the current leading theoretical paradigm in public management, known as public governance (Izdebski 2010, 28–30).

---

2 *Ibid*, art. 6.1.

3 *Ibid*, art. 7.1.

4 "Konstytucja Rzeczypospolitej Polskiej z dnia 2 kwietnia 1997." *Journal of Laws* of 1997, 78, item 483, art. 164.

5 "Ustawa z dnia 8 marca 1990 roku o samorządzie gminnym." *Journal of Laws* of 1990, 16, item 95 as amended, art 4 and 5.

The Theoretical Framework of Public Governance within the Field of Public Management

Since the early 1980s, we are witnessing a constant evolution of the practiced model of the functioning of public administration in all developed countries of the world. Polish administration is not an island and is also heavily influenced by these changes. These models are described in more detail elsewhere (see Izdebski 2010; Hausner 2008; Stępień 2008; Potkański 2010). Here only a few of the most important features will be referred to, pointing out their practical consequences for the subject being analyzed, including typical modes and channels of communication.

Polish local government administration, re-created 27 years ago, represents, both in a legal sense and also given its most often used tools and organizational forms, the *traditional model of public administration*, often referred to as the Weberian model of "ideal bureaucracy" (Weber 1922). It is based on a predominance of formal structures, and concentrates on fulfilling legal procedures. Communication with inhabitants is obviously recognized as important, but it is understood mostly as a one way information dissemination process, where the key aspect is the fulfilment of the legal parameters regarding the availability of information that is produced by the administration. The main tools used by administration to communicate with inhabitants will be in the form of printed or electronic information, produced by authorities and made available to inhabitants. Despite this model currently having an apparent negative meaning, it still produces a valid notion of professional public administration or civil service, as well as of rules of ethical conduct. The nature of the evolution of public administration models suggest that each newly emergent model responds to the current shortcomings and existing developmental needs of the societies that accept them. The traditional model ceased to be perceived as efficient by the early 1980s, but did not disappear entirely. Rather, a new paradigm emerged in parallel and co-existed under the name of *New Public Management* (NPM) (Hood 1991), also known as the *managerial approach*, which, in practical terms, meant implementing methods and tools imported from the private sector in the functioning of public administration. This allowed for better cost control, improvements in efficiency, the identification of clear goals and setting a measurement system to monitor their attainment, promoting competition, and the treatment of citizens as the clients of services. Communication with these clients (it is important to note that inhabitants started to be perceived as clients or customers) concentrated on identifying their needs and opinions, and responding to questions or complaints. Typically, modes of communication were firstly paper then electronic versions of reports, information leaflets, customer opinion surveys, etc.; as if this was indeed a customer-service office. The source of knowledge remained the administration, as it had been in the previous system. The approach, in its more pure form, with elements of *managing for results*, known also as *performance contracting*, was widely used in the Anglo-Saxon world (UK, USA, Australia, New Zealand) and to some extent in Scandinavian countries, while in other parts of Europe (e.g., Germany and France) this direction of thinking was exemplified by simply adding new (pro-efficiency) objectives and tools to the existing procedures within the traditional model of public administration. Not more than 15–20 years later, at the turn of twentieth century, the shortcomings of this approach (e.g., a preoccupation with the economic perspective) became apparent and the NPM gradually evolved into *public governance* (PG)[6] or the responsive/participatory governance[7] approach. This approach, without diminishing the value of economic efficiency in the functioning of public administration, emphasized the primary importance of communicating with citizens as being key partners of public authorities in decision making, and the need to seek solutions that included the perspective of civil society and the needs of the various categories of stakeholders. The latter are even expected to identify problems and provide proposals on how to solve them. The key principles of this mode of governance emphasize the need to engage stakeholders with the (declared) intention of making them partners who feel co-responsible for attaining commonly defined development objectives. On the other hand, individual citizens and other stakeholders expect public authorities to be fully accountable, open and transparent, provide equal access to public services for people with various disabilities, as well as promote sustainable development through practical activities (Hausner 2008, 24). Consequently, the modes and tools for communication were, to a large extent, adapted to this new approach, which has been additionally facilitated by the rapid development of electronic communication and ICT techniques over the last 15 years. The most important and expected feature is responsiveness (two-way communication), and tools that allow for this would certainly be in demand. Another separate feature is the gradual increase in the use

6 There is no one single term to represent this theoretical approach. In the literature on the subject there coexists such terms as "responsive governance, network governance, multilevel governance, new public service, new public governance, and even good governance." Following Izdebski (ibid.) I decided to use the most generic one—Public Governance.

7 In Germany and in other non-Anglo-Saxon, European public administrations, scholars refer to the current version of the existing model as the "Neo-Weberian State" (see Pollitt and Bouckaert 2004).

of social media by public authorities for communicating with citizens in parallel with the traditional channels.

To summarize this review of theoretical approaches in public management, it is important to state, that in the functioning of the current Polish local and regional self-governments we can easily trace the elements of these three approaches in almost every local or regional self-government unit, most often co-existing with each other. Similarly, each of these approaches is followed by its own characteristic modes of communication and specific tools that serve the needs that have been identified, and we can find them almost side by side in the communication toolbox of local government authorities.

In order to analyze the possible use of the inDialogue software, it is necessary to deepen the analysis of the current dominant approach. In the context of the wider public governance approach, the literature often mentions the notion of *OG*. This concept means that all the important data and findings possessed by the public administration should be made available to the wider public so as to enable public discussion and informed public debate. As Lathrop and Ruma (2010, xix) aptly conclude, the very meaning of the term *OG* continues to evolve; starting from the mere recognition that citizens have a right to access the information, documents and proceedings of government, and pointing out efforts aimed at safeguarding it; through reaching the realization that the engagement and participation of citizens leads to a greater accountability and efficiency in government activities; and leads as far as realizing that citizens can be the co-producers of some public services, using information provided under the OG framework (see also, Bovaird 2007, 847).

As has been made apparent in other chapters of this book, the inDialogue public consultation platform supports the implementation of OG concepts at the local level. But a question emerges as to what extent it helps? Here we shall refer to the concept of the *participation ladder*, developed by Arnstein (1969), or to *models of participation*—understood to mean distinct types of social relations emerging between (local) authorities and citizens or customers of services. In the Polish arena, Olech and Kazmierczak (2011, 103) present a similar typology of models to Arnstein, which is based on the roles played by authorities and citizens in terms of exercising their powers towards each other. They distinguish between; (a) an asymmetric model, (b) an opinion-making and consultative model, (c) a symmetric model, and (d) one where powers are delegated to citizens. The inDialogue public consultation platform clearly prevents the proliferation and prolonging of the existence of the asymmetric model (model a), but actively supports the use of the three remaining models, which are based on two-way communication (models b–d), especially when they are performed in a participatory and deliberative way.

The concept of deliberation forms one of the foundations of the PG approach, and refers to communication that is characterized by openness, reciprocity, and critical reflection of one's own arguments (see the recent paper by Przybylska 2016). Przybylska's main thesis in that paper is that the quality of consultation determines, to a large extent, the usefulness of the deliberative processes as the building blocks of deliberative democracy. The same author characterizes elsewhere (Przybylska 2010), the model of deliberative democracy and its operationalization through different channels of communication. In the next section, I will comment on how the inDialogue platform assists authorities and citizens in developing the range of deliberative activities.

The Practical Use of Consultative Processes in Polish Local Government Management

As outlined above, the use of consultative processes is defined by law, but it can be characterized from two separate perspectives.

First of all, since public authorities must operate within the parameters defined by the legal framework, the law on local municipal government provides them with the right to conduct consultations on all issues that are important for local communities (similarly for the authorities of counties and self-governing regions). This legal basis is very often used for conducting two-way communication processes. The practical applications will be, for example, defining objectives and reviewing the progress of the implementation of local development strategies; discussing priorities for multiannual investment planning; and defining budget priorities, especially with the recent popularity of participatory budgets (also called *citizens' budgets*), which is now practiced in over 15% of Polish municipalities.[8] The latter form is methodologically interesting, because this is a rare example of the practical delegation of the local authorities' powers to interested citizens, with the responsibility and accountability, however, remaining with the authorities. While these are clearly two-way communication processes, only rarely do they transform into truly deliberative processes where both sides learn from each other, thus creating new knowledge.

Second, different sectoral legislations (spatial planning, building permits, investment planning, nature and landscape protection, social assistance, local trade regulations, even cooperation with NGOs, etc.), require local authorities to conduct extensive consultations, and cases where they have not been fulfilled, or

8 Based on own research of the Office of the Association of Polish Cities.

there has been a compromise in certain technical parameters of the consultation (length of time, accessibility of information, form of response to citizens submissions, etc.), is sufficient reason for individual citizens to sue the local authorities so that the formal decisions made to the administrative court can easily become null and void, and the administrative process has to be restarted. It may easily delay formal decisions by several months or a year. In the same way, the region's central government representative may suspend the decision of local authorities if the consultative procedures were not fulfilled or were compromised. For such practical reasons, local (and county and regional) self-government authorities are under great pressure to concentrate specifically on fulfilling the legal parameters of consultative processes. The quality of consultative processes are very often compromised throughout the process for the simple reason of not possessing sufficient time or too high a workload imposed on municipal employees, or simply due to insufficient attention being paid to the issue of quality, etc. (see Przybylska, Chapter 2 in this book, for more details). Let's analyze how the inDialogue software can be of assistance in these cases.

The Advantages of the InDialogue Public Consultation Platform in Response to Existing Barriers

First of all, it should be stated that both the legal framework in Poland and general practice, conform to all formal rules existing in the EU regarding the implementation of procedures that safeguard the transparency of proceedings and decision-making at the self-government level. However, citizens' expectations grow much faster, and this is the reason for their often expressed discontent. Therefore, rationally speaking, local government authorities need new tools to assist them and their employees in streamlining these processes. Equally important, though structurally different, are the deficiencies in the consultative processes from the perspective of citizens and other stakeholders.

I will briefly summarize the main categories of weaknesses in the current consultative processes, and argue for the possibility of improving the practice by using the inDialogue platform. A wider analysis of these subjects has already been provided by Przybylska (Chapter 2) and by Stępień and Zadrożny (Chapter 4 in this volume). The text below is a summary of the arguments that define the usefulness of the inDialogue software, as seen by a practitioner.

From the local authorities' perspective, the large number of consultative processes required by law, in combination with the, usually, insufficient number of trained and technically well-prepared staff, often results in the insufficient preparation of processes. Moreover, only in the largest cities are there professionally trained teams who are entirely devoted to communicating with citizens; while in medium size or small towns, and especially in rural municipalities (which themselves constitute two-thirds of all municipalities in Poland) there are no specialized teams or communication offices, and these functions are usually assigned to individual employees as one of several of their tasks. Even more important in this respect is the fact that consultation subjects usually concern, or require, the involvement in activities of several internal units, or at least persons from these units. It often happens that patterns of cooperation between organizational units or departments leave much to be desired in terms of effectiveness, which is a typical weakness, countrywide, in the Polish public administration. When confronted with intense time pressures and internal communication weaknesses, the preparation quality of materials for consultation (background information, described decision options with elaborated consequences, maps, etc.) often becomes compromised, which is then noticed by citizens (for more information based on substantive research, see Przybylska, Chapter 2 in this volume). Another typical weakness in current consultative processes in Polish municipalities is the delayed preparation of reports and conclusions from consultations; or not publishing them at all, which damages trust; or simply, responses to individual questions that are too formal, which is important in terms of confirming the fulfilment of legal procedures, but in practice not sufficiently understandable for the recipient (Przybylska, ibid.).

These deficiencies in the public authorities, mostly arising from mounting time pressures and institutional weaknesses can, potentially, be significantly reduced by using the inDialogue software. The procedure for preparing each consultation within the software requires the careful planning of particular stages of the process, assigning roles to other employees within the municipal office or in other organizational units, and attaching previously prepared contextual information in the form of briefing materials. The software gives reminders about deadlines and provides suggestions on what should be done and when. Also, the selection of a methodologically appropriate group of citizens for a consultation can be more easily organized if the inDialogue software is used (for more details see Przybylska, ibid). However, it entails costs. The tiny resource that local administrations have—available time—has to be spent on entering data and planning the process; this is time-consuming in the first few instances, but subsequently, this time investment gets repaid, substantially improving the quality of the process on the municipal administration's side.

From the other side, citizens and stakeholders are also a source of weaknesses in the process. The majority of them also have severe time constraints on studying informational materials and attending public discussions. For this reason, it is very important that informational materials are well prepared and ICT tools are used to allow opinions to be given *after office hours*. The inDialogue software helps to satisfy both these needs. Another problem comes from the fact that citizens and stakeholders often have varied opinions. A typical example sees citizens and stakeholders express their opinions to the local administration one at a time, expecting the latter to agree, while disregarding the fact that a large proportion of opinions are in contradiction with the opinions of others. This is the main weakness of the processes of public communication in local communities—the weakness, or even absence, of deliberative processes; that is, a lack of discussion between the citizens and stakeholders themselves, with the expectation that local government authorities will satisfy all sides. The inDialogue software allows for the engagement of citizens in such deliberative processes, either in a consecutive way by participating in moderated text discussions, or by taking part in moderated voice discussions. In both cases, the inDialogue consultation platform produces reports in which arguments are categorized and exemplified using a graphical *map of arguments* (for more on this subject, see Przybylska, Chapter 2). Therefore, participants in the process are able to learn from each other throughout the consultation process, and thus, can reach, after a few rounds, an acceptable compromise or consciously choose a desired option. This is the expected outcome of the deliberation process, which has been enabled by the inDialogue software.

From the users perspective there is also a greater time investment needed compared to the typical method of e-consultation nowadays (e.g., by filling in an active web questionnaire). So if both sides are able to invest a bit more time, they can arrive at much more satisfactory results, and bring both local administration and interested citizens closer to a situation of deliberative democracy. This seems a necessary direction in which to go if we seriously want to rebuild social trust and overcome the social, economic, and ecological problems in our communities.

Another very important feature—which responds to the needs of, statistically, more than 10% of the entire population, that is people with various forms of disabilities—is that the inDialogue consultation platform has been designed for the participation of persons who have various types of disabilities. Navigation within inDialogue was designed to be as intuitive as possible from the point of view of such groups (for more details see Stępień and Zadrożny as well as Bembenik et al. in this volume).

The final argument for using the inDialogue software is the fact that it is available free of charge, and any interested local government office can install the software on their own servers. As has been mentioned by Kulisiewicz (see Chapter 7 of this volume) only some of the largest cities purchased consultation platforms on the market (though these are much narrower in terms of functionality). For most municipalities, however, this solution is out of reach due to either high investment costs or a lack of the technical skills needed to define all their functionalities. For these local governments, which make up 95% of municipalities in Poland, the free of charge and open-code consultation platform developed by the consortium headed by the University of Warsaw, is a valid opportunity. The software was tested positively in 10 municipalities altogether, and it is ready for wider use. There are also some new initiatives, such as the one by the Department of Digitalization, Geodesy and Cartography of the Marshall's Office of the Mazovia Region, which is considering offering this software on-line to download for interested municipalities from their own region, with some support.

The Potential Contribution of the InDialogue Software to the Quality of Consultative Processes

There are at least three very important fields within which the inDialogue software could find immediate and wide use. The first one concerns the specific field of participatory spatial planning. The expected introduction of the "Urbanistic & Construction Code" as a parliamentary bill, together with the expected changes in the Ordinance of the Council of Ministers on *the System of managing the development of Poland*, assume the deep integration of strategic planning with spatial planning (at the regional, sub-regional and local levels). This will require the revision of numerous strategic documents within the spatial context in close consultation with citizens and local stakeholders. Without the use of IT tools—such as the free of charge inDialogue software—such wide and intensive consultative processes will be difficult.

The second area in which consultations already take place, but at a scale that is grossly insufficient, is infrastructure investment planning. Not only is the location of new infrastructure important (see above) but also the functional program for the infrastructure, which are being designed, in order to avoid oversizing that will create higher than necessary operational costs. In EU countries, the typical planning process for an investment usually takes as long as it does in Poland because of the lengthy consultative processes with future users (at the pre-feasibility stage, and after the technical design stage), while the investment process itself is usually shorter due to the lack of changes during the investment process. This is now an important issue at a time of widely available EU investment funds, tight schedules for designing infrastructure investments, and submitting project documents for funding; while mistakes at this stage will result in suboptimal operating costs (usually too high) for running and maintaining built infrastructure over several decades (Czajkowski and Potkański 2016). Changing this pattern may be a very important contribution to safeguarding the long-term financial sustainability of local governments in Poland.

The third area to be described here is of a different character and has already been mentioned briefly in this chapter. The insufficient coordination of work across different departments in many of local government offices is clearly a universal weakness. Using the inDialogue platform for managing and supporting consultation processes, after an initial investment in time for learning how to use this new tool, will pay off by streamlining the flow of information among departments and organizational units. Improving this universal weakness, specifically in the field of public consultation, might be a substantial contribution to the efficiency of local government management, and will contribute to building social trust at the local level.

Conclusion

From this argument, the inDialogue software, understood in the wider sense, is not only a tool for delivering opinions to public authorities, but is also, to some extent, a tool for facilitating discussion among the public on issues of importance for local communities, and thus a tool for supporting the development of participatory governance in Polish local communities. It should be stated that not all participatory processes necessarily result in deliberation. Nevertheless, we shall aim at it, as it builds new knowledge and trust. The inDialogue software, if used, gives us this chance.

All these technical solutions will not, however, solve the problem of a lack of culture of discussion, which means a lack of willingness to conduct extensive public discussions and not treating others as partners. No technical solution will substitute for these soft elements; therefore, other solutions and stimuluses are also necessary in this respect.

A well-conducted social consultation process may, however, significantly contribute to building much needed social trust, and positively influence the implementation of the municipality's strategic goals. If the consultation procedure creates understanding among inhabitants, it will strengthen the sense of responsibility towards the common good and build consent regarding local policies. Initiatives such as the one proposed by the In Dialog consortium, which developed internet-based tools to assist in the process of consultation, are helpful in promoting the standards of deliberative processes in Polish municipalities (Przybylska 2016, 135).

References

Books and articles

Arnstein, Sherry. 1969. "A Ladder of Citizens Participation." *Journal of the American Institute of Planners* 35 (4): 216–224.

Bovaird, Tony. 2007. "Beyond Engagement and Participation: User and Community Coproduction of Public Services." *Public Administration Review* 67(5): 846–860.

Czajkowski, Jan. Tomasz Potkański. 2016. "Proste wskaźniki finansowe do oszacowania możliwości realizacji w najbliższych latach przez JST nowych przedsięwzięć. Nowa funkcjonalność na platformie BeSTi@." *Finanse Komunalne* 12: 20–50.

Hausner, Jerzy. 2008. *Zarządzanie publiczne*. Warsaw: Wydawnictwo Naukowe Scholar.

Hood, Christopher. 1991. "Public Management for all seasons." *Public Administration* 69 (1): 3–19.

Izdebski, Hubert. 2010. "Nowe kierunki zarządzania publicznego a współczesne kierunki myśli polityczno-prawnej." In *Nowe zarządzanie publiczne i public governance w Polsce i w Europie*, edited by Adam Bosiacki, Hubert Izdebski, Aleksander Nelicki, Igor Zachariasz, 11–30.Warsaw: LIBER.

Lathrop Daniel, and Laurel Ruma. 2010. *Open Government*. Sebastopol, CA: O'Reilly Media Inc.

Olech Anna, and Tomasz Kazmierczak. 2011. "Modele partycypacji publicznej." In *Partycypacja publiczna: O uczestnictwie w życiu wspólnoty lokalnej*, edited by Anna Olech, 100–111. Warsaw: Instytut Spraw Publicznych.

Pollitt, Christopher, and Geert Bouckaert. 2004. *Public Management Reform. A Comparative Analysis*. Oxford: Oxford University Press.

Potkański, Tomasz. 2010. "Profesjonalizacja zarządzania w samorządzie terytorialnym." In *Rozwój lokalny: Bariery i stymulanty. Wybrane zagadnienia, V Kongres Obywatelski*, edited by Cezary Trutkowski, 57–76. Gdańsk: Instytut Badań nad Gospodarką Rynkową.

Przybylska, Anna. 2010. *Internet i komunikowanie we wspólnocie lokalnej*. Warsaw: Warsaw University Press.

Przybylska, Anna. 2016. "The need for a qualitative change in municipal public consultations." *Przegląd Europejski* 41(3): 123–137.

Stępień, Mateusz. 2008. *Responsywna administracja Publiczna*. Toruń: Wydawnictwo Adam Marszałek.

Weber, Max. 1922 (1968). *Economy and Society: An Outline of Interpretive Sociology.* New York: Bedminster Press.

Legal sources

"Konstytucja Rzeczypospolitej Polskiej." *Journal of Laws* of 1997, 78, item 483.

"Ustawa z dnia 8 marca 1990 roku o samorządzie gminnym." *Journal of Laws* of 1990, 16, item 95.

Anna Przybylska

Conclusions: Factors for the Absorption of Innovation

Despite enthusiastic announcements at the turn of the twentieth and the twenty-first century by scholars, followed soon after by international and national public institutions, the transformative potential of ICT tools in politics has not been fully utilized; or, to put it differently, the use of ICT to encourage civic participation has serious flaws. As Coleman and Moss (2012, 14) point out,

> There exist more opportunities than ever before for citizens wishing to have their say, via the media or directly to local and national governments, but there is a more pervasive sense of disappointment than ever before that citizens are outside the citadels of power, and that those within do not know how to listen to them.

The perspective that we have adopted in the In Dialogue project, and that has been presented in this book, requires us to start thinking about the design of ICT using an empirically grounded analysis of the problem. Only after this examination can the model of intervention, and the role of ICT in it, be proposed. The diagnosis of the lack of responsiveness by decision-makers or the inconclusiveness of the communication between them and citizens is nothing new. But, as the problem persists, it demands new approaches and resolutions, taking into account the system at large (Mansbridge et al. 2012) as well as particular democratic institutions and mechanisms of participation (for an in-depth analysis of one method see Fishkin 2009; for a comparative framework of institutions and methods see Gastil 2008).

The attempts at creating new ICT tools remain relevant, even in view of their limited success up until now. The original, applied projects have brought in experiential knowledge, and if they also include the research and data analyses that allow an evaluation of the results of the intervention, they are a valuable source of information about the factors pertinent to the absorption of democratic innovations by institutional users and citizens (for methodological approaches to evaluation in projects on civic participation, including e-participation see Macintosh and Whyte 2008; Loukis and Wimmer 2012; Spada 2014; Aichholzer, Kubicek, and Torres 2016). These aspects should be taken seriously in order to produce a more systemic change.

The aim of the In Dialogue project has been to diffuse the knowledge about deliberative public consultations and their methodology, through the use of the *inDialogue* software. We have focused on public consultations as a mechanism for civic participation in decision-making due to the fact that it is an institutionalized, established channel of communication in local politics that should allow citizens to express their opinions on the directions in which their communities develop. Our purpose was to ensure the openness and inclusiveness of the public consultations organized using the inDialogue platform, for example, by addressing the standards of WCAG 2.0, as well as drawing the attention of the consultation's organizers to the issue of the targeted selection of citizens who may not be in the habit of participating in politics.

The inDialogue application has been designed to be implemented in local governments, where the decision-making process is closest to the citizens and where politicians have responsibilities towards them regarding many public policy areas as described by Potkański in Chapter 10. Local governments also attempt to demonstrate their Europeanization (being a synonym of modernization, see Bartkowski 2015) in regards to the model of governance, for example, using the public consultations or participatory budgeting; the latter in its mostly plebiscitary rather than deliberative form.

In these concluding remarks, I share some of the findings that have resulted from our tests (2016) and pilot studies (2017), and which concern some of the factors that are important to the uptake of the inDialogue software by the local government administrations. These are reflections on the experience gathered during several years of action research. We hope that they may be useful as they are relevant to a discussion that crosses the boundaries of our R&D project. The evaluation, which is based on the collected data, is forthcoming. I have also sketched out the steps the project team plans to take in regards to inDialogue's implementation as well as research and development of the software's functionalities and features.

The factors that cannot be ignored while planning the diffusion of ICT, which introduces new procedures and demands new practices, are not only structural, but can be dependent, at least to a certain degree, on the project team's engagement. I will bring up especially these aspects of the project's conduct in the following paragraphs.

Establishing Partnerships

The Polish governmental administration is divided into the three tiers: central, regional and local. In developing the inDialogue software, we considered local governments to be the most important partners and beneficiaries of the project. Establishing a partnership with a city or town hall is a key factor of success for the action research project. Prior cooperation with local government administration, a database of city and town halls that participated in our survey, online voice debates and applied case studies; all facilitated the recruitment of municipalities to the project.

We started the project with twelve partner city and town halls while aiming at a stable group of eight. It is also worth mentioning that in the first two years of the research phase we lost two-thirds of our partner cities but, with success, looked for replacements. The two cities who withdrew from the project sent us letters of explanation; the reasons presented in these letters did not refer to the model of public consultation planning and conducting that we support. We were informed that the city halls had developed their own methodology of public consultation and tools to conduct them. Participatory budgeting and polls, as well as the ICT applications supporting them, were given as examples. Some cities did not officially withdraw from the project, but before we lost working contact with the clerks responsible for public consultations, we learnt that they had joined the In Dialogue project in search of inspiration to be able to set off on an independent initiative; or, alternatively, they had expressed concern for the proposed methodology (mainly the selection of participants). Obviously, there were also political issues involved (reorganization after local elections) that could have overlapped with other motives in two city halls.

Research and Action

Within the frame of the In Dialogue project, we closely collaborated with the people working in city or town halls, which is characteristic for action research projects. And at the same time, we emphasized the need for building a broader network of social partners, experts, the mass media, and social media, which is in line with an approach represented by Mansbridge et al. (2012). Below I describe in some detail the procedure and interactions with partner institutions, as I consider them to be an important element of projects like ours.

During the research phase of the project we used multiple methods and techniques for collecting information from clerks; first, about the model of public consultation that we wanted to be supported by ICT, and then about the prototype of the inDialogue software. After receiving the decision-makers' formal acceptance of our invitation to join the project, we organized a conference and workshops to explain the aims and the plan of action, as well as to discuss the issues that we understood to be controversial such as representativeness and anonymity in social sciences and politics. We invited experts like the General Officer of Data Protection in Poland whose opinions have to be respected by the representatives of local government administration in performing their tasks. We consulted on the model for the ICT application using an open-ended questionnaire. Then we visited each partner city and town hall to meet the teams of people involved in public consultations in whatever role (including IT people). Lastly, we discussed the functions and features of the prototype during webinars as well as a face-to-face meeting organized at the university to collect the feedback on the progress of the prototype's development.

During tests in two municipalities, we assisted clerks at the different stages of public consultation preparation and conduct. We prepared workshops for clerks, NGOs, and local activists as well as workshops for people with disabilities. We offered our help during the preparation of briefing materials and reports, took the role of observers during moderated face-to-face consultation discussions, or were ourselves, moderators.

After some fixes in the software, the pilot study kicked off. We offered support in organizing public consultations using the inDialogue application in eight municipalities, repeating the procedure of the previous phase. This time we involved students who help us in coaching and advisory roles. The clerks received feedback from the students on briefing materials and moderation, while Marta Kołodziejska from the project team offered feedback on reports.

We had planned this type of support during the implementation phase. This is why we consider organizing the internships for students wishing to learn through practice on a larger scale. A system where MA students are supported by PhD students who get their feedback from team members has proven to work well.

Evaluation and Software Amendments

The pilot studies allowed us to collect information on errors as well as recommendations for the implementation version of the software. Each error report met with appropriate and immediate action. All recommendations for adjustments were considered, and the majority of them were accepted. Priority was given to the improvements requested by Częstochowa's City Hall regarding data protection and WCAG 2.0. These two issues were treated with special care in our project from the very beginning, but the remarks by clerks, especially a data protection officer, were invaluable.

Some recommendations were contradictory, in which case, wherever possible, we attempted to reconcile them by allowing the choice between different solutions, for example, the public anonymity of users or the lack of it. We were also flexible regarding the use of maps or an unfolding list to define the territorial boundaries of public consultations and the categories of information introduced into information materials etc. But, there were also preferences for solutions that we could not accept as they were inconsistent with the model of public consultation that we planned to apply in practice.

None of the municipalities participating in the pilot study has informed us while replying to our paper questionnaire or answering our questions during an interview, that they will not be implementing the inDialogue software. However, it is rather unlikely they will all utilize the platform, as some clerks made the implementation conditional on changes to the application that we cannot support due to their inconsistency with the model of deliberation. Once we prepare the inDialogue implementation version, we will be able to receive accurate feedback from the city and town halls on its further use.

An Umbrella or a Network?

By the end of 2017, the implementation version of the inDialogue software will have been prepared. The fact that the software has been developed in communication with potential institutional users facilitated the amendments to it. But, the R&D projects require the pilot phase to be followed by an implementation that is carefully prepared, monitored and evaluated. Even if the local governments were unanimously willing to accept our ICT solution for better planned and organized public consultations, they have to consider servicing and its potential development in line with changes within the legal and institutional environment.

This task is easier for local government administrations with larger budgets and dedicated IT units for which the commercial sector, with its offer of stable ongoing support, is a better partner than a consortium with a project that will end at a certain point in time. We addressed this problem by attempting to create strategic partnerships with regional and central administrations that could develop and amend the inDialogue software in the long run. The Marshall's Office of the Mazovia Region (one out of sixteen in Poland) was the first to sign a contract for the non-commercial use of the inDialogue software in at least several dozen municipalities. It will connect with the software already in use by the public administration. As the inDialogue application has an open license, it can be modified and adjusted to suit the special needs of particular institutions.

Several other marshal offices responded positively to our query about the use of inDialogue in their regions. But, the motivation to use the free software to support public consultations does not seem strong enough to bear the costs of its implementation, particularly at the municipal level. Their preferred solution is to organize a pilot implementation, financed with a grant, and with the In Dialogue consortium as leader. Although, but with less enthusiasm, they also considered financing of the inDialogue software's implementation using contributions from interested marshal offices that would cover the costs of one office that would then take on the responsibility for the service and development work.

Finally, the marshal offices have not rejected an option that takes into account the involvement of the Ministry of Digitalization. Talks with the ministry have not yet reached a conclusive stage. The inDialogue software has been designed as a multiple instances software to be installed independently on the server of each unit of a local public administration. To facilitate the support of the software for many institutional users at the regional or local level of public administration, the ministry discussed with the inDialogue team, the possibility of one, centralized installation for multiple users. On the one hand, it takes the financial and organizational burden off local governments, but on the other hand, it makes them dependent on the central administration.

Public Sphere and Scaling-up

The public sphere, including the pluralistic media system and non-politicized NGOs, is relevant to several aspects of public consultation practices and would influence the use of the inDialogue software. The institutions in the public sphere can provide education about the procedures for public consultations; encourage participation in them, especially the most vulnerable groups; and control and evaluate the performance of administration against a set of standards. They involve the broader circle of citizens in debates, even if they do not directly share their opinions with decision-makers. Unfortunately, this is not necessarily the case, and should be treated with care as an important issue.

During the tests and the pilot study, we prepared databases of the NGOs and the media in each city or town, and encouraged clerks to use their databases to contact them for workshops on the inDialogue software and recruitment for debates. The software itself can, to certain degree, contribute to better information on public consultations by its linkage with the institutions of the broader public sphere, for example, information can automatically be sent to the media and NGOs—as they are sent to registered citizens—on the subject and methodology of public consultations, registration, briefing materials, and reports. In such cases, maybe the media could provide information, not only about the controversial issues in public consultations but also on the practicalities that equip inhabitants with knowledge useful in exercising their civic roles. Knowing how the media and the circulation of information work, especially in small towns, whenever needed, we prepared media briefs and posters as we were concerned about the availability of information on public consultations and the subject involved.

Distribution of Roles

Recognizing the people within the city or town halls that wanted to be partners with the research team throughout the project, is important. The same goes for the implementation. The efficient use of time, achieving good results, and the project's progress requires good communication. Changes in the positions of clerks who are assigned tasks concerning the new application's implementation in a city or town hall are disruptive, and can stand in its way. However, the inDialogue software can come to the rescue here. It allows for the distribution of roles in public consultations, including the role of the main organizer who is responsible for internal and external communication. The inDialogue software supports internal communication that is not only managerial but also reflexive through a system of comments on the methodology of public consultations and briefing materials.

Another equally important thread under the same heading concerns the distribution of roles in public consultations between politicians and clerks. Public consultations, although managed by clerks working in public administration, are initiated and followed by decisions made by politicians. The visibility of the actions taken by politicians is low in the inDialogue software. We think that if it were higher, it could make politicians more responsible for the treatment of the data that has been collected. This experiment is worth the effort. Thus, we will think about an extension of inDialogue's functions. Consultations using the inDialogue platform could start with the publication of a letter from a mayor or president stating their aims, the expected input from inhabitants, its impact on the decision, and they could end with a document informing about how the results of consultations have been included in the decision. We expect it to have a positive impact on the involvement of citizens.

Thresholds of Participation and Incentives

This experience shows that the availability of ICT tools does not necessarily create a demand for its use (Przybylska 2010). Neither does it makes citizens feel empowered in their relations with power systems (Coleman and Moss 2012). The users have to be convinced of the purposefulness of their actions. If ICT tools are supposed to include citizens in the decision-making process, citizens should know what their input will be and what (re)actions they can expect from the city or town hall (i.e., public consultations are just an advisory mechanism, but their results should be treated seriously and competently).

It seems that in underestimating the role of the methodology of public consultations as an incentive for inhabitants to participate in public consultations, clerks overestimate the importance of registration as a possible factor in discouraging participation. People do not complain about registration that is required in commercial services as they know what purposes it serves. Thus, I would start searching for factors that discourage participation elsewhere, in, for example, missing information that is pertinent to a problem discussed, the unclear purpose of consultations, late announcements concerning the possibility of joining debates, missing or inconclusive results, or the lack of linkage between these results and the decision.

Again, it has to be verified in a quantitative study, how many citizens support registration and how many do not, but based on our qualitative research we can tell that their opinions are divided and supported by different arguments. The hypothesis is that those who participate in public consultations to solve local problems for the benefit of the community understand the positive aspects of registration, or they would understand it once it was explained to them. They can be unsure about how their personal data could be used. Then, only good practice can be a real incentive for people to become active citizens—and this is most likely to be a snow-ball effect that requires patience and repeated positive experience. The internet, far too often, is used by politicians as a safety device for allowing the control of emotions.

References

Aichholzer, Georg, Herbert Kubicek, and Lourdes Torres, eds. 2016. *Evaluating e-Participation. Framework, Practice, Evidence*. Cham: Springer.

Bartkowski, Jerzy. 2015. "Samorządy i europeizacja Polski lokalnej. Aspekt pragmatyczny, socjologiczny i polityczny." *Politeja* 33: 9–42. DOI: 10.12797/Politeja.12.2015.33.02.

Coleman, Stephen, and Giles Moss. 2012. "Under Construction: The Field of Online Deliberation Research." *Journal of Information Technology & Politics* 9 (1): 1–15.

Fishkin, James S. 2009. *When the People Speak. Deliberative Democracy and Public Consultation*. Oxford: Oxford University Press.

Gastil, John. 2008. *Political Communication and Deliberation*. Los Angeles: SAGE.

Loukis, Euripidis, and Maria Wimmer. 2012. "A Multiple-Method Evaluation of Different Models of Structured Electronic Consultation on Government Policies." *Information Systems Management* 29: 284–294.

Macintosh, Ann, and Angus Whyte. 2008. "Towards an Evaluation Framework for eParticipation." *Transforming Government: People, Process & Policy* 2 (1): 16–30.

Mansbridge, Jane et al. 2012. "A system approach to deliberative democracy." In *Deliberative Systems. Deliberative Democracy at the Large Scale*, edited by John Parkinson, and Jane Mansbridge, 1–26. Cambridge: Cambridge University Press.

Przybylska, Anna. 2010. *Internet i komunikowanie we wspólnocie lokalnej*. Warsaw: Warsaw University Press.

Spada, Paolo. 2014. "The Diffusion of Participatory Governance Innovations: A Panel Data Analysis of the Adoption and Survival of Participatory Budgeting in Brazil." Working Paper. Accessed November 8, 2017. https://www.researchgate.net/publication/273774248_The_Diffusion_of_Participatory_Governance_Innovations_A_Panel_Data_Analysis_of_the_Adoption_and_Survival_of_Participatory_Budgeting_in_Brazil.

About the Authors

Robert Bembenik, PhD, works at the Institute of Computer Science at the Warsaw University of Technology, email: r.bembenik@gmail.com.

Jacek Haman, PhD, is head of the Department of Statistics, Demography and Mathematical Sociology at the Institute of Sociology, University of Warsaw, email: jhaman@uw.edu.pl.

Marta Kołodziejska received her PhD at the Institute of Sociology, University of Warsaw, email: kolodziejskam@is.uw.edu.pl

Tomasz Kulisiewicz, PhD, is an analyst of the electronic communication and IT market in Poland and, Eastern and Central Europe, email: tomasz@kulisiewicz.eu.

Tomasz Potkański received his PhD in Ethnology and Cultural Anthropology at the University of Warsaw. Currently Deputy Executive Director of the Association of Polish Cities. Cooperates with the Institute of Public Policies of the Collegium Civitas, email: tomasz.potkanski@zmp.poznan.pl.

Anna Przybylska, PhD, is manager of the In Dialogue Project, assistant professor and head of the Centre for Deliberation, Institute of Sociology, University of Warsaw, email: a.przybylska@uw.edu.pl.

Maja Sawicka received her PhD at the Institute of Sociology, University of Warsaw, email: maja.sawicka@gmail.com.

Radosław Sierocki, PhD, researcher and lecturer at the Faculty of Social Sciences, University of Warmia and Mazury in Olsztyn, email: rsierocki@wp.pl.

Bartosz Stępień is an expert in ICT accessibility for people with disabilities, email: bs@spoldzielniafado.pl.

Aneta Świercz received her PhD from the Faculty of Electronics and Information Technology at the Warsaw University of Technology, email: anes@ire.pw.edu.pl.

Klementyna Świeżewska is a Ph.D. student at the Institute of Sociology, University of Warsaw, email: kl.swiezewska@gmail.com.

Paweł Tymiński is a programmer. He graduated from the Faculty of Electronics and Information Technology at the Warsaw University of Technology majoring in Computer Science (Computer Systems Engineering), email: ptyminsk@gmail.com.

Jacek Zadrożny is a graduate of the Social Policy Institute at the University of Warsaw, and founder of the Forum of Accessible Cyberspace, an organization working for the digital inclusion of disabled persons, email: jaczad@gmail.com.

Warsaw Studies in Politics and Society

Edited by Radosław Markowski

Vol. 1 Izabela Handzlik / Łukasz Sorokowski (eds.): Found in Multiculturalism. Acceptance or Challenge? 2014.

Vol. 2 Radosław Markowski / Michał Kotnarowski / Michał Wenzel / Marta Żerkowska-Balas: Democratic Audit of Poland 2014. 2015.

Vol. 3 Stephen Coleman / Anna Przybylska / Yves Sintomer (eds.): Deliberation and Democracy: Innovative Processes and Institutions. 2015.

Vol. 4 Michał Wenzel: Labour Protest in Poland. Trade Unions and Employee Interest Articulation After Socialism. 2016.

Vol. 5 Lenka Dražanová: Education and Tolerance. A Comparative Quantitative Analysis of the Educational Effect on Tolerance. 2017.

Vol. 6 Anna Przybylska (ed.): ICT for Dialogue and Inclusive Decision-Making. 2017.

www.peterlang.com

www.ingramcontent.com/pod-product-compliance
Ingram Content Group UK Ltd.
Pitfield, Milton Keynes, MK11 3LW, UK
UKHW041828100926
8556IPUK00002B/72

9 783631 748107